THE MEDIA AND THE MAKING OF HISTORY

For Françoise, Tom, Ana, Joe, Alice and Marianne

The Media and the Making of History

JOHN THEOBALD
Southampton Institute, UK

ASHGATE

Published by
Ashgate Publishing Limited
Gower House
Croft Road
Aldershot
Hants GU11 3HR
England

Ashgate Publishing Company
Suite 420
101 Cherry Street
Burlington, VT 05401-4405
USA

Ashgate website: http://www.ashgate.com

British Library Cataloguing in Publication Data
Theobald, John, 1946-
    The media and the making of history
    1.Mass media and history 2.Literature and history
    3.Historiography
    I.Title
    907.2

Library of Congress Cataloging-in-Publication Data
Theobald, John, 1946-
    The media and the making of history / John Theobald.
        p. cm.
    Includes bibliographical references and index.
    ISBN 0-7546-3822-7
        1. Mass media--Political aspects. 2. World politics--20th century. I. Title.

    P95.8.T49 2004
    302.23--dc22

                                                                    2003057015
ISBN 0 7546 3822 7

Printed and bound in Great Britain by MPG Books Ltd, Bodmin, Cornwall

Contents

Preface   *vii*
Acknowledgements   *ix*

1. Moments of Untruth   1

2. Radical Media Critics. The Four Generations   19

3. The Great Discursive Illusion – 1914-1918   55

4. No Word that Fits. Media Discourse and the Rise of Fascism   67

5. Comics and Communism. Tintin Fights the Cold War   79

6. Consuming Reality. Mutually Assured Destruction and Routines of
    Embedded Deception   91

7. Acting as if … Resistance to Dominant Discourses of Anti-Communism
    and Nuclear Escalation in the 1980s   111

8. A Collapse of Hegemonic Discourse. Resistance in Eastern Europe   129

9. Cold War Victory and the Selling of German Unification   141

10. The Longevity of Wartime Discourses and Identities. The Case
    of Britain and Europe   153

11. The Balkans Revisited   167

12. Twin Towers of Babel. 'War on Terrorism' and 'Anticipatory
    Pre-emption'   179

13. Conclusion – For an Active Audience   205

Bibliography   *209*
Index   *217*

Preface

People who 'make history', or 'make the news', are in everyday language those who have a transforming impact by their actions on a flow of events of public significance or interest.

They may, seen in the narrower terms of the historian's or journalist's craft, also be the recorders of events, those who produce or edit texts which bring to their readers or audiences a meaningful account of the past or present.

It is not commonly perceived or thought through that the first category, seen as people of action, might be less influential in determining the course of past and future events, as the public and decision makers come to understand them, than the second – the scribes. The authors and purveyors of the versions of events which become identified with 'what happened', and are thus subsequently reacted to with further actions by people of action, are habitually positioned on the sidelines of reality.

This book sets out to cross-examine two linked hypotheses. First, that the all-important battle for reality, the established truth about what is going on, and how citizens and decision makers should interpret events and situations, is crucially a discursive one, to a much greater extent than normally assumed in the hands of story-tellers rather than actors. Second, that discourses which gain hegemonic status do not arrive at this position because they are full, accurate and unbiased, but because they function in the political and economic interests of power elites. In this perspective, corrupted story-tellers, that is, journalists and high-profile popular historians, whose craft in Western society has (with few exceptions) long been swallowed into large, and in some cases globally influential media enterprises, move from the periphery to an indispensable position of close enmeshment with the centres of power.

In positing that the role of the media and their discourses in the 'making of history' (in both senses) has been seriously underestimated, this book does not wish to overreact by inflating that role in reductionist fashion at the unreasonable expense of other key factors. Rather it wishes to advance its hypotheses, examine their concepts, and test them in a series of exemplary case studies.

Within the conclusions to be drawn may be sought some answers to key cultural questions about why the age of mass media and mass information, which were supposed to have led to greatly enhanced public knowledge and awareness, has also been the age of the most extreme and widespread barbarism that humankind has committed. Indeed, many of the worst cases have emanated from, or happened under the scrutiny of the most media-saturated societies.

From the conclusions may, I hope, be drawn stimuli for envisaging a future in which such a diabolical synchronicity will not continue to be produced.

Acknowledgements

Thanks unlimited to the close family – Françoise, Tom, Ana, Joe, Alice and Marianne.

Thanks to many friends and colleagues. My preoccupation with the themes of this book goes back for decades, thus dozens – too many to list, dating from periods in Vienna, Leicester and Southampton – will recognise their association with parts of it.

Thanks for comment and support in the latter months and weeks to David Berry, Patrick Burke, David Cromwell, Patrick Stevenson, John Sandford and Priya Varghese.

Thanks to the students who really showed interest.

Thanks to institutions – particularly Southampton Institute and the AHRB – for indispensable time and space.

Thanks to Caroline Wintersgill and colleagues at Ashgate for helping the project through to publication.

I have taken from each, including the numerous unnamed, according to their patience, resources and critical insight, and I thank each according to their generosity, encouragement and good humour.

Chapter 1

Moments of Untruth

My words fly up, my thoughts remain below:
Words without thoughts never to heaven go.
Hamlet Act 3, Scene 3

Moments of Untruth

The words of King Claudius, reflecting on the fateful consequences of the separation
between words and meaning, provide an apt starting point for a critique of the role of
mass media discourse in key historical events and processes of European and Western
history since the outset of the age of mass communication – the central project of this
book. Shakespeare's couplet captures an individual moment of what George Steiner
expands into the broader 'break of the covenant between word and world' (Steiner
1989:93). This defines a process of cultural disintegration in the course of which
'words without thoughts' multiply into an immense, ever growing media tapestry of
what I am calling here 'moments of untruth'.

To those entering the discourse based vision of the historical process in the media
age, which is elaborated here, is offered a disturbing contribution to the cultural
understanding of what Eric Hobsbawm has called 'the most murderous century of
which we have record' (Hobsbawm 1994:13). In this perspective, media discourse, the
way in which an event or issue is presented to masses of citizens on the newspaper or
web page, and on radio or television, moves from the footnotes to become a central
object of analysis. *The story/l'histoire/die Geschichte*, with all the connotations of
these words, becomes the pivotal point and door of perception (we should recall here
that in both French and German 'story' and 'history' are expressed by the same word,
and that in all three languages, the expression 'telling stories' can mean 'telling lies').
The frequently unnoticed and unquestioned historian's and journalist's task might be
habitually construed in the public mind as a functional process of searching out and
portraying as accurate and true a depiction of events as possible, and showing how they
fit in with other salient events in a given time frame. The project here is to highlight
untruth and *half truth*, and to focus on the complex interaction between genealogies of
lies as purveyed to the public via the media, and the events which precede and follow
them. In this account, we shall test the hypothesis that journalists, and those who rely
on them to mould our historical and current assumptions are in fact not our guides, but
our great misleaders.

Explicit here is an astringent critique of mass media practice within its ideological
and economic context and the societal structures which it helps to uphold. Chapter 2

will enter further into this, grounding the critique, and the intellectual tradition it belongs to, within a broader mapping of mass communication history.

The project's uniting concept of 'moments of untruth' draws on a conceptualisation of the *difference* of the twentieth and early twenty-first centuries (particularly in the technologically developed Western world) as far as the distribution of information and ideas is concerned. It works with the view that something *revolutionary* happened towards the end of the nineteenth century into which was woven a transformation of our culture, our ways and means of seeing the world. At the core of this was the impact of the development of mass communications technology and networks on language, within the context of liberal-capitalist structures and energies. It is clear that, as the channels through which discourses could be spread diversified, and the speed with which this could happen multiplied, so whole new possibilities of using language emerged. As part of this process, language became a valuable and exploitable commodity, and in this new commodified form, a tool to communicate specific kinds of information and discourse to ever larger publics. Political and economic elites rapidly saw the importance of mass mediated discourse in the exercise and expansion of their power and wealth. Subsequently, and particularly in times of pre-war, war, and post-war, into which one can easily slot Europe's entire recent history (see Hobsbawm 1994, Carruthers 2000), mass communications, and the kind of instrumentalised discourse they enabled, became the dominant feature of Western culture.

In this context, George Steiner's striking rhetoric speaks of 'the tidal mendacity of journalism and the mass media, the trivialising cant of public and socially approved modes of discourse' which 'have made of almost everything modern urban men and women say or hear or read an empty jargon, a cancerous loquacity' (Steiner 1996:23). Elsewhere, he designates the already mentioned separation of 'word' and 'world' as 'one of the very few genuine revolutions of spirit in Western history' (Steiner 1989:93). This gigantic assertion is not made lightly.

With comparable breadth and eloquence, Armand Mattelart makes the equally striking observation that 'communication serves first of all to make war' (Mattelart 1994:xiii). In his trenchant view, 'confining the notion of communication to the entertainment industry in peacetime is merely the latest way of stifling examination of the relation between communication and war. [...] War and its logics are essential components of the history of international communications and of its doctrines and theories, as well as its uses' (ibid).

Startling as these assertions from the end of the twentieth century may seem, they are not new. Chapter 2 will look at their genealogy more closely, but two short examples may point here to the existence of their intellectual hinterland. In 1918 Austria, Karl Kraus wrote of the 'loyal bond' which he saw to have operated through the First World War between *Tinte, Technik*, and *Tod* (ink, technology, and death, or, translated more freely, to maintain the alliteration, mass media, machine, and massacre) (Kraus 1918a:29). George Orwell, in his essay *Politics and the English Language* (1946) saw war as the consequence of the development of a language which 'name(d) things without calling up mental images of them' (Jackall 1995:432). With that, we spiral back to Claudius's 'words without thoughts'.

The contentions so far are: (i) that 'words without thoughts' – dislocations of language and meaning – are key factors in Western history in the media age, and particularly in its ceaseless wars and barbarisms; (ii) that mass communication, and its most influential discursive offspring – modern journalism – are the chief purveyors of this dislocation. If these are to be substantiated, then the processes bringing about the corrupt interactions between mass media discourse and historical events must be *demonstrated.* We must elucidate how mass media journalistic practice has not just reported and portrayed the century's history falsely as it went along; it has also, through doing so, *created consequences*, chains of further events (equally falsely mediated) which could not have happened, or at least not in the way they did, without the intervention of initial misleading mass media discourses.

It is examples of such trails, rooted in 'moments of untruth', such 'genealogies of lies' that the body of this book sets itself to trace, weave together, and evaluate.

Concepts of truth and untruth, and hence the 'moments' attached to them, are culturally and discursively determined and centrally associated with words and images. It is within this *literate* framework that the present narrative offers a perspective on central aspects of the twentieth and twenty-first centuries, in terms of their having been crucially shaped by 'moments of untruth', key moments at which false discourse has played a decisive role in forging the future. More bluntly, it examines the processes and consequences of Western culture's failures in coming to terms with the impact of public discourse in the media age. As discourses of technologically mediated journalism and distraction have expanded to global proportions, largely eclipsing or swallowing other contenders for discursive hegemony, those on the receiving end, it is suggested, have been exposed to a new historically defining mixture of persuasion and seduction whose motivating energy has been power and profit. A first hypothesis to be examined here is that, while the purveyors of these discourses have proclaimed that they have been the bearers of truth, and have been believed, they have in fact brought us a cocktail of illusions in the form of corrupted and self-interested discourses, mingled with and disguised as truth. These have, it is further suggested, built into citizen-consumers, over time, false structures of perception, false historical consciousness, and a false, passivity-inducing sense of powerlessness. From all of these it is possible, but difficult and risky, to liberate themselves, and easy and enjoyable to comply with, especially when they are well convinced, by means of those same discourses, that they are operating on the basis of free choice between a genuine plurality of options.

The key image to be investigated and tested here is thus one of a twentieth century which set out on a, from the public's or citizen's standpoint, disastrously false path in its radically new relationship with public discourse. This started with the nineteenth century introduction of mass production, communication and distribution processes such as rotary presses, the telegraph, and railways, and, in tune with the guiding mentality of the age, developed and expanded according to free market processes and values. The discourses of public information via mass media were thus from the start subject to market forces and ideology, and 'owned' by powerful entrepreneurs for whom the maximising of accuracy and objectivity was, ultimately, subordinate to the business of accumulating wealth and power. It must be added that there never was a golden age or utopia in which neutral reporting and public information were as one; other ages, places, and socio-economic systems were, and are, subject to other forms of discursive manipulation. But the development of communications technology through the twentieth century under the aegis, in the Western world and those it dominated, of free market economics and perceived military imperatives can with justice be perceived as having opened up opportunities of exponentially increasing proportions for the distribution of lies. The extent to which these opportunities have been taken will be a measure of the plausibility with which the twentieth century can be construed as a period of ever increasing massive accumulation and distribution of wilfully distorted information, and success in the management of deceit. A version of the most provocative and unwelcome of questions is thus posed here again, for it is one which has never been properly answered: 'Looking back at the twentieth century, must we conclude that the Western world lived through a period in which the commodification of public discourse led to an accumulation of "moments of untruth" which had a determining noxious influence on events and history, and which have a continuing dominating impact on current accepted constructions of our global context?'.

History, Common Sense, and Illusion

Common sense tells us that contemporary history, properly done, describes and bequeaths a series of decisive events, things which really happened, linking them into a narrative of which every element is true and verifiable from on the spot accounts and contemporary documentation. In doing so, it locates us. By showing us reliably where we (and the collective 'we' usually refers to a nation) have been, 'our' history gives us understanding of an ongoing continuum of events, incorporating them into itself as they roll inexorably by. Those of us who seek context, meaning and progression in our lives would be hopelessly disorientated without it. A structured series of 'moments of truth', providing a sense of identity is thus what mainstream historians traditionally deliver. From time to time interested parties and media audiences are made aware of academic disputes of theory and factual detail, ideology and historiography, but ultimately, and cutting a long story short, we can take these as variations on a theme or supplementary features, enrobing, but not fundamentally changing the established core and explanatory framework via which we can see significant real actions leading to visible consequences and reactions. In this process, plain words play the simple role of reporting these moments of truth, and setting them down in their most natural order. In our minds, such words have no autonomy, they are the neutral servants of fact. We believe that the key events of, say, what happened in the Second World War, or of technological development in the second half of the twentieth century, can, without serious controversy, be described; dates and figures can be ascribed to events, set out in charts and maps, and integrated into salient narrative. No-one in their right mind doubts the key events of the holocaust, or of the moon landing.

There is in our individual minds and social consciousness a self-evident distinction between a substructure of really existing facts and events, described by words which we forget are words since they are totally identified with the truth of their events or actions, and a superstructure of more or less reliable communication about them. The smarter we think we are, the more we are convinced that we can distinguish between the two.

But, however credulous or sophisticated we may be, we, as citizen-consumers, will mostly live our practical lives with the common sense that, in past and present, events precede the corresponding discourse. Something happens, *then* it is described, we discuss it, tell stories about it, analyse it, form opinions about it. Even when we talk about the future, we are only capable of doing so in terms of how we formulate the past, and what we believe to be true about it, that is, in terms of experience, personal or collective.

As with our understanding of the past, the habit of reading, hearing or watching the present, the news, confirms this. 'News' is constantly blended into historians' narratives. Locally, nationally, globally, things happen, *then* they are reported to us. The news is credible and believed, or it is not news. The late twentieth century even established virtually instantaneous global communication networks whereby the event and the report on it were often simultaneous, with word and image describing an event being produced and broadcast as it happened. The suicide attacks on the twin towers of the World Trade Centre in New York on 11 September 2001 are an example of this. But still, common sense tells us, the event produces its image and its report; this is the sequence which the whole framing of 'the news' presupposes, and on which the trust relationship between news media and audience is based. The news media's overt pact with their audiences is to provide as full, balanced, realistic, rapid and 'true' an account of significant events as possible, while the audience undertakes to accept and believe it. Event precedes report which precedes belief. Evidence creates credibility which creates truth. Our view of the wider world, beyond that of our immediate experience is thus, from this perspective, crucially constructed of a myriad of tiny written or broadcast packets of 'moments of truth', which we, members of the audience, help to link together into a more or less coherent narrative with the aid of experience, history, media presentation and reactive conversation. From this develops an understanding or opinion via further contacts with the media and with the immediate social environment, upon which decisions at big 'moments of truth' are based.

In other words, we, the publics of the mediated world, *accept*, for everyday purposes, and for our interpretation of the world about us, *first*, notions of sequence, (from event to report to reception), and *second*, notions of truth (reception accurately interprets report which accurately interprets event). This is surely as it should be: something firm and real on which to base our view of the world, and by which to fulfil our personal and democratic responsibilities.

But another model challenges this. It is already clear that the intention here is to interrogate these two 'normal' acceptances, and to put forward premises which upturn them and investigate the extent to which a more sceptical model, with its radical consequences, offers a viable critique of, and persuasive alternative approaches, from the receivers' standpoint, to 'mediatised' popular history and journalism.

Key questions here are: to what extent in the first hundred years of the media age, broadly congruent with the twentieth century, have less translucent and worthy processes been at work, undermining the model just outlined? To what extent have the media been *actors* or *agents* in the events and processes which they purport only to be describing? To what extent have the media themselves had an impact on the course of historical events, and been a significant ingredient in their development? Furthermore: what if trust in the media has been misplaced? What if the present that history has given us, as it has filtered through to the public via media output, contains (deliberately or accidentally) serious elements of distortion and lies? What if the narrative continuum of public events from past to present, chiefly provided by the media, is a tangled hybrid tissue of moments of truth and *untruth*, which has led to falsely based life and death decisions by governments, organisations, publics and individuals? What if this has actually created or influenced events further down the continuum, and *changed* the course of history? What if corrupt narratives have led to false perspectives and conclusions such that the 'lessons of history' and the justifications for future actions are, at crucial moments, based on misapprehensions or deliberate misappropriations? Should we look again at the public's pact with the media, and ask, on the one hand, to what extent the media keep their side of the bargain by providing accurate accounts, and, on the other, what the consequences are if the public questions mass media discourse to the extent of losing faith in it, seeking out its own 'truth' elsewhere?

'Newstoriography' and 'Passivication'

Such questions are not new, but they are persistent. As questions, they may, to specialists in the field, seem evident to the point of naivety, but answers to them are contested not only within the wordplay between theorists, but also in the confrontations between the common sense and everyday practice of journalists and public on the one hand, and the findings of engaged practical critics and analysts on the other.

Two neologisms will help to conceptualise the approach taken here:

Newstoriography

Pierre Bourdieu has stated cogently, but in relation to *legal* discourse, that it is 'a creative speech which brings into existence that which it utters', going on to say that it 'creates what it utters in contrast to all derived, observational statements, which simply record a pre-existent given' (Bourdieu 1991:42).

While these statements may be easily understood when referring to legal discourse, they are more contentious when applied, as is the intention here, to journalistic discourse. It may surely be agreed that journalism should precisely be seen as 'derived, observational statements, which simply record a pre-existent given', for this is what liberal minded common sense tells us, and what mainstream reporters and news purveyors would assert and wish us to believe of their products. The concept of newstoriography upturns such assertions. A derivative of 'historiography', it names the undertaking of charting and analysing news discourses within their ideological and political contexts, just as historiography does for historical discourses. The importance of historiography is an established ingredient of historians' debates, and there is widespread, if by no means universal, recognition among the interested public that historical narratives of major past events vary substantially between nations, ideologies and periods. The application of the same criteria to serious journalistic output in one's own country or region, with its *prima facie* claims to immediacy and authenticity, is, however, far less common, and can meet with heated opposition. There is widespread acceptance that, while *others* are victims of propaganda or falsified views of events, *we* are in receipt of reliable, balanced information, and *we* are alert enough to recognise any attempts to subject us to 'spin' or propaganda.

Newstoriography thus involves the work of unmasking news creation, approaching media discourse as something which predominantly 'creates what it utters', rather than 'records a pre-existent given', and deals in 'moments of untruth' (half truth, distortion, distraction) more often than 'moments of truth'. It envisions public understanding of local, national and global environments as substantially dependent on individually absorbed and semi-digested accumulations of constructed media stories, and thus attributes a manipulative power to the language of journalism which is substantially greater than that usually accorded to it. This can be seen as a specific application of Bourdieu's more general statement which concludes the passage cited above:

> One should never forget that language, by virtue of the infinite generative but also originative capacity [...] which it derives from its power to produce existence by producing the collectively recognised, and thus realized, representation of existence, is no doubt the principal support of the dream of absolute power (ibid).

A link must also be established between newstoriography and historiography insofar as the former blends into the latter and eventually becomes part of it. In the twentieth century context, it may be argued, historiography is to a considerable degree *old* newstoriography, and newstoriography can be perceived conversely as largely a continuation of historiography. Except when revolutions take place, new lies are transformed with time into old truths, which act as the reference points for newer lies in a process of constantly self-replicating distortion or mendacity. Moments of untruth reproduce further moments of untruth, thus corrupting the future as well as the past. One of the key tasks of newstoriography is thus to trace genealogies, family trees of untruths across the generations, demonstrating their ongoing influence on the perceived historical process.

Passivication

There is no inevitability about the receivers of journalistic discourse accepting the product which is purveyed to them. Quite apart from all the (unsurprising) evidence that audiences do not absorb news in the same form as it is put out (for example Morley 1992, Ang 1996) there are significant examples (to be referred to later) of non-acceptance of, or active resistance to, journalistic versions and framing of events. Journalistic discourse thus does not have automatic power to control or influence the minds of its consumers. Media decision makers can and do misjudge the malleability and credulity of their public. If they are to gain, maintain and increase their audience or readership, they have to work constantly to do so by using a range of discursive mystifications, devices and techniques to ensure that the consumers will 'buy', literally and figuratively, what they market to them. This is done directly, in terms of advertising, or indirectly, in terms of headlines, images and stories that 'sell' and convince as accounts of events which fit into the newstoriographical framework.

The expectation here is that most media audiences, who are also citizens, would *want* to be active, to feel that they were taking part in society and in democratic processes. Most, if asked whether they would like to participate in public decisions and processes which affect their lives, would reply in the positive. Yet only a small minority is actually active in this way, between one election and the next, with the rest being caught in indifference, alienation, resignation, evasion ('doing other things'), and feelings of powerlessness or isolation. In other words, it may be argued, they are subject to processes of anti-democratic 'passivication'. Something takes place which diverts their will from even minor 'public sphere' activity into actual passivity. In trying to locate and define this, the roles of media structures, patterns of communication, and discourse need to be carefully examined.

Four factors come into play here. First, media organisations, private or public, have a vested interest in preserving the societal and economic power structures of which they are a key component. Second, media contact with and supply of information to the public has become largely a top-down process, in which individuals define their social posture (their knowledge base and position within the spectrum of acceptable opinion) more in relation to their newspapers, TVs, radios, or web-based information (of which only a token amount is counter-hegemonic) than to their likewise media-influenced peers or to local or alternative socio-political organisations or movements. Third, media discourse successfully conveys to individuals that they are free to form and voice their opinions, but that the 'experts' and 'authorities' know best and are in charge. Fourth, there is constant media encouragement to spend time on consumption, distraction and self-gratification, mostly and increasingly supplied by the media – 'staying in is the new going out', as recent BBC self-promotion has it. Where these factors can be observed, an effective system of passivication can be shown to be operating.

Certainly, factors such as the education system, forces of law and order, employers and work conditions, economic and class status, and non-media-based distractions also play key roles, which take their due place in any comprehensive analysis. There is no wish here to understate their importance. But it is nevertheless posited that, in twentieth and twenty-first century Europe, as in the USA, and to an increasing extent globally, a central influential role in public passivication has been played by the media, and particularly by journalistic discourse. In the body of this book, arguments and cases are exposed which develop and test this hypothesis.

The well-worked combination of newstoriography and passivication make up a potentially powerful set of instruments for manufacturing public consent to the will of economic, political and economic elites, and it becomes more plausible and therefore effective as its pedigree lengthens and its genealogies of untruths become increasingly complex and unfathomable. The longer lies are believed, and the more effects they have had, the more difficult they are to disbelieve. In pragmatic terms, the more engrained they become, the 'truer' they become, as long as the *status quo* prevails.

Some readers will have initial reactions to what has preceded along the lines that exaggerated or overstated assertions with regard to the media, media discourse and mainstream journalism are being put forward. Certainly, there have been intentionally provocative statements, and in the course of the coming narrative, some hard edges may need to be rounded off. The challenge of the series of case studies to be presented here is, however, to test this 'exaggerated' hypothesis without prejudice. It will be the readers' task to determine whether that testing delivers convincing conclusions, and whether they ultimately confirm, modify or contradict the hypothesis.

The Critical Pedigree

Chapter 2 establishes a genealogy of the hypothesis itself. By tracing key formulations of components of the kind of radical media critique proposed here across the decades of the twentieth and early twenty-first centuries, it will demonstrate that there is a strong and distinguished tradition of 'exaggerating' media power and 'overstating' criticism of journalistic practices. Starting with Kraus, Tönnies and Tarde at the outset of the century, it includes Gramsci before following the ideas of Frankfurt School writers across the Atlantic, absorbing the case of McLuhan, and moving on to Chomsky, Herman, Postman and McChesney. Back in Europe, it quotes the work of the Glasgow Media Group and of Critical Linguists and Discourse Analysts (Fowler, Fairclough), as well as Cultural Studies theorists (Hall) and radical journalists (Pilger). It also assesses the key importance in this context of the French thinkers, Foucault, Debord, Bourdieu and Mattelart, and of Habermas in Germany, and concludes by looking at the work of Martín Barbero and others in Latin America, and of Castells in Spain and the USA. The above list is indicative, but it suffices to outline from the outset the extent and diversity, as well as the increasing complexity of the intellectual tradition which is being drawn on here.

Methodology

There is significant resonance between the ideas formulated so far and the growing body of work which emerged from the late 1980s onwards under the name of Critical Discourse Analysis (CDA). In terms of both ideas and methodology CDA builds on previous work to draw together and propose more systematic frameworks for thinking and research which places at the centre, and investigates relationships between, discourse, ideology and power.

There is by now a substantial academic cottage industry and body of writing which elucidates the theory and demonstrates the practice of CDA, but it is not the task here to summarise this. Suffice it to say that works by Norman Fairclough in Britain (Fairclough 1992, 1995) and Ruth Wodak with her collaborators at the Viennese School of Discourse Analysis (Wodak *et al.* 1999) *inter alia* present clear expositions of the field. A section in Chapter 2 locates CDA specifically within the longer genealogy of radical media criticism, although media discourse analysis is only one branch of CDA. The case studies in this book from Chapter 3 onwards concur with and are indebted to the CDA paradigm, both in terms of attitude and in terms of analytical approach, while at the same time, I believe, extending a customised understanding of CDA into places where it has not yet been. In terms of attitude and ideological perspective, the current project acknowledges key formulations to be found in the work of Wodak and Fairclough; it will be clear how these statements dovetail with positions already described. In his book *Media Discourse*, Fairclough, who in turn acknowledges intellectual roots in the British and French critical traditions (especially Critical Linguistics, Foucault) recognises the power of mass media discourse in processes of social change:

> Given the focal position of the mass media in contemporary social systems, there can be little argument about their relevance to the study of socio-cultural change. What will be less obvious to many social scientists, and more contentious, is that analysis of the *language* of the mass media can make a substantive contribution to such research (Fairclough 1995:7).

Elsewhere, Fairclough makes clear his belief that those wielding media power, with its 'linguistic-discoursal nature' can and do abuse that power through concealed and misleading practices. In *Discourse and Social Change*, he writes: 'The news media can be regarded as effecting the ideological work of transmitting the voices of power in a disguised and covert form', and goes on:

> The media generally purport to deal in fact, truth and matters of knowledge. They systematically turn into 'facts' what can often be no more than interpretations of complex and confusing sets of events [...]. Newspapers tend to offer sometimes contending [...] versions of the truth, each of which is based on the implicit and *indefensible* claim that events can be transparently and categorically represented, and perspective can be universalised. This myth underpins the ideological work of the media, offering images and categories for reality, positioning and shaping social subjects, and contributing for the most part to social control and reproduction (Fairclough 1992:160-61).

Wodak situates the Vienna School 'within Critical Discourse Analysis as well as within the philosophical and sociological tradition of Critical Theory' (Wodak et al. 1999:7). Thus, highlighting influence from the German tradition, she and her team see CDA as a means of emancipatory social engagement:

> The aim of Critical Discourse Analysis is to unmask ideologically permeated and often obscured structures of power, political control, and dominance, as well as strategies of discriminatory inclusion and exclusion in language use. In contrast to other types of discourse and conversation analysis, Critical Discourse Analysis does not pretend to be able to assume an objective, socially neutral analytical stance. Indeed practitioners of Critical Discourse Analysis believe that such ostensible political indifference ultimately assists in maintaining an unjust status quo. Critical Discourse Analysis, which is committed to an emancipatory, socially critical approach, allies itself with those who suffer political and social injustice. Its aim is therefore to intervene discursively in given social and political practices (Wodak *et al.* 1999:8).

In terms of analytical approach, a merging of Wodak's and Fairclough's schemes also serves as a guideline for this project. Wodak proposes a triangulation of historical, socio-political and linguistic perspectives when tackling a given theme or issue, and an approach to the text for analysis which involves a further triangulation between its extra-linguistic social setting, its co-text or semantic environment, and its intertextual or interdiscursive references (see Wodak *et al.* 1999:10). Fairclough's three-dimensional conception of discourse is comparable to the above, with its division into social practice, discursive practice, and text, whereby micro-analysis of the structure and salient features of the text is linked to its means and mode of production, distribution and reception. These in turn are shown in their necessary interaction with the macro-analytic level of the broader socio-political and ideological context. While the approach of this project assimilates the spirit and framework of CDA into its methodology, it also appropriates these into its specific historical dimension, its tracing over time of 'moments of untruth', 'genealogies of lies', cumulative newstoriographies and perpetuated processes of public passivication. It is this further admixture which constitutes the new direction taken here.

Moving Goalposts?

In a study of this range, covering examples over the time span of a century in which the media or mass communications age developed from possessing a single mass medium, the newspaper, through the advent of radio, the development of television, and its evolution from national terrestrial to global cable and satellite, and finally to the impact of computer networks and the world wide web, the question clearly arises as to whether the same interpretative concepts can possibly cover this series of explosions of technological revolution and exponential geographical expansion. What did Alice Schalek, reporting from the trenches in 1915 for the Viennese *Neue Freie Presse* with her pen, notebook and occasional dispatches via field telephone have in common with the BBC's Kate Adie with her satellite broadcasting equipment in the Iraqi desert in 1991, supposedly beaming instantaneous words and images around the world? What did the Viennese First World War news consumers reading their twice daily editions, with their week old reports, have in common with war news consumers around the turn of the twenty-first century to whom 24-hour news from several rival channels, instantaneous TV images, incessant radio and newspaper loquacity, and mushrooming websites were all accessible from their armchairs?

The initial answer would seem to be 'very little'. Nick Stevenson puts it this way in his 1999 book *The Transformation of the Media*:

> The transformation of the media at the end of the twentieth century is one of the most important social changes currently facing advanced industrial and indeed global societies [...]. Our culture is more profoundly mediated than any other that has existed within human history [...] if we compare our 'common world' to those that lived at the end of the nineteenth century then one of the major differences we could point towards would be the genuinely mass development of public systems of communication. It is indeed hard to imagine what our lives would be like without the mass media. News from the world's four

corners taking months rather than seconds to arrive, politicians escaping the visible public scrutiny of the cameras [...]. Yet as we come to the century's close, these shared networks of communication are arguably undergoing a change as deep seated as the initial provision of mass television. The emergence of new technologies in respect of digital television, video recorders, the internet and a host of other features are reshaping our shared cultural landscape (Stevenson 1999:1).

The implication here is that, thanks to technological progress, media audiences could get a far more realistic, detailed and accurate account of what was going on in the world around them in 1999, when the above passage was written, than was conceivable a century previously.

Yet while the changes are self-evident, and both the public and media analysts were and are confronted with a bewilderingly rapid pace of development, in which each innovation brings its own socio-cultural issues and subjects for research, one may still argue, along with Steiner, that, in terms of the use and abuse of discourse, the *deep* change took place towards the end of the nineteenth century. In this perspective, subsequent technological transformations may dazzle with their scope, speed and reach, but it could be said that their main achievement has been the more rapid, comprehensive and ubiquitous dispersion of the same lies, distortions and deceits with the same, only expanded, economic and political motives. If this can be convincingly argued, the vital focus for research and analysis – *the point where it has the capacity to influence cultural change* – is not the power of glittering innovations in media technology itself. Rather, it is the way in which new technologies have been continually and effectively subjugated to the blinding power of the corrupted word and image within hegemonic struggles to maximise control of consumer thought patterns and routines in the interests of those power elites wishing to uphold their dominant position in a fundamentally unjust socio-economic system.

The passage quoted above from Nick Stevenson alludes to the big *contrasts* in the media landscape between 1900 and 2000. Let us now confront ourselves with six big *likenesses* which may equally serve as reference points through the case studies which follow:

1. A context in which all, or virtually all, public information – be it true, false, partial or distorted – on the place, people and issues involved, is derived, directly or indirectly, from the media, and in which a regular flow of media output virtually monopolises discourse on the subject.

2. A context in which the media are operating in and with the criteria of a market economy and the primacy of business interests. News is treated as a commodity, the public as consumers. 'Choice' is offered within a limited 'acceptable' spectrum of opinion (where 'acceptable' means that which may contradict, but does not upset the dominant propaganda).

3. A general readiness of the media to be censored, or to self-censor – that is, to lie and manipulate discourse and images – in the interests of the power elites of which they form a part, or at least to acquiesce in what is manifestly one-sided and falsifying.

4. A context in which the public is to be persuaded of the desirability or necessity of war, and in which, as a consequence, the barbarity of war, and the motives behind it,

must be concealed – that is presented and edited, or otherwise manipulated so as to be rendered acceptable – while at the same time preserving the public illusion of free choice.

5. A cultural linguistic context in which the great majority of customers are ready to accept that what is propagated to them as 'news' is true, and to suspend their critical faculties, imagination and humanity with regard to warlike and exploitative actions perpetrated in their name for the duration of those actions, and when constructing their memories of (or forgetting) them.

6. A cultural linguistic context in which the great majority of consumers have been led to believe through media discourse that they are powerless to bring about change, and that their expected role is to remain at the very least passive and consenting. Token opposition may be tolerated to the extent that this consensus is not disturbed, and to the extent that it can be held up as proof of freedom and pluralism.

These observations may seem over-deterministic and over-ideological – especially to those detained by hegemonic media self-definitions or indulging themselves in the hall of mirrors of post-modernism. However, the issue in the present context is whether their credibility will be sustainable through the case studies that follow; particularly whether or to what extent they may need to be modified in the face of the analysis of relatively 'successful' counter-hegemonic discourses – that is those which brought about, or at least threatened to bring about, their own transformations against all expectations (see Chapters 7 and 8).

The Power of Hegemonic Discourse

Chapters 3, 4, 5, 6, 9, 10 and 11 are comprised of specific discourse-based case studies relating to mass media power at key moments of the twentieth century. The first two of these centre on critical approaches to selected writings of the Austrian critic and satirist, Karl Kraus on the subject of the role of the press in the 1914-18 war, and in the rise of National Socialism. Although Kraus's writings are little known in the anglophone world, his status as the first to recognise, and devote the major part of his life's work to demonstrating the impact of media discourse on events, history and cultural consciousness is advanced here, and cannot be disputed. Central aspects of his Vienna-based satirical dramatised documentary account of the 1914-18 war, *The Last Days of Humanity*, are analysed here from the perspective of his ironic, self-confessed 'exaggeration' of the role of the press in creating the possibility of the war's outbreak, the initial public euphoria surrounding it, and the acceptance of its continuation throughout the four years.

Kraus's writings of the 1920s and 1930s then form the basis for an examination of the role of media corruption of language in the rise of German and Austrian fascism. Kraus expounded passionately, and with a vast accumulation of evidence, that it was corrupt journalistic discourse which was at the cultural root of the descent into Nazi barbarism of the German-speaking world. In placing media discourse at the centre of his cultural analysis, he opened, at the outset of the century, a debate which was still controversially alive, and just as relevant, at the end of it. Krausian formulations, and the challenges they pose, are central to the narrative of this study.

The following two chapters are set within the framework of the 'Cold War' (itself a highly dubious journalistic designation which passed into common parlance and accepted historical discourse). The modalities of public discourse during this period (still hovering at the time of writing at the interface of newstoriography and historiography) in East and West, are far from having received a full and just analysis, and these chapters represent no more than microscopic, but, for all that, not superficial, and perhaps symptomatic, cases. The first examines Hergé's cartoon story *Tintin au Pays des Soviets*. Appearing originally in serialised form, starting in 1929, in the children's section of the Belgian daily *Le Vingtième Siècle*, it appeared again in a bound facsimile edition in 1981, and was reprinted in 1988. It thus represents one way among many in which young people in a particular corner of the Western world were exposed to crude anti-Soviet propaganda, presented as entertainment, in popular culture, via the media, first in the earlier years of Stalin's rule in the Soviet Union, then at the beginning of the Reagan era with the escalation of the nuclear arms race, and finally right up to the end of the 'Cold War' period, and the collapse of the Soviet bloc. A further edition was also published for the new millennium.

The Western hegemonic view of the Soviet bloc to which virtually all young people in Britain and the rest of the Western world were exposed was not fundamentally different from that of the Belgian comic strip. The results of a survey carried out by the present author in the mid 1980s are analysed in the next chapter. Here, questionnaires responded to by students in higher education in Britain, whose courses included studies of a member of the 'enemy bloc', the German Democratic Republic, provide evidence both of propaganda-based negative predispositions of the sample towards the communist bloc, of which almost all participants had no direct experience, and of the relative lack of power of the education system, when weighed against other discursive influences, to counter prejudices and change inaccurate images. Although the 1980s was a period of significant resistance to dominant anti-Soviet discourse in the West, as will be shown in a later chapter, it may be seen that propaganda in the print and broadcast media preserved, if with some difficulty, sufficient public consent to Anglo-American escalation of the nuclear arms race by maintaining and strengthening distorted images of the Soviet threat.

Western 'Cold War' victory, bringing the collapse of Soviet control over Eastern Europe, and of the Soviet Union itself in 1989-1990, together with the events leading to German unification, provide manifold opportunities to debate the interplay between historic events and the active role of media images and discourse in them. Chapter 9 again focuses on the pivotal German situation, as emblematic of the broader transformations, attempting to delineate the particular use that was made of the media in creating the story of the demise of the German Democratic Republic and the 'inevitability' of a German unification which was far from most German minds in November 1989 at the opening of the Berlin Wall.

Next, in Chapter 10, the role of the mass media in provoking nationalism and xenophobia in the European geopolitical context is highlighted, using the case study of Anglo-German relations. In the UK, the issue and implications of German unification, combined with polarised negative positions on Britain's role in the European Union, taken up by sections of the media in alliance with a powerful section of elite opinion, provided in the 1990s the pretext for a wave of xenophobic anti-German discourse, based on clichéd constructions of history and national character, in both print and broadcast media. The image of the European Union was constructed as an undemocratic German conspiracy for achievement of its historic ambition of European domination. The chapter analyses how images of Germany and 'the Germans', with repeated references to the Nazi period, were deployed over the decade to fuel the anti-EU case being made by the UK's europhobes. Working with sympathetic multinational media corporation bosses, they attempted to block at every stage the further integration of Britain, also constructed in terms of distorted history, into the European project.

One of the concluding major events of the century was the war over Kosovo. Just as the initial case study in this series covered war sparked off in the Balkans, so this one, demonstrating the power and historic role of dominant media discourses, returns to the same area, where conflicting regional historiographies and newstoriographies may be seen to have played a key role in the perpetuation of conflict and violence. Chapter 11 concentrates, however, less on the discursive causes of the Kosovo war itself, than on the 'mediatic' means used to convince the public that this was a clean and justified conflict against a Hitler-type dictator whom it would have been folly to appease.

The Potential of Counter-hegemonic Discourse

To have confined the argument to a demonstration of mass media power would have put an excessively deterministic gloss on the ability of hegemonic media discourse to influence minds and events. While it has been argued that elite controlled mass media discourse, and particularly mainstream journalistic discourse, needs to be given its due place as a key powerful actor in twentieth century events and history, it has also been stated that such power is not inevitable. The image of the public as captive consumers whose thoughts and activities (or passivities) are at the mercy of manipulated media discourse can, depressingly enough, be sustained in many settings and circumstances, but as well as such instances of the power of untruth, there are also occasional, if often temporary and geographically limited 'emancipatory moments', and, more frequently, moments of doubt and uncertainty when power elites themselves are genuinely split or otherwise weakened (as opposed to giving the illusion of pluralism by emphasising their differences on secondary issues), or when counter-hegemonic forces muster themselves into progressive social movements which discursively and politically challenge top-down control. The refined power structures of entrenched free market 'liberal democracy' are generally well equipped to see off or accommodate such threats, but that does not mean that the threats are not real. It is the habitual view of power elites that the collective public mind is there to be controlled or 'passivised', and in the twentieth century, media discourse was instrumentalised to bring this about; but a public which becomes wise to discursive manipulation, and perceives the gap between lived experience and the story being spun to it (as did the majority of East European populations in the run up to 1989, when faced with somewhat cruder propagandistic methods than Western audiences are normally confronted with) can be open to accepting radically different discourses which it sees as 'truer', and which pose fundamental challenges to the *status quo*. The ability to distinguish between authentic, emancipatory challenges and those built on further dimensions of 'untruth' depends on individual and collective development of ethical vigilance and critical discursive sensitivity, and the effective operation of counter-hegemonic public sphere networks.

Chapters 7 and 8 examine two such challenges which developed in late twentieth century Europe, again via the analysis of specific alternative discourses which they created.

The first of them looks at how 'alternative thinkers' in the German Democratic Republic developed their discursive and political challenge to established power in the 1980s, and at how they developed alternative media in a discursive cat and mouse relationship with the enforcers of an authoritarian regime. In many ways, the GDR government's behaviour was, from a Machiavellian standpoint, a textbook example of how *not* to accommodate or assimilate forces of radical reform from within; its leaders were, it seems, so caught up in existential fears for the survival of their state and conception of society that they were unable, until far too late, either to be receptive to Gorbachev's discourses of change, or to distinguish between genuine dissident messages from within and Western ideological interference. The regime could not survive, but the subsequent irony was that the majority of the East German populace, having been perceptive enough to see through the distorted discourse of its own state, utterly failed at crucial moments to see through that of its Western benefactor turned predator.

Following this, an aspect of Western critiques of global East-West ideological conflict, and particularly the underpinning of this divide in Europe by closed frontiers and massive nuclear and conventional military confrontation, is considered. The peace movements of Western Europe, at their strongest in the United Kingdom and the Federal Republic of Germany in the 1980s, successfully developed and propagated counter-hegemonic discourses, in the face of the dominant media, to the extent of gaining the support of a substantial active minority of citizens, and of being perceived as a genuine threat by established power elites. Although the ultimate impact of the peace movement in the 1980s is still subject to claim and counter-claim in subsequent (unequal) struggles for historiographical and newstoriographical hegemony, there can be no doubt that it brought into being alternative discourses which helped to bring about mass citizen activism and caused, however one views it, substantial political disturbance by its undermining of 'Cold War' strategic orthodoxy. Selected texts emanating from the organisation END (European Nuclear Disarmament) furnish the materials for this case study.

The Outset of the Twenty-first Century

The final case study, Chapter 12, observes the processes of hegemonic persuasion, and resistance to it, in the early years of the twenty-first century, and particularly in the aftermath of the events of 11 September 2001. Looking particularly at examples of European reactions, and focusing on BBC *Panorama* programmes, as well as press coverage and oppositional activity, it examines the presentation of concepts such as the 'axis of evil' and 'anticipatory pre-emption' in relation to the 'war on terrorism', and efforts, on the one hand, to create support for, and, on the other hand, to oppose the US-led invasion of Iraq.

Aims and Contours

It is essential to this book that it focuses, through specific symptomatic discursive examples, on *decisive* events, conflicts and issues of central concern to the Western world in the media age, and this has led to an initial concentration on materials concerned with Germany and, in the post-1945 period, on central Europe and the East-West fissure. The later case studies then cover contemporary issues over a wider geographical and thematic range. The subject matter is as limitless as grains of sand, each of which may contain a universe, and the choice, ultimately, has been subjective. In terms of traditional scientific criteria, the narrative cannot offer 'proof', but it does seek to demonstrate recognisable discursive processes, draw out their cultural and historical significance, and contribute to an accumulation of evidence concerning the key and constant relationship between mass media discourse and historic events across the ceaselessly developing and expanding media environment that characterised both the twentieth century and the early years of the twenty-first.

If the period's most traumatic and grotesque events and processes have been substantially more the result of false or distorted mass mediated discourse, moments of untruth, than is habitually recognised, then this must have consequences in any diagnosis of the tragic failings of what stands out as humankind's most barbaric era. The failure of citizens and consumers to understand, be sceptical about and see through the discursive manipulation to which they have been subjected on the one hand, and the corruption of discursive manipulators and their paymasters on the other, take their place more prominently than has been normally supposed among the key factors in the insanities of recent and current generations.

Chapter 2

Radical Media Critics.
The Four Generations

There corresponds to the capitalist mode of production a type of intellectual production quite different from that which corresponded to the medieval mode of production. Unless material production itself is understood in its specific historical form, it is impossible to grasp the characteristics of the intellectual production which corresponds to it, or the reciprocal action between the two (Karl Marx 1959:82).

Introduction

One of the spurs to undertake this project was the thought that radical mass media criticism is almost as old as the mass media. Whether or not they derived their positions from Marx's insights or elsewhere, in every decade of the twentieth century major social critics and cultural analysts had formulated *fundamental* critiques of the role played by the mass media. Yet the significance, substance and implications of this were neglected. Doubtless the media themselves were actively involved in the maintenance of the muted reaction. As the Norwegian historian Hans Fredrik Dahl has said:

Most media themselves tend to function in a way which plays down the very notion of a media past. History or historical events are of course quite often displayed by the media, but rarely in the way showing that they themselves have one. Intrinsically they hide their clues (Dahl 1998).

Academic writing around this subject also remains fragmented. Mattelart observes that the sociology of communications is 'far from having thrown itself into the cross-fertilising approach', stating:

As the third millennium draws near, this conception of history is still very much in the minority, and indeed more and more isolated, when it comes to approaching the evolution of technologies and systems of information and communication (Mattelart 1996:ix).

Likewise, Vogel and Engell point out: 'Mediology is still in the process of constituting itself. A history of mediology has thus not yet been written, and will for the time being remain unwritten' (Pias et al. 1999:8-9. Translation JT).

Correspondingly, in the corpus of media history writing, neither could a comprehensive account of this radical critical tradition be found, nor had the major historical and socio-cultural implications of the radical critiques been gathered into a coherent narrative across the decades. While the case studies in the coming chapters start to fulfil the latter task, it is the aim of the current chapter to provide a concise sketch of the former. This will serve as a frame within which to weave radical critical discourses with the complex continuum of reported current affairs – a key base material of twentieth century history writing. For it is only with constant dialectical awareness of the radical critical perspective that the generations of 'moments of untruth' can be traced.

What is meant here by *radical* media critics? A working definition runs as follows: radical mass media criticism situates the mass media, as they operated in the liberal, free market societies which dominated the twentieth century and continue into the twenty-first, close to the pinnacle of power. As an integrated element of the elite of these societies, top media entrepreneurs and managers, and thence the organisations they controlled, had, and still have, the job of ensuring, in their own interests as well as in those of the rest of the elite, through mass media distribution and content, that the public was and remains compliant, and that the status quo remains intact. Thus such *de facto* consequences of the liberal, free market system as mass destruction in war, and extremes of poverty and wealth, have been continuously rendered acceptable and accepted by the majority of consumers. In short, according to radical critiques, the mass media have through their history been operated by key members, and have functioned in the interests, of the ruling elites in inherently violent and unjust systems, and have thus served to undermine the freedom they have loudly claimed to be representing and upholding. We are used to hearing such media roles attributed to authoritarian or totalitarian dictatorships. For radical media critics, precisely because the mass media have acted in disguise, they can be seen to have functioned most successfully in societies claiming liberal, democratic credentials. A striking expression of this position comes from Eduardo Galeano:

> The communication media are monopolised by the few that can reach everyone. Never have so many been held incommunicado by so few. More and more have the right to hear and see, but fewer and fewer have the privilege of informing, giving their opinion and creating. The dictatorship of the single word and the single image, much more devastating than that of the single party, is imposing a life whose exemplary citizen is a docile consumer and passive spectator built on the assembly line following the North American model of commercial television (Herman & McChesney 1997:vi).

The tradition of radical mass media criticism is being presented here, with good reason, as a contemporary history rooted in nineteenth century developments. However, Mattelart's warning in *The Invention of Communication* concerning the archaeology of knowledge about communication needs to be taken into account:

> The mediacentric perspective causes us to forget that the history of communication possesses a trunk that existed long before the appearance of modern mass media. The media tropism engenders a reductive vision of the history of communication. Worse, it

provokes a historical amnesia that prevents us from discerning where the truly important stakes lie in the current and rapid transformation of our contemporary mode of communication. It is this rejection of history that explains why the debates on contemporary communication are so meagre, so banal, and so mired in dualistic visions and impossible dilemmas [...]. Paradoxically, we learn more about the uncertainties of the future by asking why, four centuries ago, the modern notion of communication emerged alongside the ideals of Reason and Progress, and how they became embodied in the visions of nineteenth century utopian thinkers, than by listening to the latest speech on the thaumaturgic virtues of digital superhighways, arteries of twenty-first century 'Global Information Infrastructure', and to the latest manifesto for the conquest of the natural-technological frontier through the development of private enterprise. This is all the more true in that our contemporary era is pervaded by the crisis of the ideals of Reason and Progress, the offspring of both the Enlightenment and liberal capitalism (Mattelart 1996:x).

With this in mind, we may also, in placing criticism of media discourse at the centre of this analysis, think back to Jonathan Swift's *Proposal For Correcting, Improving and Ascertaining the English Tongue* (1712), in which he posited that reform of language was a vehicle for social and political change (see Crowley 1996:59).

The First Generation

While other names can be put forward, and definitive genealogies have yet to find general acceptance, it is suggested here that the German Ferdinand Tönnies, the Frenchman Gabriel Tarde, and above all the Austrian Karl Kraus stand out as principal seminal thinkers in the lineage of radical mass media criticism. All three produced relevant work around the turn of the twentieth century and during its opening decades.

These figures lived, spent their formative years and worked at a period in which the enterprise of mass gathering, production and distribution of news and information – mass public discourse presenting a particular view of the world – was in its infancy. The technological, economic, demographic and educational factors behind this only need indicative mention here. Europe's nineteenth century industrial revolution and all that is associated with it in the field of communications – railways, telegraph and telephone, photography, industrialised paper manufacture and mechanised printing processes, the growth of the cities and urban culture, the rapid increase in literacy, the demand for news and advertising in a competitive business environment – all these combined to open up the possibility and concept of daily or twice daily newspapers as viable commercial propositions, and integral features of liberal capitalist society. Newspapers had, of course, existed before, but the fundamental difference was that now they became big business. The task of public information passed into the hands of successful entrepreneurs, and became subject to the rigours of commercial priorities. More precisely, the presentation of public discourse, thus the use of language itself, and any ethical commitment to accuracy, impartiality or truth were at this point subordinated to the rules of marketing and the compulsions of profit making. If an untruth (or distorted or half truth) was more saleable, or more in the commercial or political interests of the owner (his class or his representatives) than a truth, then the untruth would be printed. This was the crucial first step in breaking the pact between 'word' and 'world' in mass consumed public discourse that Steiner meant when he spoke of a 'genuine revolution of spirit'. It was no longer a *fundamental axiom* that language should be there to communicate meaning about the world (even if it did not always succeed or live up to this); instead, the basis or *raison d'être* of discursive practice was selling and propaganda in the interests of the investors in the enterprise. This, logically, had to be kept from the readers themselves by concealment or distraction, for if it became apparent, they would be less inclined to consume the product unquestioningly. In this context, ideological and economic forces effectively snuffed out independent and radical journalism.

Tönnies, Tarde and Kraus spent their formative years at the moment when all this was happening for the first time. Several generations later, it requires an imaginative leap to immerse oneself in the newness of what they were experiencing. If, however, at the turn of the twenty-first century we felt the transformative impact on our lives of the computer, the internet, and globalised mass communications, now, for increasing numbers, already assimilated into 'normality', and if we have been concerned that deep cultural and ethical issues raised around these developments have been brushed aside in the headlong rush to create and exploit consumer demand, then we might gain half an insight into the far more radical revolution that confronted critical thinkers around the turn of the twentieth century.

Before turning in more detail to these three seminal figures, brief mention should be made of significant forerunners and early contemporaries. The Danish theologian Sören Kierkegaard (1813-1855), in the 1840s and 1850s, was the earliest, as well as one of the most vicious of early critics of journalists and the daily press, acknowledged later by Kraus as a kindred spirit in this respect. What Kierkegaard holds against the press is not so much that it prints lies as that it elevates the trivial into the important, distracting and entertaining rather than informing, peddling sophistry and ready-made opinion in the guise of thought:

> People complain that now and again an untrue article appears in a paper, but that is just an insignificant detail. No, the whole essential form of this kind of information is false. Back in the times of antiquity, the masses were distracted with purely sensuous pleasures, with the help of money, bread and circuses, but the press now distracts the minds of the middle classes. What we need is a Pythagorean silence. There should be many more abstinence societies, helping people out of addiction to newspapers rather than addiction to brandy (1847) (Kraus 1925:1-28. Translation: JT).

Furthermore, Kierkegaard continues, the press traps readers in the sensational instant, and provides a succession of these such that it becomes impossible to see what is happening in perspective:

> The evil of the daily press lies in the fact that it is concerned to inflate the moment and make it a thousand or ten thousand times more important than it actually is. But the task

of all moral education is above all to wean people away from a life of instant gratification. Just as Chinese civilisation came to a halt at a particular stage of development, so European civilisation will come to a halt on account of its press, stopped in its tracks as a reminder of the fact that here a discovery was made which finally overwhelmed it (1848) (ibid).

Journalists come off no better in Kierkegaard's polemic: 'If Christ returned to the world today, there can be no doubt that it would not be the high priests that he pilloried, it would be the journalists' (1849) (ibid).

In 1863, Ferdinand Lassalle (1825-1864), founder of Germany's first independent labour party, his ideas associated with the revisionist wing of what, five years after his death became the united German Socialist Workers Party, identified the point at which the press was transformed into a speculative enterprise whose primary aim was profit:

From that moment on, the newspaper became a highly lucrative investment for those with a talent for making money or for publishers wanting to gain a fortune [...]. *From that moment on*, then, newspapers, while still retaining the appearance of being campaigners for ideas, changed from being educators and teachers of the people into lickspittles of the wealthy and subscribing bourgeoisie and of its tastes; some newspapers thus have their hands tied by their current subscribers, others by those whom they wish to gain, but both are always shackled by the real financial foundation of the business – advertisements. *From that moment on*, therefore, newspapers became not only the commonest of vulgar commercial operations, no different from any other, but also they became something much worse, namely *totally hypocritical* businesses, run with the pretence of fighting for great ideas and the good of the people (Lassalle 1874:14. Translation: JT).

As for journalists and their work, Lassalle saw them as pen-labourers, a proletariat of the mind, the last resort of failures in other professions, a standing army of newspaper scribes who create public opinion, and inflict deeper, more harmful, mental wounds on the people than the physical brutalities of the actual army. Workers sell their time and labour to their bosses, but journalists sell their souls, prostituting themselves by writing what the newspaper owners and editors require:

Whether they are sufficiently informed, or indeed have the slightest understanding of what they are writing, or not – the subject must be written about, the newspaper must be filled, the business requires it! To this is added the lack of time to study the subject more closely, to research appropriate books and sources, even just to reflect and collect one's thoughts. The article must be finished, the business requires it. All ignorance, all lack of acquaintance with the facts, everything, everything must be concealed as far as possible behind the devious, clichéd turn of phrase (ibid).

The rousing conclusion to the polemic runs:

Be sure to remember this: the true enemy of the people, its most dangerous enemy, and the more dangerous since it appears in the guise of a friend, is today's press! Be sure to remember with burning soul this motto which I hurl at you: hatred and contempt, death and destruction to today's press! (ibid).

In 1875, twelve years after Lassalle wrote this, Heinrich Wuttke's book *Die Deutschen Zeitschriften und die Entstehung der Öffentlichen Meinung (German Journals and the Creation of Public Opinion)* appeared. Amid a more general critique of the corruption and corruptibility of contemporary press enterprises, he singled out the Viennese press as by far the worst case and central example. This is significant for the key importance accorded in this study to the Vienna-based press criticism of Karl Kraus. Wuttke wrote:

> Berlin, Munich and other great centres too are riddled with this cancer, but nowhere has it been worse than in Vienna. [...] Vienna became the site of the worst abuses of the press. Any outstanding public figure who could be harmed by the pressure of dominant public opinion was put under surveillance by newspaper owners and producers to see if they could entrap him into their control (Wuttke 1875:405. Translation: JT).

The Viennese press itself was, Wuttke established, in the hands of the financial and business elite. He stated that the Viennese daily press had become dependent on the power of the Viennese Stock Exchange, and functioned as its tool.

We turn now in more detail to the three seminal figures identified above. **Gabriel Tarde** (1843-1904), in Mattelart's account, produced his major work in the last ten years of his life. Having come to Paris at the age of 51 from a position as magistrate in the Dordogne, he was appointed to the chair of contemporary philosophy at the *Collège de France* in 1900. His key work in the current context was *L'Opinion et la Foule* (1901).

Tarde's analysis is situated at the pivotal point between the pre-mass communications era and the media age. As the founder of social psychology, he realised the revolutionary nature of the socio-cultural changes which were occurring. It was the same 'revolution of the spirit' that Steiner has pointed to, but Tarde's focus was less on language, or, in Stuart Hall's late twentieth century terminology, the 'encoding' facet of communication, than on audiences, or 'publics' at the 'decoding' end of the process. Previous work on audiences had placed the emphasis on the crowd – a physical gathering of people – and its psychology. Tarde's contemporary, LeBon's, *Psychologie des Foules* (1895) exemplified this, portraying a threatening image of the crowd as 'delirious', subject to 'mental contagion', and consisting of 'automatons no longer guided by their will'. Although LeBon was describing mass society, and of course physical crowds by no means faded out in the mass media age, his model (apart from other failings) is still limited by this conceptualisation. Tarde, on the other hand, observed the formation of new kinds of audiences, which he named 'publics'. These were virtual crowds, without common physical location or interaction, made possible and united by the new processes of mass communication, and particularly the mass media. Tarde called journalism a 'suction pump of information', an increasingly powerful force which then disseminated its information across the world:

The winged words of the papers easily cross borders which were never crossed by the voice of the famous orator, or the party leader. Certain large newspapers, the *Times*, the *Figaro* and certain journals have their public spread throughout the entire world (Tarde 1969:286).

'Publics' in Tarde's sense are an inevitable consequence of this dissemination, created by 'regular communication of those associated by a continual flow of common information and enthusiasms' (ibid).

Tarde thus identified in the relation between mass media (at that time, the press) and 'publics', a control by the former of the latter, given the publics' inclination to 'imitation'. Public opinion is here seen as an imitation of ideas propagated by the media. It follows from this that he perceived problems concerning the power of the media in mass democracy. Tarde's ideas met with limited immediate resonance on the French scene, but they crossed the Atlantic with Robert E. Park, who specialised in the study of the role of the press in the formation of public opinion, and raised questions about the *conflictual* relationship between media and democracy. Tarde is also seen as an influence on fellow Frenchman Jules Rassak, whose book *Psychologie de l'Opinion et de la Propagande Politique* appeared somewhat later in 1927. Rassak took up a critical position with regard to commercialised news, and noted how publics saw through and rejected didactic messages, and that the most effective propaganda *disguised* itself successfully as fact. He thus pointed to the most successful manipulative technique of mass media discourse in 'free' societies through to the present.

Finally, one may look back to Tarde as an originator of debates on media effects, on the nature of audiences, and on the reception of media messages – debates which gained new currency in the 1990s.

Karl Kraus (1874-1936) lived and worked in Vienna, not as an academic or theoretician, but as a satirist, essayist, playwright, performer, poet and cultural critic. Between 1899 and 1936 he produced, and largely wrote himself, the magazine *Die Fackel (The Torch)* which, in its 922 numbers, contains the most sustained attack on the press, journalism and the journalistic corruption of language that any individual has ever produced. While he was both acclaimed and detested in Vienna for his devastating political polemics against individual journalists, editors and cultural figures, his more threatening underlying critique of media discourse and long-term cultural effects takes his writing beyond ephemeral satire and into a radical, language-based cultural criticism which transcends the time and place of its production. Kraus grew up through the founding years and rise to prominence of the first German language mass medium. Journalism in this context was a transformed profession, engendering new genres, new styles of writing, new kinds of discourse, and a new powerful elite of owners, editors and writers with potentially greater influence over mass publics than had ever been conceivable before. Kraus belonged to the first generation to be socialised in a society in which the first mass medium, the press, was an established fact of life, but an as yet unanalysed cultural presence.

Kraus's press criticism covers a period which includes both the inglorious massacre of the 1914-18 war, and the rise of fascism in Germany and Austria, with

Hitler's take-over of power. His writings on these events figure importantly in the coming chapters. The linking of the possibility of these barbaric events with his view of the destructive socio-cultural role played by the mass media is central to Kraus's position, built not so much on theory as on the massive accumulation of evidence, which rests on the conviction that journalism had risen to become the real power in the land, subjugating all other influences. In 1905, he wrote:

> Someone – was it Burke – called journalism the *fourth* estate. In his time, that was doubtless true. But in our time, it is actually the *only* estate. It has gobbled up the other three. The lay nobility says nothing, the bishops have nothing to say, and the House of Commons has nothing to say, and says it. Journalism rules us (Kraus 1905:12).

In Kraus's language-based perspective, the first mass medium rose to control its public through a stealthy process of gradual confusion and erosion of faculties by its substitution of the pure water of information with the seductive perfume of the cliché. Once the cliché, or resonant phrase takes over, Kraus argued, then a gap has opened up between language and the communication of unadulterated news; the link between the event and its understanding by the public has been broken. Once this has happened, the lie or the distortion can be presented and believed; comment, propaganda and titillation can be subtly mixed with fact; values and priorities can be surreptitiously intermingled with description such that, over a period, readers' perceptions are able to be moulded, their views of the past, present and future shaped through the linguistic hegemony of those maintaining control of the dominant medium. Kraus's work was known to the 'Frankfurt School' writers, Walter Benjamin, Max Horkheimer and Theodor Adorno, and Benjamin makes explicit their debt to him. In his essay on Kraus, he acknowledged him as the one who first posited that 'journalism is the prime expression of the changed function of language in the capitalist world', and that 'the cliché is the trademark which turns the thought into a commodity'. In the same passage, Benjamin also recognises Kraus's insight that:

> The newspaper is an instrument of power. It can derive its value only from the nature of the power which it serves. It is the expression of that power not only with regard to *what* it represents, but with regard to *how* it expresses it (Benjamin 1969:106).

There are also strong and acknowledged contemporary overtones of Kraus's work in George Steiner's formulations, already mentioned. In addition, one can see clear echoes, whether direct or indirect, in the work of British critical linguists, and of critical discourse analysts such as Norman Fairclough in Britain and Ruth Wodak, back in Vienna. Chapters 3 and 4 of this book make more detailed reference to Kraus's work.

There are considerable areas of overlap between the ideas of Tarde, Kraus and **Ferdinand Tönnies** (1855-1936), but if Tarde can be seen predominantly as the originator of the audience, or 'public' centred approach, to the mass media, and Kraus can be seen above all as the founder of the language, or 'discourse' centred analysis, then Tönnies can be situated particularly as the precursor of the 'political economy' centred perspective, although his later work can also be seen as a critical reaction to Tarde's writings.

One of the founders of modern sociology, Tönnies is best known for his development of the opposing concepts of *Gemeinschaft* (community) and *Gesellschaft* (society), the latter being the contemporary, modern development from the former, rooted and traditional social organisation. Tönnies made initial reference to public opinion and the press in his first major work, *Gemeinschaft und Gesellschaft* (1887), but returned to the subject in detail much later in his *Kritik der Öffentlichen Meinung* (Critique of Public Opinion) (1922).

For Tönnies, public opinion takes over in modern society the role played by religion in traditional communities, that is, it becomes the guiding force which defines and determines values. The press is the main organ for the formulation of public opinion, and thus editors and journalists take over in *Gesellschaft* the role previously played by priests and shamans in *Gemeinschaft*. Since the press itself in modern society is owned and controlled by the entrepreneurial middle classes, it follows that these classes dictate dominant public opinion – *the* public opinion, as he calls it. In an ideal society, public opinion would emerge from the public (the public sphere); as things are, citizens acquiesce in opinions disseminated by the articulate in positions of power – a modern secular priesthood which assures internal cohesion and the suppression of external dissent. *Kritik der Öffentlichen Meinung* was partly written during the 1914-18 war, and chapters 3 and 4 contain a 'provocative analysis of the relationship between public opinions and the role of propaganda, political parties and the press in the formation of public opinion' (Gollin & Gollin 1973).

Tönnies observes, prefiguring Noelle-Neumann's 'spiral of silence' (1984), that dominant opinion, once formed, is intolerant of opposition. Recognition of the pressure exerted by media-propagated opinions and beliefs coerces individuals and groups into self-censorship and the repression of their dissent out of fear of ostracism or punishment: 'To label deviant opinion as sin is a characteristic of the genuine public opinion as much as of religion' (Tönnies 1922:205).

Tönnies builds on Lassalle's premise that the press is a capitalist enterprise, organised to make profits for its owners; journalists in their writing have to take this primary interest into account, respecting in particular the newspaper's reliance first on its advertisers, and second on its subscribers. Only after these pressures have been taken into account can the readers' interests, or the ethics of accurate reporting enter the equation. The corruption of discourse and the misleading of readers are thus endemic in the production priorities of the press. 'Judgements and opinion are wrapped up like grocers' goods and offered for consumption in their objective reality', he wrote (Tönnies 1963:221), and elsewhere:

Every prominent newspaper is the defender of some interest and everything it says is directly or indirectly (and most effective when indirect) in support of that interest. There is no such thing at the present time as a newspaper that defends a principle (Tönnies 1922:184-86).

The major influence on the press is 'industrial capital' because, on the one hand, control of the information flow in relation to business, politics and events is important to the economic elites, and on the other, the press itself is a capitalist enterprise to whom the priorities of industrial capital also apply. For Tönnies, a compliant or favourable public opinion is the end product of the mass media production process, in collusion with the political process, such that finally:

> A particular public opinion has been manufactured, as one manufactures any manner of merchandise [...]. The powers of capital are intent not only to bring about a favourable opinion concerning their products, and an unfavourable one concerning those of their competitors, but also to promote a generalised public opinion which is designed to serve their business interests, for instance regarding a policy of protective tariffs, or of free trade, favouring a political movement or party, supporting or opposing an existing government (Cahnman & Heberle 1971:262).

Tönnies was doubtless aware of the writings on the press of his German contemporary, the economist Karl Bücher, whose essay *Das Zeitungswesen* (The Newspaper Business) first appeared in 1906 (Hinneberg 1906), and whose *Die Deutsche Tagespresse und die Kritik* (The German Daily Press and its Critics) (1915) also took up a radically critical position. In the former piece, he wrote of the influence of the press:

> Day after day it directs the minds of thousands along the same lines of thought, repeating at every opportunity and in every context the same views, opinions and judgements as if they were incontrovertible truths; ultimately, the reader comes to believe that he finds his own thoughts reflected in them. [...] He does not get time to form his own opinion [...]. Everything has been thought for him in advance; in every column, in every little announcement information is mixed with value judgements, opinions and feelings. In the end, the formulation from outside is imposed on one's own judgement like a lead weight [...]. So the view which was first put forward by one or two people in the press becomes mass opinion, its morality becomes mass morality, and its campaigning becomes a mass campaign, joined by all or the great majority of readers. It is extraordinarily difficult to withdraw from this entrapment by 'what the public has decided'; anyone who exceptionally manages to diverge from this with independent thinking is seen as an eccentric and an outsider (Bücher 1906:547. Translation: JT).

This imposition of opinion takes place, for Bücher, in publications produced primarily for profit and for the benefit of advertisers. The news and information in them are just window dressing to help sales:

> This must be said absolutely categorically. The news and editorial office is for the profit making capitalist enterprise no more than a tiresome added cost which is needed to get the advertisements in front of the eyes of people on whom they might have an effect (Bücher 1915:377).

Exactly what Tönnies and Bücher knew and thought of each other's work is less important in the present context than showing their presence and common cause at this early juncture in the genealogy of mass media criticism.

Tönnies's framework prefigures the terms of reference of the 'Frankfurt School' thinkers, and re-emerges in the thinking on the mass media of the American trio of Chomsky, Herman and McChesney, as well as, in different ways, in the work of Curran, Garnham, Murdock and Golding in the UK at the end of the twentieth century. The work of Habermas within the Frankfurt tradition is clearly in the picture as an intermediary in the case of McChesney and Herman's *The Global Media. The New Missionaries of Corporate Capitalism* (1997), while references in Herman and Chomsky's *Manufacturing Consent. The Political Economy of the Mass Media* (1988) take us indirectly back to Tönnies via the different route – largely avoiding European theoreticians – of Walter Lippmann's 1922 work *Public Opinion*, in which, in turn, are to be found significant resonances with the work of Robert E. Park. We have already mentioned Park as having been influenced by Tarde, but he also studied and wrote his doctorate *Masse und Publikum* (1904) in Germany, and integrated into his thinking Tönnies's concepts of *Gemeinschaft* and *Gesellschaft*. Tönnies was himself indebted to Park in his later refinements of Tarde's definition of 'publics'.

In all three cases, Tarde, Kraus and Tönnies, it has thus been possible to start tracing genealogies which stretch to the end of the twentieth century. The following section, however, examines continuities and developments in the second quarter of the century.

The Second Generation

Amongst the most influential in the second generation of radical critics, whose salient work was produced primarily in that part of the century in which the radio and cinema as new mass media came to co-exist with fascism and Nazism, the mass slaughter of the Second World War, and the holocaust were Gramsci in Italy, Orwell in Britain, and most crucially those associated with the earlier 'Frankfurt School' – Benjamin, Horkheimer and Adorno, initially in Germany. These thinkers all belong within the Left tradition of writers and intellectuals who, in their own ways, sought to re-evaluate and increase the importance of the cultural superstructure within the Marxist framework, where Marx's original perception and metaphor, referred to in the quotation at the top of this chapter, saw intellectual production as subordinate to and dependent on material production.

Antonio Gramsci (1891-1937) was a founder member of the Italian Communist Party (1921) and member of its Central Committee. He spent the last eleven years of his life in Mussolini's prisons from where he produced the *Prison Notebooks* and *Letters from Prison*, in which he developed his key ideas.

While Gramsci is not seen primarily as a media critic, his ideas on dominant discourses, hegemony and discursive struggle, derived from his harsh political and journalistic experience, have inspired many subsequent thinkers in the field.

Important here is Gramsci's view that current bourgeois control of society, while certainly manifest in material modes of production, is culturally embedded and naturalised in the minds of the people via its hegemony over discourse. Dominating ways of thinking, speaking, assuming, hoping, and fearing – that is to say, through language – the ruling elite controls by creating normalisation and acceptance of the status quo in the minds of those being exploited by it. Gramsci's answer to this is the creation and dissemination of counter-hegemonic discourses through which the exploited become aware of their condition, and engage in struggle for self-emancipation. Within this process, it is one role of the intellectual to formulate such counter-hegemonic discourses – new ways of thinking, speaking, and feeling, leading to new perceptions of 'normality' which will challenge the old, and build the practical processes for overcoming it.

Gramsci is today a ubiquitous presence in writings on the mass media and mass communications; it is thus difficult to trace clear paths of influence. However, it is clear that his current high level of recognition can be traced back to the 1970s when the publication of his complete works was completed in Italy, and when translations of his main works appeared. From there, a particularly strong trail can be observed in Britain from Raymond Williams through to Stuart Hall, and British Cultural Studies, and to Norman Fairclough in the field of Critical Discourse Analysis.

George Orwell (1903-1950) is included here more for the fact that he is often cited as an influential figure, and for his many striking formulations, than for his originality as a thinker on language and mass media. While his interest in language and its manipulation for political and ideological purposes is well known from his brilliant allegory *Animal Farm* (the book rather than the CIA-financed animated film version), and his great visionary novel *1984*, it is in the present context his essay *Politics and the English Language* (1946) which is habitually cited. How Orwell came to produce formulations in this essay which are so like some of those made by Karl Kraus forty years earlier is uncertain, but the affinities are clear, and have already been remarked on by Steiner, who sees Orwell as 'a more pallid but rationally usable version of Kraus' (Steiner 1996:23), while nevertheless noting that Orwell 'lacks altogether Kraus's philosophic reach and apocalyptic poetry' (Steiner 1989:112). Despite Steiner's comment, Orwell's essay does contain some resonant material, and, at least in the anglophone world, posterity accorded him greater fame than it has Kraus. Significant for this narrative are Orwell's formulations on the self-perpetuating attributes of linguistic corruption and decadence through which a downward spiral of separation of language from meaning occurs:

> Now, it is clear that the decline of a language must ultimately have political and economic causes: it is not due simply to the bad influence of this or that individual writer. But an effect can become a cause, reinforcing the original cause and producing the same effect in an intensified form, and so on indefinitely (Orwell 1946, Jackall 1995:423).

The catalyst for linguistic decadence is, for Orwell, as for Kraus, the 'phrase' or the 'cliché':

> As soon as certain topics are raised, the concrete melts into the abstract and no one seems able to think in turns of speech that are not hackneyed: prose consists less and less of *words* chosen for the sake of their meaning, and more of phrases tacked together like the sections of a prefabricated hen-house (ibid:425).

> This invasion of one's mind by ready-made phrases [...] can only be prevented if one is constantly on guard against them, and every such phrase anaesthetises a portion of one's brain (ibid:434).

It is right that Orwell does not draw out the full cultural implications of his statements in the essay, but they represent a link in the chain insofar as they were specifically taken up and debated critically in the USA by, among others, Neil Postman as an important antecedent of the arguments he presents in *Amusing Ourselves to Death* (1985), and Edward Herman in *Beyond Hypocrisy* (1992).

Much contemporary writing on mass media analysis inaccurately uses the **'Frankfurt School'** as its starting point, as if the writings of Benjamin in the 1930s and then Horkheimer and Adorno in the 1940s were the start of the theoretical debate. The formulations of these thinkers, whose ideas were formed in the context of German society and culture in the ten years preceding the Nazi takeover, before Benjamin's suicide and Horkheimer's and Adorno's emigration to the USA, are seen as heavily influenced by the use of the mass media – especially radio and film as then new media – for propaganda purposes by the Nazi party and eventual regime. The success, in its own terms, of the Nazi propaganda machine is seen to have induced in the Frankfurt Critical Theorists a deterministic view of the power of the mass media, or 'culture industries' over the public mind, and hence to have led them into an impasse of cultural pessimism. Some subsequent critiques of what is presented as the 'Frankfurt School' position set it up somewhat simplistically to represent an extreme point of view, superseded or discredited by the results of more recent thinking and research. A typical account of this kind of packaging can be found in Graeme Turner's book *British Cultural Studies* (1996). Here, it is reported:

> The *first* phase of media research (from the 1920s to the 1940s) can be exemplified by the work of the Frankfurt School [...]. Researchers in this phase saw the media as a powerful and largely unmediated force that had entirely negative effects on mass culture [...]. The Frankfurt School's warnings about the manipulative potential of mass culture were *made redundant* by pluralism' (Turner 1996:184-85. JT's italics).

In the present narrative, it becomes more appropriate to see the work of the early Critical Theorists as part of a complex intellectual continuum to the present, with its antecedents and its successors and modifiers. In this light, it is the more optimistic and superficial work of those who have set out to minimise and relativise the power of the mass media out of existence which (unfortunately) needs revising in the face of a more powerful analysis and recalcitrant evidence.

The 'Frankfurt' thinkers, of whom much has already been written, synthesised, within a critical Marxist framework for their historical moment, chains of ideas brought to prominence in their own ways and places by Tarde, Tönnies and Kraus, in particular through their formulations about the structure, mechanisms and processes of the 'culture industries'. The tradition they contributed powerfully to is further discussed below.

The Third Generation

The later work of the 'Frankfurt' thinkers, here particularly Herbert Marcuse, who remained in the USA while Horkheimer and Adorno returned to Frankfurt in the post-war period, impinges on and interacts with that of the third generation of radical thinkers, both within and outside the Marxist tradition. Here, among the most important, are Althusser, Barthes and Foucault in France, Günther Anders in Germany, Raymond Williams in Britain, and Marshall McLuhan in Canada. The third generation coincides with the arrival of television, and its growth to become the dominant mass medium. In terms of communication technologies, it also takes us into the era of nuclear weapons, the 'Cold War', intercontinental ballistic missiles, mass car ownership, and space travel. As mass media and other fields of communication developed, so writing, analysis and reflection on their implications multiplied, as did the scope for their dissemination. The 'chain of influence' metaphor no longer suffices to describe the movement, dispersion and development of ideas; instead, one has to envision ever more closely meshed fibrous networks within which influences *may* still occur through the selective reading of primary printed sources and dialogue, but increasingly *do* occur through any number of mediations and at least partially random, and often misleading, indirect routes. The golden threads through the mesh identify themselves for present purposes by their radicalism, original contribution to debate, and influence.

The first trail to follow here is that of those close to or engaging with the Frankfurt thinkers, and their responses to criticisms of cultural pessimism and determinism. A first response is to uphold, or largely uphold, the early Frankfurt critique, and to confirm the pessimistic analysis in the post Second World War context. The West German philosopher **Günther Anders**'s (1902-1992) 1956 essay *Die Welt als Phantom und Matrize. Philosophische Betrachtungen über Rundfunk und Fernsehen (The World as Phantom and Matrix. Philosophical Observations on Radio and Television)* (Pias et al 1999:209) is an early and precocious example of this in the television age. Anders's vision is of mass media consumers as not just passive, but induced to enjoy their passivity, *and* made to pay for it by the media industry. The new mass media – radio and television – isolate and atomise consumers, who willingly digest their pre-packaged cultural fodder.

For Anders, news and information are pumped into households via mass media in the same way as electricity or gas; raw events, like raw energy, are converted into prepared commodities which no longer resemble the source material; they arrive as a constantly available stream which has become an everyday necessity.

The achievement of the mass media is that people now no longer go outside to discover the world; they go inside and have what they are told is the world delivered to them behind locked doors. As a result of this, they come to be voyeurs of an off-the-peg phantom world which is presented to them without the possibility of dialogue or interaction. The very nature of the process means that they are silenced. This phantom world is ultimately one composed of lies. Thus Anders posits a culture in which untruth has triumphed – untrue statements about the world have become 'the world', and it is impossible for the consumer to see around this. If only sliced bread is available, you buy it, and it is both superfluous and impossible to try to unslice it; so you end up eating it, and enjoying the convenience. 'Sliced bread' becomes simply 'bread'.

Anders' conclusion is pessimistic. Mass media audiences are trapped into the phantom world without the realisation that they are there, and that they have given up their freedom to see outside it. They cannot step out of it, and what is more, they do not *want* to.

Max Horkheimer (1895-1973) and **Theodor Adorno** (1903-1969) had already rejected the expression 'mass culture' as manifest in the 'mass media' in 1947 in their *Dialectic of Enlightenment*, preferring 'culture industry' as a clearer formulation. If 'mass culture' could be construed as referring to an authentic culture of the people, 'culture industry' left no doubt that what was being referred to was, first, a business, and second, culture propagated by, and in the interests of, the economically and politically powerful. Adorno sets this out with great clarity in his 1963 essay *Résumé über Kulturindustrie (Summary of the Culture Industry)* (Pias et al. 1999:202).

For Adorno here, as for Anders, culture industry consumers are literally 'stuffed' with its products, in which considerations such as truth or quality are of second rank. The primary motive is to maintain the socio-economic status quo by creating a conformist, uncritical public. The masses should 'see and accept the world in exactly the way that the culture industry has constructed it for them' (ibid.:208. Translation: JT). For Adorno (and Horkheimer) the overall effect of the culture industry was to bring about 'mass deception' and the 'imprisonment of consciousness'. If anything, Adorno is yet more pessimistic than Anders in that he does not just portray a public which, in its search for gratification, is unaware of its deception, he also sees people who actually desire and see through the deception, accepting fabrications in full knowledge of the motivation behind them, while closing their eyes to them in a kind of self-contempt.

Herbert Marcuse (1898-1979) deserves mention here, but more because of the wide audience he reached, and the resonant formulations he produced than because he had much original to say about the media. His 1964 book *One Dimensional Man* reiterates points about monopoly capitalism's power to control the formulation of public desire for commodities through language; consumers are seen as manipulated objects; the rhetoric of individualism is seen as a deliberate concealment of underlying patterns of *imitation* (see Tarde); the rhetoric and experience of 'pluralism' is in fact 'repressive tolerance' in which circumscribed permitted freedoms disguise underlying control.

The difference in Marcuse is his belief in the possibility of emancipatory escape from the perceived one-dimensional society, the impasse into which the earlier Frankfurt thinkers had been driven. He saw a revolutionary potential in an alliance between intellectuals who have been able to step critically outside the system, and various groups of the oppressed who were never bought into it. One-dimensional consumers can eventually be led to break away from the repressions which hold them captive. It was his formulation of this revolutionary potential which thrust Marcuse into the limelight and turned him into a guru of the student movement of the late 1960s.

Louis Althusser (1918-1990) operated from the French structuralist tradition in territory similar to that of Gramsci and the 'Frankfurt' thinkers in that he adapted Marx to allocate a *relatively autonomous* rather than a subordinate role to the cultural superstructures and to ideology. Ideology thus becomes in itself a determining, consciousness-shaping force. This, however, does not imply independent choice of ideology by individuals, seen as free, self-determining agents; in practice, people's consciousness is determined by 'ideological state apparatuses' – including the mass media. In Western capitalist societies, ideological discourse leads individuals to perceive themselves as autonomous, when in fact they are shaped by ideological processes. This resembles Adorno's position, which sees the manufacture of individual consciousness to be like the manufacture of Yale locks, each one differing by only a fraction of a millimetre from the rest. Despite this virtually closed system (intellectuals like Althusser saw themselves as observing and analysing it from outside), Althusser's thought was the catalyst not only for further developments in France, through to Baudrillard (see Stevenson 1995:145-6), but also in Britain, through to Stuart Hall.

Although he cannot be so specifically delineated as a 'radical media critic', **Michel Foucault**'s (1926-1984) work is salient here insofar as discourse, history and power are central to it. Foucault relates to Marx and the Western Marxist tradition in that he finally turns Marx's metaphor of foundation and superstructure upside down. He takes the step, which others already mentioned here only partially took, of placing language, the discursive/cultural 'superstructure', beneath the technical/economic 'foundation'. Returning to the vicinity of Kraus's language-based historical perspective, Foucault sees that Marx's structure is precisely that, a structure or discursive formulation, a truth of its time and place within a genealogical process which comes down to our present through the linguistic archive which it has generated. With discourse at the centre of our historical perspective, knowledge and consciousness, it follows that control of discourse brings power. Those with power operate 'regimes of truth' which sustain them; power struggles are ultimately discursive struggles:

> Discourse is not simply that which *translates* struggles or systems of domination, but it is the thing for which and by which there is struggle, discourse is the power which is to be seized (Foucault 1971.Translation in Shapiro 1982).

The relevance of such a position to *media* discourse is self-evident. Along with Gramsci, Foucault's work was a key influence on the development of the theorisation of Critical Discourse Analysis by Fairclough, Wodak and others in the 1990s.

The *évènements* of 1968, which emanated across Europe from Paris, and led to Marcuse's celebrity in California, also led to the expression of revolutionary thoughts on the mass media. One of the several 1968 posters which highlighted mass media power, produced by students in the Paris art and design schools – the *Atelier Populaire* – showed a human being crouched on all fours like a sheep, the body divided up by dotted lines, as in butcher's shop posters showing the different cuts of meat. The various 'cuts' are labelled 'radio', 'television', 'press' and 'sheep'. The eye is in the form of the Gaullist *Croix de Lorraine.* The caption is *'On vous intoxique'* ('They're poisoning you'). Countering the hegemonic power of the mainstream mass media in Paris 1968 were revolutionary wall newspapers in the streets and in the *metro*, read and discussed in public by the crowds which gathered around them. One of the key cultural forerunners of the 1968 events was **Guy Debord** (1931-1994), prominent among the 'situationists'. Polemically branding grand structuralist theorists, for example Althusser, as 'anaemic gods' (the disrespect was mutual), and drawing inspiration from the Dada and Surrealist movements, Debord promoted a liberating anarchism which would bring about spontaneity and a genuinely innovative state of mind. In his book *La société du spectacle* (1967) he expressed a radical critique of the affluent, mediated society, applying an early Marxian economic analysis to cover culture and the media. Debord's society of the spectacle is one in which the commodification of mass media and culture (the culture industries) has the effect of alienating their consumers from reality rather than connecting them with it. Ahistorical image production, supposedly informing us about events, in fact makes them unreal, inducing the spectators of all sorts of atrocities and inhumanities to be, precisely, spectators – passive, distracted, and unaware of the concealment of the social relations which produce what they are watching. Debord perceives social power elites, in the form of capital, the nation state and media professionals as creators of a one way discourse, from them to us, constantly maintaining us in a state of organised 'ignorance of what is about to happen, and immediately afterwards, the forgetting of whatever has nonetheless been understood' (Debord 1990:13-14. See also Stevenson 1995:148). The situationist way out of this entrapment starts with the artistic and cultural, envisaging the production of alternative images through posters, street art, graffiti, etc. which inspire resistance to and rebellion against the dominant imagery. In many ways reminiscent of Kraus, Debord's perspective can also be detected in Pierre Bourdieu's 1996 essay *Sur la télévision* (On Television and Journalism). It can certainly be maintained that, alongside a genuine critical position, the qualities of humour, polemic and the unexpected combine (as with Kraus) to inspire and attract in a way which is absent from the heavier theoretical contributions.

The German poet, critic and thinker **Hans Magnus Enzensberger**'s 1970 essay *Baukasten zu einer Theorie der Medien* (Pias et al. 1999:264), published in *New Left Review* (12/70) as *Constituents of a Theory of the Media*, emerged from a similar *zeitgeist*, although it distances itself from some of that moment's simplifications. Building on Brecht's 1932 *Speech on the Function of Radio – Der*

Rundfunk als Kommunikationsapparat (Pias et al. 1999:259), Enzensberger here promotes public action to convert the existing one way, top-down communication system into an interactive communication system controlled by its users. He envisages the electronic media themselves as 'a mobilising force', where, he emphasises, 'to mobilise' means to make people literally more mobile, not in the sense of imposed marches and propaganda, but 'free, like dancers, alert like footballers, surprising like *guerrillas*' (Pias et al. 1999:265. Translation: JT). Like Debord, Enzensberger sees media structures and flows, as currently constituted, to be hindering rather than promoting communication, and ascribes this not to technical limitations, but to the kind of provider-consumer relationship desired by the industrial and political power elites. Enzensberger does not, however, see the operations of what he calls the 'consciousness industry' as totally hermetic. It is too complex to be able to achieve total control, and subversive activity is thus possible. He criticises the media-phobia of the New Left as quaintly atavistic, counter-productive, and contradictory in that for the most part it relies on the media as much as everyone else at the personal level. He blames the political left's negative position with regard to new media for the depoliticisation of counter-cultural activists who wish to exploit new technology and its communicative opportunities. His view is that it is for the people to treat the opportunities offered by the media as an emancipatory challenge, to use them democratically rather than reject them. Genuine publicly or community owned media can produce a view of society and the world which reflects ordinary *people*'s reality rather than that of the elites. Enzensberger foresees left wing movements taking over broadcasting frequencies and building their own emancipated counter cultures, taking into account genuine popular interests, needs and desires.

In Britain, the pivotal figure of this generation was **Raymond Williams** (1921-1988). His work provided the impetus to shift critical studies away from high culture and a literary-moral approach towards the acceptance of popular culture – as manifested in particular in the mass media – as a legitimate object of study, and towards an anthropological-historical approach. Where previously the text centred approach associated with F.R. Leavis had dominated, Williams's approach involved seeing the cultural process as a whole, and thus conducting textual analysis – which remained crucial – in the context of analysis of the institutions and socio-historical structures and processes which produced them. In the 1960s and 1970s Williams assimilated ideas from mainland Europe in the form of Lukács's and Goldman's Marxist literary criticism, Saussure's and Barthes's semiology, and the key influences, which later passed through to the Birmingham Centre for Contemporary Cultural Studies – those of Althusser and Gramsci. If Althusser left Williams, and contemporaries Richard Hoggart and Edward Thompson uneasy with what they saw as an over-rigid structuralist approach, it was Gramsci's ideas which enabled them to reconcile critical Marxist ideas with their 'culturalist' position. They needed to find space for individual experience and the complexities of actual life, whose contradictions they could not see as always fitting into theoretical structures. The complexity and dynamism of Gramsci's formulations, and his conception of the hegemonic struggle as continuous, perpetual, and at the every day level, provided them with the sought-for link between theoretical structures and space for individual action and initiative, free from the hegemony of state or capital. Comparisons may be made here with Enzensberger, as well as with Habermas, who will be considered in more detail below. Williams's particular way out of the impasse of determinism, as just briefly described, was an important resolution which opened up a way forward for subsequent thinkers and critical practitioners, particularly in the British tradition.

Williams was dismissive of the work of the Canadian **Marshall McLuhan** (1911-1980), levelling at it the frequent criticism of 'technical determinism'. What the two men did have in common, however (although in different ways) was the formative influence of F.R. Leavis. Other influences, from whom McLuhan picked selectively, included T.S. Eliot, Lewis Mumford, and Harold Innis. We see from this that with the eclectic McLuhan we move away from the Marxist tradition, and even from those non-Marxist thinkers who nevertheless defined themselves in relation to it. In fact, McLuhan was more of a radical mass media *visionary*, who saw revolutionary cultural change taking place and articulated it with resonant formulations, than a radical mass media *critic*. After an initial critique, it is often argued, he ultimately welcomed the transformation of world society into his 'global village' by media technology. Moreover, he is criticised for accepting the control of society by a (post-)industrial elite capable of directing a progressive, technology-led socio-cultural revolution which would outflank and outmode ideological conflict.

However, to dismiss McLuhan precipitately from the current narrative is to miss significant areas of debate which he raised. Like Kraus in this specific respect, McLuhan has been a marginalized and awkward figure in some recent analyses because his work defies dominant classifications and expected logics. Although it can be argued that the determining importance of technological change is inherent to the whole historicised debate on mass communications and the mass media, it should also be clear that it was McLuhan who popularised and refocused attention on this basic facet of the socio-cultural significance of mass media, and their transforming effects on people's perception of the world in terms of time and space. His shift from a critical 'technological humanist' perspective in *The Mechanical Bride* (1951) to a celebratory 'technological determinist' one in *The Gutenberg Galaxy* (1962) thereafter becomes a field for making judgements on his position on ideological or other grounds. Beyond that, McLuhan's somewhat hit-and-miss dispersal of ideas from the ludicrous to the insightful, from the emancipatory to the reactionary may be seen as symptoms of, as well as comments on, the fragmentation and confusions of individualistic mass media based, rather than more historically and theoretically based, apprehensions of reality. McLuhan did have big, fundamental, stimulating thoughts about mass communications and the mass media, but it is hard to argue that they add up to a systematic and credible alternative non- or anti-Marxist standpoint, which functions at the level of those who sharpened their teeth either within, or in reaction to the critical Marxist tradition. His influence can be seen in Postman's work (1985), and in the work of some 1990s writers who provide interesting re-assessments (Stevenson 1995, Grosswiler 1998), and perceive continuities through to Baudrillard, but these threads are of limited significance for the current narrative.

The Fourth Generation

As with any genealogy, the picture for radical mass media criticism becomes ever more complex as generations succeed each other. Not only are inherited ideas recycled and refined in a range of different directions by a larger number of people, but environmental factors, for example, new technologies, and new kinds of exploitation of them, change the locations and terms of debate, and the situation being debated. In addition, the subject becomes increasingly global, multi-lingual and multi-disciplinary, thus containing several 'archives' with limited cross-referencing. Well-known figures are read, known, or known of, by sizeable academic publics, many of whom themselves write, research or organise. Within the academic sector, large conferences and a range of journals serve the expanding productivity of adjacent intellectual cottage industries. A few works also reach a broader public, and link into, as well as being informed by, a myriad of organisations, magazines, electronic networks and actions.

Yet while a critical public sphere has developed, with its dialectics, arguments, wisdoms, stupidities, humour, vanities, and narcissisms, with its pessimists, optimists, theoreticians and practitioners, and while all these lives and energies are being spent, the objects of all the radical criticism, the mass media themselves, flourish, expand, and consolidate positions of huge global power. Between 1975 and 2000, home satellite and cable TV, video recorders, home and workplace PCs and the internet, and the flows of information, entertainment, lies and distraction that they enabled for the hundreds of millions able to access them, spread, intensified and embroidered many times over the critical issues identified earlier in the century.

Faced with all this, it is impossible to attempt a comprehensive overview here. Rather, I will present a brief framework, before, with apologies in advance, making subjective emblematic choices which will serve to underpin the narrative of the rest of this book. The already selective thumbnail portrayals of the first three generations have at least provided signposts to the main historical and thematic parameters of the debate. Future historians will eventually arrive at their well-considered selections for this fourth generation. For now, the following criteria have been behind my choices.

First, they cover between them the salient range of issues. Second, those chosen express and contextualise their positions clearly and accessibly. Third, and this is the central reason for privileging them here before others, they do not just spectate and theorise, they are not exclusively academics, they enter into various kinds of political-cultural practice; more than that, they engage radically in public debate and action. That is to say, they are *thinker-activists* who respond to a current sense that enough laps of the theoretical circuit have now been run; players and spectators, equipped with their (ongoing) analysis should also be moving out from the inward looking arena, which so easily becomes narcissistic and self-absorbed. There is no intention here to personalise or set up individual icons. While the figures placed in the foreground are there on account of their personal qualities, they are used as valuable conduits into the cultural-political environment that concerns us here.

Before situating these key thinker-activists, a very brief contextual survey is necessary.

In the last quarter of the twentieth century, the *overall* conceptual framework did not change. It was necessary for writers to reformulate, for the new generation of the public, critical reflection which was in step with current technological development, and which promoted intelligent radical critical standpoints at a time when they were meeting with opposition that needed to be refuted. Indeed, it was vital that a sense of urgency should be propagated. But, despite the volume, it can be argued that only a relatively small amount of what was startlingly original was produced, or needed to be produced. The rationales for optimism or pessimism were transferred easily from the less new to the brand new technologies. The four interweaving fields of investigation continued to develop and interweave, although in terms of polemic, post-1989 triumphalism placed all approaches which could be loosely associated with opposition to the US-dominated world order, or with 'Marxism', as defined by its opponents, on the defensive, and lent confidence and credibility to those, masquerading as progress, which emphasised the benign nature of current dominant structures and practices. Thus, in the new atmosphere, radically critical positions could be dismissed with impunity, 'consigned to the dustbin of history', as the phrase went, without their arguments being refuted, superseded, or even seriously challenged intellectually by theories or evidence of equivalent depth.

While the intertwined and synergetic development of the four fields cannot be overstated, and we are constantly dealing here with questions of relative emphasis rather than divisive pigeonholing, or polarising argumentation, the following categorisations do help the tracing of genealogies and the organisation of ideas.

Those most prominent in continuing the line in which *political economy* is at the core of analysis were James Curren, Graham Murdock, Peter Golding and Nicholas Garnham in the UK, Dallas Smythe and James Winter in Canada, and most resonantly, the trio of Noam Chomsky, Edward Herman and Robert McChesney in the USA. It is these latter three who are considered in more detail below.

Those whom one may associate more closely with analyses centred on *language, discourse and culture*, range from George Steiner, Norman Fairclough and Bob Franklin in the UK, Neil Postman, Edward Saïd and Douglas Kellner in the USA, and Pierre Bourdieu in France, to subversive journalists John Pilger in the UK and Günter Wallraff in Germany. Some attention was already given to Steiner and Fairclough in the previous chapter. Here, Bourdieu and Pilger will be considered, with brief further reference to Fairclough.

Those representing a radical critical standpoint in relation to the *audience and the public sphere* are Stuart Hall at the radical edge of the BCCC, and Greg Philo and John Eldridge of the Glasgow University Media Group in the UK, Jürgen Habermas in Germany, Jésus Martín Barbero in Colombia, and Nestor García Canclini in Mexico. Here, we shall concentrate on Habermas and Barbero.

Those emphasising critically the primacy of *technology* are Manuel Castells in Spain (and the USA), and, quite differently, Jean Baudrillard in France. We shall look here at the work of Castells.

Finally, the best overviews of the scene to date are provided by Mattelart (1994, 1996, 1998) in France, whose original analysis goes well beyond the description as 'overview', Stevenson (1995, 1999) in the UK, and the anthology assembled by Claus Pias et al. (1999) in Germany. Although none of these last is comprehensive, a reading of them will reveal and supplement the inevitable lacunae and subjectivities of the current minimalist account. While Pias et al. take a balanced, comparative approach, Stevenson (1999) moves towards a more urgent moral-ethical critique. Armand Mattelart's outstanding series of books (some written with Michèle Mattelart) are extraordinary both for their historical scope and for their radical incisiveness.

The first figures to be singled out within this framework are **Noam Chomsky**, **Edward Herman** and **Robert McChesney**, who have worked together in different combinations, and have produced substantial popular academic and publicistic work. Prominent among these is Herman and Chomsky's *Manufacturing Consent. The Political Economy of the Mass Media* (1988). Chomsky followed this, amid his extensive written output and political activity, with, among many others, *Necessary Illusions. Thought Control in Democratic Societies* (1989), *Deterring Democracy* (1991), and the pamphlet *Media Control. The Spectacular Achievements of Propaganda* (1991). The documentary film *Manufacturing Consent – Noam Chomsky and the Media*, made by Peter Wintonick and Mark Achbar, which follows Chomsky round the lecture and interview circuit, appeared in 1992 (despite Chomsky's initial reservations about its personalisation of the issues), and achieved world-wide success, not just at film festivals, where it won several awards, but in that it was televised and shown in independent cinemas across the world. A companion book of the same title, edited by Mark Achbar, appeared in 1994. Chomsky points out critically that while Edward Herman wrote most of the book *Manufacturing Consent* he, Chomsky got most of the publicity, but he also acknowledges that the film succeeded in bringing key issues raised by radical mass media critics to mass audiences.

Herman and Chomsky had already collaborated on books in the 1970s, and Herman produced a series of books and articles on corporate power and propaganda through the 1980s. In 1992, he made a polemical and satirical excursion in the tradition of Kraus and Orwell with the popular *Beyond Hypocrisy. Decoding the News in an Age of Propaganda*, which included the *Doublespeak Dictionary*. The latter is a glossary of political euphemisms for which Herman provides definitions. Thus, for example, 'Politics' is: 'The art of winning investors, and then voters' (Herman 1992:64); 'Safety Net' becomes: 'A porous mesh made from the guts of the deceased welfare state, through which will fall the Undeserving Poor' (ibid:172); 'National Interest' means: 'The demands and needs of the corporate community' (ibid:156); and 'Search for Peace' translates as: 'Public relations ploys that will allow us to continue to pursue war' (ibid:174). Following this, Herman returned to political economy-based work, and collaborated with Robert McChesney to produce, in 1997, the book: *The Global Media. The New Missionaries of Corporate Capitalism*. This was followed, in 1999, by *The Myth of the Liberal Media*. McChesney himself has written, among much else, the pamphlet *Corporate Media and the Threat to Democracy* (1997), and the book *Rich Media, Poor Democracy. Communication Politics in Dubious Times* (1999), as well as, with John Nichols, *Our Media, Not Theirs. The Democratic Struggle against Corporate Media* (2002).

All three writers see the mass media corporations, or more precisely, the global industrial corporations which include mass media ownership and operations, as well as media-related hardware and software, in their portfolios, as expanding world powers which have already eliminated most of the competition. They also note, as does Mattelart, that advances in peacetime information and entertainment technology are invariably spin-offs from technologies originally developed for military purposes. Finally, they all lay blame on the commercialisation of the media for the massive distortion of discourse, and consequent intention to mislead the public, which has become so routinised in media production that its operatives either just accept it as coming with the job, or no longer even notice it. This emerges from the five filters in Herman and Chomsky's Propaganda Model, described in *Manufacturing Consent*. McChesney puts the by now familiar perspective as follows:

> In the final analysis, this is a thoroughly commercial system with severe limitations for our politics and culture [...]. The present course is one where much of the world's entertainment and journalism will be provided by a handful of enormous firms, with invariably pro-profit and pro-global market political positions on the central issues of our times. The implications for political democracy, by any standard, are troubling (McChesney 1997:23).

'Such a dark vision of our future should give us pause', McChesney continues later in the same essay:

> In accepting (and encouraging) widening class divisions, the glorification of profit, greed and commercialism as the necessary cornerstones of our age, it portends grave damage to the human spirit and our ability to live together in viable communities (ibid:74)

We are thus confronted here with a reiteration for the USA of the late 1980s and 1990s of positions demonstrating a pervasive influence over the minds of media consumers by elite-controlled mass media operations. As with previous writers, only a limited optimism with regard to individual or organised resistance is expressed, and relatively few positive examples and prospects are pointed out. Replying to criticisms of the 'determinism' of the Propaganda Model, Herman stated that 'while putting forward a "powerful effects model", we admit that the system is not all-powerful, which calls into question our determinism' (Herman 1996:4). Likewise, having painted their bleak, corporation-dominated picture, Herman and McChesney underline in their conclusion the porosity and vulnerability of the system:

> For the short and medium term, we expect both the global market and global commercial media to strengthen their positions worldwide [...] but beyond that the future is very unclear, and remains the subject of human political control [...]. The

system may be far more vulnerable and subject to change than appears to be the case at present […]. If it is to change, and in a positive way, it is important that people who are dissatisfied with the status quo should not be overcome and rendered truly powerless by a sense of hopelessness and cynicism. As Noam Chomsky said, 'if you act like there is no possibility for change, you guarantee that there will be no change' (Herman & McChesney 1997:205).

What remains noticeable in the current context is the lack of reference to or acknowledged link with the largely European critical tradition traced so far in this section. It is true that Herman and Chomsky make occasional reference to Orwell, and cite Curran and Seaton's portrayal of nineteenth century British radical journalism in *Power without Responsibility* (1985), and that McChesney refers to Habermas's concept of 'the public sphere' (see below), but one searches their indexes in vain for mention of most of the figures named so far in this survey. In the index of Herman and McChesney's *The Global Media* one finds Mickey Mouse and Rupert Murdoch under 'M', but no Mattelart, or even Marcuse or McLuhan; Adorno and Althusser do not appear under 'A', but Atari does; under 'G' one finds Goofy, but no Gramsci. Given the subject of the book, this may be unfair comment in detail, but the deeper point is sustainable, and can probably be traced back to the influence of Chomsky's scorn of theorists in this field. In his own work, Chomsky reserves the words 'theory' and 'research' for his output in the field of linguistics. In his political writing and media criticism he sees himself rather as applying easily accessible data to a working model; there is no place, or need for a theory. Like Bertrand Russell, whose picture hangs in Chomsky's office, he chooses to keep a clear separation between his academic life and his social/political engagement. It would appear that his own engrained radical libertarian socialism (see Chomsky's 1992 interview with John Pilger), and his deeply rooted faith in the individual's ability to resist, which predate his encountering of, particularly, French theorists, are so naturalised in his mind that he finds their formulations obfuscating, superfluous, and in some cases positively harmful. In a 1995 letter to his biographer Robert F. Barsky, he wrote:

> Doubtless there is a power structure in every speech situation; again, that is a truism that only an intellectual could find surprising and seek to dress up in appropriate polysyllables. As honest people, our effort should be to unmask it and diminish it, as far as we can, and to do so in association with others, whom we can help, and who can help us in this necessary libratory task. Will it ever end? (Barsky 1997:197).

There are echoes here of the British culturalists' reaction against structuralism, and it is similar considerations which have led the current narrative to focus on 'thinker-activists' rather than on certain theorists of the 1980s and 1990s whose effects are less evidently radical. However, the longer historical view taken here does demonstrate that earlier collections of theoretical polysyllables across the twentieth century, where genuinely radical, did also contribute valuably to the genealogies being traced here, and to the creation of a critical dynamic to which the contributions and insights of Chomsky, Herman and McChesney are indebted.

One of the putative objects of Chomsky's critique of French theorists was Pierre Bourdieu, but it is the intention here to draw out similarities between the two on specific points rather than to seek their differences. We thus now move on to those whose media critiques centrally involve an unmasking of journalistic discursive practice, making the at first glance unlikely juxtaposition of French intellectual Bourdieu, and the British radical journalist John Pilger, whose work in the field can in turn be linked to the applied academic work of critical discourse analysts such as Norman Fairclough, and to the German critical writer and documentarist Günter Wallraff.

Only a corner of the extensive sociological work of **Pierre Bourdieu** (1930-2001) refers specifically to the mass media, but it may be noted that, as in the case of Chomsky, his decision in the 1990s to step beyond his highly distinguished academic career and publicly take up critical positions on social issues was accompanied by writings expressing a radical critique of the media. Here, selective reference will be made only to the more theoretical collection *Language and Symbolic Power* (1991), which brings together in English an otherwise uncollected range of work from the 1980s, and to the three shorter, more polemic texts: *Sur la télévision* (1996), *Contre-feux* (1998), and *Contre-feux 2* (2001).

While Bourdieu fits his thoughts on language and power into his own elegant sociological structures and terminology, he joins Chomsky (and many others) in his observation of language as 'an instrument of action and power' (Bourdieu 1991:37). Consequently, as J.B. Thompson comments mildly: 'His relentless disclosure of power and privilege in its most varied and subtle forms [...] give(s) his work an implicit critical potential' (Bourdieu 1991:31). As with most other thinkers considered here, there is a tension in Bourdieu's work between his variant of determinism – a thought system which effectively analyses the human condition into a predictable, historically and theoretically underpinned state of domination by hegemonic forces – and a search for formulae or practical courses of action which allow for ways out of the determinist impasse. As we have seen, the barb of 'determinism' is one which argumentative scribes enjoy launching at each other, and it is one that Bourdieu too has had to counter. For example, Richard Jenkins (1992:96-97) writes: 'The charge of determinism is, in Bourdieu's case, justified [...]. His model of practice, despite all of its references to improvisation and fluidity, turns out to be a celebration of (literally) mindless conformity.'

Subsequent positions taken up by Bourdieu, however, contradict this, or at least show him acting as if it were not the case. The previous baggage that Bourdieu brought to *Sur la télévision*, and *Contre-feux* does indeed bear traits of determinism. In *Language and Symbolic Power*, writings dating from 1982, for example, he writes:

> Integration into a single 'linguistic community', which is a product of the *political domination that is endlessly reproduced* by institutions *capable of imposing* universal recognition of the *dominant language*, is the condition for the establishment of relations of linguistic domination (Bourdieu 1991:46. Italics: JT).

While Bourdieu posits a complicity of the dominated in being dominated – conforming and playing the linguistic game for their own purposes – the rules of the game are nevertheless set from above, formulated in the interests of the powerful, and executed by a class of educated apparatchiks (e.g. teachers, lawyers, media workers). Writing of the discursive 'dispossession' of the dominated classes, he says: 'The fact remains that this dispossession is inseparable from the existence of a body of professionals, objectively invested with the monopoly of the legitimate use of the legitimate language' (Bourdieu 1991:59).

These have the function of naturalising dominant discourse, such that a process of mass self-censorship becomes normal, even unconscious. As Jenkins puts it: 'The ultimate success of censorship is to be found [...] in its apparent abolition' (Jenkins 1992:156). The only way out of this is clearly to recognise the game for what it is and to question it, a process which those in possession of linguistic domination constantly strive to suppress. Their success is not inevitable, but, logically, they *should* succeed:

> The legitimate language no more contains within itself the power to ensure its own perpetuation in time than it has power to define its extension in space. Only the process of continuous creation, which occurs through the unceasing struggles between the different authorities who compete within the field of specialised production for the monopolistic power to impose the legitimate mode of expression, can ensure the permanence of the legitimate language and of its value, that is, of the recognition accorded to it (Bourdieu 1991:58).

Sur la télévision (1996) (references given from the English translation *On Television and Journalism* (1998a)), however, takes a different tone. The short book contains the texts of two televised lectures, given 'because I wanted to reach an audience beyond the usual audience at the Collège de France' (Bourdieu 1998a:10 – the Collège was Bourdieu's workplace). In the first lecture, *On Television*, he expounds his view that 'television poses a serious danger for all the various areas of cultural production' and 'poses no less of a threat to political life and to democracy itself' (ibid). In the second lecture on *The Power of Journalism*, he examines 'how the structural pressure exerted by the journalistic field, itself dominated by market pressures, more or less profoundly modifies power relationships within other fields' (ibid:68). In confronting these themes, he does not claim originality, but he does see a specificity in his current environment which contains new elements. We thus have here a specialist speaking in lay terms to a broad public, expressing insights and concerns arising from his specialist work – a socio-cultural intervention – with the presumed aim, and belief in the possibility, of influencing that public through the expression of counter-hegemonic discourse – not the act of a determinist. This is underlined in the opening words of the book's prologue:

> It should go without saying that to reveal the hidden constraints on journalists [...] is not to [...] point a finger at the guilty parties. Rather it is an attempt to offer to all sides a *possibility of liberation*, through a conscious effort, from the hold of these mechanisms, and to propose, perhaps, a *programme for concerted action* by artists, writers, scholars,

and journalists – that is by the holders of the (*quasi*) monopoly of the instruments of diffusion (ibid:1. Italics: JT).

Here, he is advocating an organised subversion by the normally loyal (or if not, marginalized) of the central instrument of established power.

In *Contre-feux* (1998) (references here to the translation *Acts of Resistance. Against the New Myths of Our Time* (1998b), he deepened his position. A slim collection of short essays and articles, this book shows us Bourdieu as a politically engaged intellectual, hoping that he is providing 'useful weapons to all those who are striving to resist the scourge of neo-liberalism' (Bourdieu 1998b:vii), entering the public arena, not with a banal optimism that he can exercise some kind of automatic influence, but out of civic anger: 'I would not have engaged in public position-taking if I had not – each time – had the – perhaps illusory – sense of being forced into it by a kind of legitimate rage, sometimes close to something like a sense of duty' (ibid).

The promulgators of the dominant neo-liberal discourse, particularly in the media, are central objects of Bourdieu's rage. His target here is not so much the working journalists who are ensnared in the web of constraints which determine their output and livelihood, as the more senior players and their bosses who operate the market-based system and the processes of mind-control over the public. It is through their actions, he asserts, that 'television enjoys a *de facto* monopoly on what goes into the heads of a significant part of the population and what they think' (Bourdieu 1998a:18). Looking at television's discursive practice, he argues that it:

> [...] can hide things by showing something other than what would be shown if television did what it's supposed to do, provide information. Or by showing what has to be shown, but in such a way that it isn't really shown, or is turned into something insignificant; or by constructing it in such a way that it takes on a meaning that has nothing at all to do with reality (ibid:19).

Bourdieu sees as a role for critical writers the ceaseless unmasking of such false constructions and discourses, an emancipatory task designed to teach the many, who have not yet seen through these processes, how to read and view critically:

> There is a need to invent new forms of communication between researchers and activists, which means a new division of labour between them. One of the missions which sociologists can fulfil perhaps better than anyone is the fight against saturation by the media. We all hear ready-made phrases all day long. You can't turn on the media without hearing about the 'global village', 'globalisation' and so on. These are innocent sounding words, but through them come a whole philosophy and a whole world-view which engender fatalism and submission. We can block this force-feeding by criticising the words, by helping non-professionals to equip themselves with specific weapons of resistance, so as to combat the effects of authority and the grip of television, which plays an absolutely critical role. It is no longer possible nowadays to conduct social struggles without having a specific programme for fighting with and against television (ibid:57).

With such formulations, Bourdieu is clearly aligning himself amongst the media critical thinker-activists of the 1990s. It is interesting that in his essay *La culture est en danger* (Bourdieu 2001) he, in reminding his readers of the difficulty of the struggle, refers back admiringly to one of the great thinker-activists of the 1980s, Edward Thompson, and his *The Making of the English Working Class*. Still perhaps intellectually convinced of his old quasi-deterministic stance, he nevertheless refuses pessimism. The essay finishes:

> The position of the most autonomous producers of culture, gradually being dispossessed of their means of production and, above all, distribution, has doubtless never been as weak and under threat, but it has also never been as rare, useful and precious (Bourdieu 2001:8.Translation: JT).

In the UK, both **Norman Fairclough** and **John Pilger** would agree. Bourdieu's project, as expressed here, synchronises closely with Fairclough's Critical Discourse Analysis as applied to the mass media, and more broadly to his call for *action* on language in the new capitalism. Language, Fairclough argues, is:

> [...] important in imposing, extending and legitimising the new order; for instance the pervasive representations of 'globalisation' as a natural and universal process – disguising ways in which it is based on choices by business corporations and governments which can be changed. The project of the new order is partly a language project – change in language is an important part of the socio-economic changes which are taking place. And challenging the new order is partly a matter of challenging the new language (Fairclough 2000).

Fairclough rightly sees this challenge as being much broader than one concentrated on the mass media, but clearly the pervasive role of the mass media, as his own earlier writings show, is crucial.

Despite several honorary doctorates from UK universities, John Pilger is no theoretician. Over the last quarter of the twentieth century, and more, he has been a radical investigative journalist, reporter and documentary film maker, who has also gathered his writing in several books, two of which will be considered here: *Distant Voices* (1992) and *Hidden Agendas* (1998). A glance at the references in these books shows that almost all of them are journalistic. The strongest link to the intellectual genealogies being traced here are those to the writings of Chomsky and Herman – Pilger reprints a short and admiring article on Chomsky in *Distant Voices* – and to the Glasgow University Media Group. There are also brief references to Orwell, to Bob Franklin's 1997 book *Newszack and News Media* and to Australian David Bowman's book *The Captive Press* (1988). Unlike Fairclough therefore, who acknowledges significant influences in Foucault, Gramsci, and others, Pilger's is a largely practice-based critical perspective with intellectual links to the anglophone radical tradition. His highly literate and passionate journalism from the sites of the world's most horrific atrocities could be advanced as a prime example of Chomsky's assertion of the superfluity of theory in this field, but then, as in Chomsky's case, theory may have been less relevant for Pilger because the radical perspective was passed on to him as an engrained assumption from a very young age. From his own account, on his mother's side, his great grandfather had been deported to Australia from Ireland for 'making political agitation', and his father was one of the early members of the Australian Socialist Party.

Pilger describes *Hidden Agendas* as 'something of a *J'accuse* directed at a journalism claiming to be free', and as a 'tribute to those journalists who, by not consorting with power, begin the process of demystifying and disarming it' (Pilger 1998:15) – a truly Krausian mission. While eloquently demonstrating the immense and increasing power of media corporations in the media age, with its discourses conforming to 'hidden agendas' which 'often prevent us from understanding the meaning of contemporary events' (ibid:4), Pilger also perceives widespread, if concealed, popular resistance, '…a subterranean world of the mind where most people think what they want to think, and their thoughts are invariably at odds with and more civilised than those of their self-appointed betters' (ibid:10).

While this may be an unquantifiable article of faith and hope, it does bear witness to the undoubted resilience of critical and oppositional discourses in the face of ubiquitous media messages promoting conformism and passivity. Correspondingly, Pilger perceives the present order 'built on money, electronic technology and illusions' as 'chronically insecure' (ibid:13). As we shall see below when looking at the work of Barbero, Canclini, and others in Latin America, atomised resignation and fatalism may not be *appropriate* responses, just the ones that suit those in positions of power:

> In almost every country today […] people's solidarity with each other in the form of vibrant grass-roots organisations enables a form of democracy to function in spite of and in parallel with oppressive power often dressed up as democracy. The anarchist Colin Ward called this 'the seed beneath the snow' (ibid:14).

Pilger thus sets up an energetic challenge to hegemonic mass media discourse and the powers that control it which counters the pessimism of more determinist thinkers and sees an important role for the critical, independent journalist as part of this challenge. For example, his essay 'A Cultural Chernobyl' in *Hidden Agendas* makes a radical attack on the Murdoch empire, and its manipulation of facts, stories and language, particularly by the UK tabloid *The Sun*. In another essay, 'The Guardians of the Faith' (ibid.:485), he attacks the journalism of a world-renowned bastion of impartiality, the BBC, and others at the supposedly responsible end of the journalistic market. Here he argues that, far from acting independently:

> Serious journalism in Britain, dominated by television, serves as a parallel arm of government, testing or 'floating' establishment planning, restricting political debate to the 'main centres of power' […] and, above all, promoting Western power in the wider world (ibid:488-89).

Vital to this role is the manipulation of discourse:

One of the most effective functions of 'communicators' is to minimise the culpability of this [Western] power in war and terrorism, the enforced impoverishment of large numbers of people and the theft of resources and the repression of human rights. This is achieved by omission on a grand scale, by the repetition of received truths and the obfuscation of causes (ibid:489).

Thus, corruption of language is a central issue:

Popular concepts like 'democracy', 'freedom', 'choice' and 'reform' are emptied of their dictionary meanings. This has long been standard practice, but in the late twentieth century it is reinforced by the facility of technology and the illusion of an 'information society', which in reality means more media owned by fewer and fewer conglomerates (ibid:490).

Pilger, of course, does get his documentaries broadcast on television, his articles published in the mainstream press, and his books accepted by a major publisher; it is thus to be expected that, consequently, he will be dismissed by some as, at its kindest, an unreliable eccentric, and seen by others as primarily one who is 'licensed' to criticise by the UK's hegemonic powers in the sense of Marcuse's 'repressive tolerance' – one of those few whose criticism it is in the interests of the authorities to permit as powerful evidence of *their* democratic tolerance and *his* paranoia. Although such appropriation of radical discourses for reactionary purposes has many times proved to be far more effective than other more oppressive options, it is unfair to Pilger's work to judge it on the tactical terrain of its enemies. Writing such as his more importantly plays an empowering and emancipatory role for those seeking and working for alternatives to the current dominant ideology. As a working journalist himself, who knows the processes of the job from the inside, and has witnessed at first hand the barbarism which he reports, he also cannot be denied a respect and credibility which mainstream journalists and defenders of the system habitually deny to more desk-based and theory-orientated radical critics.

The massive global public opposition to the Anglo-American invasion of Iraq in 2003 led Pilger to discern and further promote a sea change away from power elite and media control of the minds of the public (see Chapter 12). Certainly at this moment there could be seen spectacular evidence of a new and powerful counter-hegemonic activism and the appearance of a global public sphere.

Jürgen Habermas's concept of the *public sphere* takes us on to critiques and alternatives to the status quo which focus on audiences, seen as *citizens* rather than *consumers*, genuine *resisters* rather than active or passive, system-complicit *dopes*. In this section, consideration of Habermas's work in Germany will be followed by a look at the work of Barbero in Colombia and Canclini in Mexico, insofar as these can provide fresh perspectives on old European-led debates.

Habermas's concept of the public sphere was first formulated in his 1962 work *Strukturwandel der Öffentlichkeit* which, since it was only published in English translation in 1989 as *The Structural Transformation of the Public Sphere*, had a delayed international impact. Seeking, like Marcuse, a way out of the more deterministic, pessimistic conclusions of the earlier 'Frankfurt School' thinkers,

Habermas loops back to a pre-Marxian Enlightenment environment to locate a model for a public sphere – a social space, free of government and economic influence, for rational, democratic public debate and opinion formation leading to civic action – in the eighteenth century coffee house. Not unlike Chomsky's appeals to principles stated in the US constitution, or his statement to the effect that, judged by the principles of the Nuremberg Trials, every US President since 1945 would be found guilty of crimes against humanity, Habermas uses the strategy of adopting mainstream, non-controversial, apparently harmless sources to underpin radical positions which subvert current practice. If, as Pilger says, the commercialised mass media, or culture industries, to return to Frankfurt School terminology, separate words like 'democracy', 'freedom', 'choice' and 'reform' from their full meaning (Steiner's separation of 'word' from 'world' again) then it is in Habermas's public sphere that that meaning, with all its implications for social practice, can be restored.

Some of Habermas's most accessible more recent writings were collected in the volume *Die Normalität einer Berliner Republik* (1995) – available in English as *A Berlin Republic. Writings on Germany* (1998). Within this collection of essays and interviews he discovers a striking and alarming continuity between populist mass mobilisation on the fascist models of the early part of the twentieth century, and a more concealed post-totalitarian mass manipulation of the 'electronically interconnected network audience' (Habermas 1998:144). He argues that:

> The images of the totalitarian state appear to have vanished, but the destructive potential of a *new* kind of massification has remained. In the public sphere of the media as well there are still structures that block a horizontal exchange of spontaneously taken positions – that is the use of communicative freedoms – and simultaneously make the isolated and privatised viewers susceptible to an incapacitating collectivisation of their conceptual worlds (ibid).

He contrasts, then, a public sphere *shaped* by the mass media and susceptible to mass arousal (recalling Tarde's 'publics'), to a *liberal* public sphere which offers 'a vehicle for the authority of a *position taking* public. Once a *public* starts moving, it does not march in unison, but rather offers the spectacle of anarchically unshackled communicative freedoms' (ibid). Those who have been active in social movements will know what he means – the experience of free debate and active citizenship is a liberating one; but it brings with it the knowledge that there is still a huge uninvolved majority which it is hard to engage. Even in a society whose ostensible structures enable a degree of space for discussion of vital issues, and participation in organisations, there are other forces to hand which powerfully encourage – virtually determine – the opposite, and subvert Habermas's promotion of 'radical democracy': 'Dispositions continue to exist that make a considerable proportion of an overstressed population susceptible to the LePens and Schönhubers, to nationalism and xenophobia' (ibid:145).

But, although he expresses himself regularly as a public intellectual, he does not see it as within the philosopher's realm or possibility to create the active citizen or to make various gesticulations telling people what they *ought* to be doing, or as he put it, to 'further a postconventional consciousness'. How that possibly utopian step is to be made remains unclear.

Concrete Latin American circumstances have generated perspectives which have led to dynamic radical critical debate and action there. While space here is too limited to do more than provide the briefest of summaries, at least a signpost can be erected to an area as yet little treated in Europe and the USA, and some personal comparative thoughts and impulses can be expressed which may encourage critical debate in globalising countries to let itself be inspired by insights from those on the receiving end of the process.

Two Latin American contrasts to the Europe-based tradition stand out. The first is that in Latin America, practice precedes research, which in turn links back into action (investigación – acción), whereas in Europe the research-theory axis has been dominant. The second is that in Latin America the prime emphasis is on identifying, setting up and working with real alternative channels of communication or 'mediations', rather than dwelling on the almost insuperable power of the corporate forces to be resisted. Within the discourses of the thinker-activists at the forefront of Latin American communications research, the words 'culture' and 'communication' are constantly coupled with the word 'change', and are *centrally* associated with processes of democratic socio-political transformation, whereas in Europe and the USA, they tend to be primarily associated in thinkers' minds with control, and processes of conservation of the status quo.

An important reference point for these perspectives is the Colombian **Jesús Martín-Barbero's** book *Communication, Culture and Hegemony. From the Media to Mediations* (1993). Martín-Barbero suggests entry into communications issues via social movements rather than via analyses of media power; via the particular, concrete local situation rather than via confrontation with vast homogenising global corporations. Thus, building on Freire's work in pedagogy, he is emphasising 'horizontal' and 'dialogical' rather than 'vertical', top-down models of communication. In this context, the fields of art, religion, popular music, and even the counter-hegemonic decoding of mass media products, appropriating them for subversive purposes, are all seen as sites of social change.

In a recent interview with Adelaida Trujillo of the 'Communication Initiative', Barbero speaks of his own work in Bogotá, but also draws attention to other Latin American centres of activity. He refers particularly to the work of **Nestor Garcia Canclini** in Mexico City, whose research has fed directly into national policies on culture and communication, and looks at ethical and political concepts in mass communication, suggesting how they can link in with ideas of democratic culture. Barbero also draws attention to Rosario Raguillo's work in Guadalajara, analysing 'communication events', that is to say putting together the whole fabric of communication that is created around a (local) event, from its discursive shaping in various ways, to its exploitation or neglect by different parties, to different political and popular actions it provokes, and secondary events arising from it. Elsewhere in Latin America, this time in Peru, Barbero foregrounds Rosa Maria Alfaro's grass roots work in the Barrios, the squatters' settlements of Lima. Again in the tradition of linking research and social action, Alfaro's local consciousness-raising work with women creating alternative community information networks exemplifies the way in which research is fed by and feeds into practical emancipatory action and politics.

Although the Latin American context may have circumstances, spaces and opportunities for action which are already closed or unworkable in 'First World' contexts, countless alternative culture and media initiatives and movements do operate in the public spheres of Europe and the USA. Yet overall the climate of debate and activity emerging from the more difficult Latin American environment exudes a radical optimism and revitalising energy which challenges recurrent temptations to cynicism and resignation in the 'developed' world.

The final reference point in this selective set of 'fourth generation' representatives is **Manuel Castells**, who foregrounds in his writing critical responses to challenges posed by transformations in media and communications technology, and what he calls the 'informational economy'. After all, the issue remains that, however strong the democratic and critical impulses, and however lively the public sphere, the pace and impact of technological change at the end of the twentieth century and the beginning of the twenty-first may be just too overwhelming for people to understand properly, let alone resist or control in their own civic interests. To highlight Latin American grass roots initiatives may be just a nostalgic throwback to a previous political culture, lost forever to the 'developed', networked world. To expect people to undertake counter-hegemonic decodings of media discourses may be illusory in a fast moving culture of instant images, 24-hour news, or no news by choice, running on globalised, multi-channel, interactive digital information, entertainment and communications systems. Under these circumstances, surely the term 'couch potato' – and the people it refers to – will have achieved its full realisation. As Castells puts it: 'We are not living in a global village, but in customised cottages globally produced and locally distributed' (Castells 1996. Quoted in Stevenson 1999:172).

In Castells's perspective, which we can trace back through the 'Frankfurt' thinkers to Kraus, the apocalyptic visions of the earlier analysts and prophets are virtually realised over the ever expanding sections of the world that globalisation has reached. The electronic information revolution has at one stroke *both* provided a massive shot in the arm and increase in economic power for the techno-capitalist elites (358 people own as much as the poorest half of the world, foremost among them the 'information age' tycoons), *and* created a system which provides the means of reaching and controlling the minds, in ever more differentiated and localised ways, of global consumer audiences of billions of people. Extending this vision, it thus may seem that, where the escalation of nuclear weapons technology already some decades ago brought the world to a state where it could destroy its civilisation and most of its life systems dozens of times over, now, the escalation of media communications and information systems is coming to the point where they can turn people and citizens into quasi brain-dead, willing vegetables dozens of times over, as Neil Postman pointed out, by Huxleyan gratification rather than Orwellian coercion.

Castells (1997) however, like most other previous thinkers, leaves the door open to alternatives. He identifies space for autonomy, or a public sphere, a porosity in the system of the 'informational society' where a critical paradigm can operate. He shows that oppositional and critical social movements can and are appropriating the potential of new global information networks to create their own information flows and worldwide publicity for their causes. It is thus an optimistic evaluation of the ability and potential of democratic social movements to work effectively in the cracks of the dominant media communications system which is the emancipatory touchstone in Castells's perspective.

Castells himself seems to remain in the role of definer and analyst rather than ethical guide or activist, but we may take from his analysis that even couch potatoes contain the seed of resistance, and, kept in a half darkened, heated room (their favourite habitat), will, eventually, miraculously sprout. Indeed, to pursue the metaphor, that process may be accelerated if they come to see the advertisements for potato crisps, uniformly stacked in cylindrical packs, as grotesque attempts to persuade them into cannibalistic consumption of themselves as junk.

Conclusion

This skeletal hundred-year survey of radical mass media criticism has attempted to do the opposite of what academics habitually find it rewarding and useful to do. Rather than setting one thinker critically against another, pointing out fine theoretical distinctions and arguing the pros and cons of different positions, it tries to weave strands of thought together, emphasising points in common, to produce a tapestry which tells a story from which practical things can be learnt. In many cases, I have left it to critically active readers to note for themselves the numerous similarities across time, space and intellectual discipline which are present, and to follow up ideas and references.

A brief account such as this inevitably lays itself open to criticisms, not least for its omissions, its selectivity, its lack of attention to the 'narcissism of small differences', and its structuring around the work of individual thinkers who represent only the tips of icebergs of other writing and activity.

For the purposes of this book, however, it hopes to have:

1. Provided a robust pedigree for the critical perspectives adopted in the coming case studies.
2. Established that throughout the twentieth century the rapidly developing technical systems of gathering and providing accurate information in European and other 'advanced' societies were, in the view of major thinkers throughout the period, constantly corrupted in the interests of commercial gain, and the gaining or retention of power for elites, regardless of the interests of the people.
3. Shown that, consequently, populations can be seen to have undergone continuous cynical manipulation via false or distorted media discourses and subsequent constructions of history.

4. Indicated that critical thinkers and activists have a vital role to play in unmasking and resisting these endemic, system-inherent processes which are destructive of human lives and welfare, accurately informed participatory democracy, and authentic cultural and critical expression.

The case studies which follow form the main body of the book. They are grounded in material which demonstrates rather than conceptualises abstractly about historical processes. While they are microscopic, they should also be seen as emblematic of, and thus directly linked to larger processes – ones which show that the big battles for discursive hegemony, and our critical consciousness of them, have a real role in our everyday lives, and in those of our increasingly networked counterparts and fellow denizens of the globalised information society across the world.

Chapter 3

The Great Discursive Illusion – 1914-1918

He, who would presumably have had the bitterest of scorn for the academic label 'Sociology of Language' sharpened the strict and precise experience of language into a means of critical social theory [...]. Language becomes for him, first, decisive evidence of socially produced 'dumbing down' which brings people to a position where they let themselves comply with whatever the power elites of the world think up, and, second, decisive evidence of the brutalising action which envelops everyday expression before realising itself in the form of wars, dictatorships and concentration camps. When catastrophe occurred, it merely confirmed what Kraus had already deduced from language (Max Horkheimer 1955).

Introduction

John Pilger began an article in November 1998 with the following anecdote:

In 1917, the Prime Minister, David Lloyd-George, confided to C.P. Scott, editor of the *Manchester Guardian*: 'If people really knew [the truth], the war would be stopped tomorrow. But, of course, they don't know and can't know'. The Guardian's C. Montague described how the wartime truth was inverted; a massacre became 'quite a day – a victory really'. Montague's great-grandson, Simon, believes that when the soldiers returned home and discovered the extent of the lying and omission, they never again trusted journalists. I think he has a point. What has changed is that we now have the illusion of information saturation – when, in fact, we have media saturation, most of it politically repetitive, shallow and safe (Pilger: 1998).

Pilger quoted the anecdote in order to illustrate the fact that now, as in the 1914-18 war, journalists tell lies in order to make acceptable that which would not be acceptable, or *accepted*, if instead the truth were told. In other words, in the 1914-18 war, lies changed history, and cost the lives of millions of young men. The false version of events, where a 'massacre' became a 'victory', was what the public read in their newspapers, and the daily lies added up to an image of the war, as perceived at home, which made it acceptable. Untruth masquerading as truth did not just provide the public with a wrong account of what had just happened at the front, it ensured that as a result of that false story, the massacre continued; it *determined future events*.

It did so not only on the level of mass death, physical mutilation, psychological scarring, and the loss of loved ones which blighted so many subsequent lives, but also on the level of the broader historical process in which the First World War led to the rise of Nazism, and then to the Second and the shadow of 'Cold War' insanity that it threw forward onto the succeeding decades.

We may comment further on the Lloyd-George anecdote, for it tells of a prime minister of the mother of democracies, whom conventional British history treats as a distinguished and victorious war leader, conniving with a leading and most respected newspaper editor, in a country priding itself on its free press. Lloyd-George *knew* the truth, and had the power to have it conveyed to the public, and thus, in his own estimation, to change history, but he did not. C.P. Scott, along with his fellow editors, had the influence, resources and journalistic duty to get at the truth and print it, and likewise change history, but they did not. Instead, corrupt prime minister and corrupt newspaper editors conspired to tell lies and withhold truth in full knowledge of what they were doing. For them, people were not just cannon fodder, but manipulation fodder; the system was such that 'they don't know and can't know', because political and journalistic elites made the conscious decision to deceive them.

Karl Kraus and the Last Days of Humanity

We cannot, it will be argued, derive the course of twentieth century history from the few words of an anecdote. Those who have absorbed Karl Kraus – *he* derived it from the positioning of a single comma! – might dispute that. But we do not need to.

The main source on the 1914-18 war to be used here is taken from the 'other side'; if power elites in Britain and the Entente powers collaborated mendaciously to send their people, against their own interests, into the inferno of the trenches, so also did the equivalent elites in Vienna and Berlin. Karl Kraus did not just write about commas; he was unique in that he not only opposed the war passionately from 1914 onwards, but he also gathered and published a voluminous record of how it was reported in Vienna, which he then turned into a monumental documentary drama *The Last Days of Humanity* (1919). This exposed satirically the specific processes of discursive deception from event to its 'mediatic' transformation to its reception and consequences, revealing the combination of economic, political and journalistic power interests that were operating it. Moreover, Kraus's seminal writing portrays the war as the culmination of a whole prior process of cultural/linguistic corruption in which the takeover of journalism and its discourse by commercial and power-seeking interests, minutely observed over the previous fifteen years in his journal *Die Fackel* (The Torch), played the central role.

Text extracts, largely from *The Last Days of Humanity*, will be analysed here, on account of their status as direct quotations and observations from the 1914-18 period (Kraus both demonstrates this and specifically confirms it in his introduction), and of the use Kraus puts them to in unmasking journalistic products, processes and contexts in a publicly accessible way for his contemporaries and for subsequent generations.

The first words of the drama are, appropriately enough, uttered by a newspaper seller. It is 1914 and the moment at which the media first bring news of the assassination of the heir to the throne to the Viennese public. Kraus presents it to us as an act of selling and buying. Rival newspaper sellers from Vienna's leading dailies of the time, the *Neue Freie Presse* and the *Neues Wiener Tagblatt*, with their special editions, vie with each other to sell more copies than the other, re-appearing five times during the short scene as its framing motif. News is thus immediately presented to us as a competitively sold commodity; the more sensational the news, the bigger the opportunity for sales and profits. The significance of the news itself – the pending outbreak of world war – is subordinate to the act of selling it.

The intervening snatches of street conversation between groups of officers, and an old newspaper subscriber talking to the oldest one, show how easily news consumers see the commercialised press as their sole and trusted source of information, education and opinion. One of the officers evidently looks up with great respect to another, whom he sees as 'fantastically well educated' (Kraus, 1919:8. All Kraus translations by JT) *because he reads the press thoroughly, from A-Z*. The oldest subscriber can scarcely wait for tomorrow's leading article; he eagerly anticipates the editor's phrases and opinions, so that he can adopt them as his own, saying: 'He'll find the right words to express it, better than ever before [...]. He'll speak to us all from the heart [...] even to those in high places – especially to them' (Kraus 1919:10). It is Moriz Benedikt, owner/editor of the *Neue Freie Presse* – Vienna's most prestigious paper – who is referred to here. *He* will find the language, and *his* words will be listened to in the very highest echelons. *His*, the journalist/entrepreneur's, discourse, in other words, sets the agenda; it will become the dominant, accepted discourse among consumers *and* decision makers.

The final snatch of conversation in the scene is between two reporters rehearsing their articles for the next day's editions. They describe the atmosphere in the streets as the momentous news breaks. Earlier in the scene, the exchanges of street conversation have shown people who have just heard the news of the assassination carrying on conversations about which café to visit, their sexual conquests, the theatre, and famous actors. The assassination of the Archduke in Sarajevo is no more than another item of gossip. The reporters' planned story, however, speaks of the feeling of deep shock which engulfed the normally joyful crowd. In *their* story, grief suffuses people's faces as they snatch up the special editions of the newspaper. The event being constructed thus bears no resemblance to what is actually happening; the journalists are far too busy mixing their metaphors and choosing the most stirring phrases for (they hope) tomorrow's front page to even think of concerning themselves with the irrelevancies going on around them. Kraus is, in miniature, illustrating the process of how eyewitness reports by those supposedly providing accurate accounts of events are, in fact, fabrications. It is not what happens, but what will sell, and what fits in with the paper's agenda, which concerns reporters, and gets chosen to appear on the pages.

This, then, is Kraus's opening scenario for the last days of humanity, which we recall, but do not recognise, as the First World War. Word and world become separate in the interests of power and profit. The public is sold distorted reports in manipulated language, and believes it is being informed and educated. Power elites are swayed by the same corrupted discourses to make life and death decisions based on them. The media mogul reigns supreme.

Given this perspective, the media mogul, in this case Moriz Benedikt, becomes Kraus's arch enemy, the diabolical source of anti-culture and 'responsible editor-in-chief of the world war' (Kraus 1919:514). Benedikt's admirers, celebrating the fiftieth anniversary of the *Neue Freie Presse*, also in 1914, praised him, *without irony*, as 'the commander-in-chief of the mind' – military metaphors were, of course, in vogue. Benedikt is the *eminence grise* of *The Last Days of Humanity*. His first appearance in person, in Act 1 Scene 11 (all references to 1919 edition) is instructive both as an insight into Kraus's working methods, and as a portrait of Benedikt himself.

Quotation, and juxtaposition of contradictory extracts from the press – most frequently Benedikt's *Neue Freie Presse* – was a major feature of the wartime numbers of Kraus's journal *Die Fackel*, as of his work in general. It was Kraus's habitual way of letting the press condemn itself with its own words, and was also an effective way of avoiding wartime censorship, since there was little sense or justification in censoring that which had already been published. The mere appearance of these extracts in *Die Fackel*, however, often with minimal or no comment, sufficed to alert readers aware of Kraus's perspective to the point he was making.

Thus, in *Die Fackel* of 5 October 1915, Kraus juxtaposed two press quotations, the first from the Pope, also named Benedikt, issuing a prayer from the Vatican, the second from Moriz Benedikt, issuing a leading article from his editor's office. *Pope* Benedikt's prayer is an impassioned plea to the governments of the warring nations to put an end to the terrible carnage which has now been going on for more than a year, reminding them of their responsibility before God, and of the price in corpses and ruins, of their destructive decisions and orders. In contrast to this, *Moriz* Benedikt's editorial, the voice of Kraus's Antichrist, gloats over the fact that the fishes, lobsters and spider-crabs of the Adriatic are able to feast so sumptuously on the bodies of the crews of enemy boats – among them the Italian battleship *Amalfi*, and the submarine *Medusa*, sunk by the Austrian fleet. By juxtaposing the two quotations, Kraus, as well as emphasising the journalist Benedikt's bloodthirsty rejoicing over enemy deaths at sea (prefiguring Murdoch's *Sun* and the sinking of the *Belgrano* in the Falklands War in 1982), is clearly making the bitter comment that in Catholic Austria, Pope Benedikt, the highest power in the Catholic Church, and thus supposedly God's foremost representative on earth, has no influence on government decision making, since it is Moriz Benedikt, the all-powerful journalist-editor, whose word holds sway.

In *The Last Days of Humanity*, exactly the same quotations appear in two consecutive scenes, the first in the Vatican, showing the Pope at prayer, the second in the offices of the *Neue Freie Presse*, with the editor dictating his leading article. Thus, base raw material from the twice-daily newspaper production is snatched from its ephemeral existence by Kraus; it reappears in *Die Fackel* endowed with new critical meaning for contemporaries by the very fact that he has used it. Kraus then plucks the self-same words from *Die Fackel*, and gives them their place in more durable literary form by including them in his drama, which, generations later, is still as powerful an analysis and condemnation of the journalistic manipulation of language and public perceptions in wartime as has been written in the media age.

As well as the war's editor, Kraus portrays an array of star war reporters and behind-the-lines media consumers existing among the profiteers, officers safely billeted away from the action, draft dodgers and warlike clerics, none of whom have any real idea of, or concern for, the butchery and its victims at the front line. Interspersed with these portrayals is a series of scenes consisting of conversations between a character named 'The Optimist', and another, representing Kraus's standpoint, named 'The Grumbler' (elsewhere translated as 'Kraus, the Grouse'). These last frame the tapestry of very specific scenes and characters within Kraus's broader analysis of the war, and his passionate opposition to it; they are thus central to an understanding of the work.

Through them, as well as through polemics in *Die Fackel*, we see how Kraus viewed the war from the start as a commercial operation, desired and run by those who could profit from it – a diabolic materialist elite of techno-capitalist entrepreneurs, opportunistic traders, corrupt journalists, and the military leadership, who all conspired to control and overcome the aged, distant, regretful emperor, whose dynasty and paternalistic value system was about to collapse for ever. In December 1914, in his first great polemic following the outbreak of the war, Kraus wrote:

> Humanity is just the client. Behind the flags and the flames, behind the heroes and helpers, behind all fatherlands, an altar has been set up, from which the holy wisdom of the market is handed down: God created the consumer! But God did not create the consumer so that he might prosper on earth, but rather for a higher purpose: so that business might prosper on earth [...] (Kraus 1914:5).

Kraus clearly saw the link between the rise of international capitalism and the development of new military and communications technologies and equipment, now being manufactured, sold and used for real. His wartime writing on the subject uses such concepts as the 'techno-capitalist world view' (Kraus 1918a:31), and, in the words of The Grumbler, his *alter ego*, 'capitalist world destruction' (Kraus 1919:91). Following a report of a submarine sinking an enemy troop transporter in the Mediterranean in just 43 seconds, the Grumbler envisions an ultimate technical war of depersonalised mass destruction, with a crippled individual destroying cities by pressing buttons in his office:

> For there's a cripple sitting there at work,
> Presses the button, gives the switch a jerk,
> And London just went up in smoke [...] (Kraus 1919:493).

In this scenario, ordinary front line soldiers on both sides are no more than fodder, transported to the abattoirs of the trenches, for hungry arms manufacturers, themselves portrayed as international capitalist entrepreneurs, supplying to customers on either side of the battle lines. In one of many examples, the Grumbler contrasts Bethlehem, birthplace of the saviour of the world in the Christian tradition, with Bethlehem, USA, home of America's largest arms manufacturers. His counterpart, The Optimist, states that this then, is a place from which Germany's enemies are supplied with arms. The Grumbler agrees, but adds that this is being done not just by German-Americans, but by Germans from Germany – the head of the Steel Trust is a German-American, and, according to the Wall Street Journal, 20 per cent of its shares are German owned (Kraus 1919:233-4).

To Kraus/The Grumbler, just as international arms manufacturers, military suppliers and war profiteers treat the war as a business opportunity, so press enterprises are an internationally harmonised force, which manipulate the minds of the publics on either side into supporting the start and perpetuation of the war, in their financial interests, and those of their advertisers and fellow entrepreneurs in the market place. Within this unsavoury collaboration, the press plays *the* key role, for it delivers public opinion, based on its hegemonic discourse, to the economic power elites and their political fig leaves. For Kraus, the war is just one lucrative episode in a larger, long-term process; the press did not suddenly switch to such a propagandistic role because of the outbreak of war. Rather, this was part of its structural function, which it had been practising for years. Correspondingly, it had not only long since gained control over public thought patterns and attitudes, it had also by 1914 created the cultural climate in which war became possible, acceptable, even desirable. He wrote in 1914:

> One might one day realise what a small matter such a world war was relative to the spiritual mutilation of humanity through its press, and how the war was basically just one manifestation of that self-mutilation [...]. If one only reads a newspaper for information, one does not learn the truth, not even the truth about the newspaper. The truth is that the newspaper is not a place for information to be given, rather it is just hollow content, or more than that, a provoker of content. If it prints lies about atrocities, real atrocities are the result. There is more injustice in the world because there is a press which has falsely reported it and which complains about it! It is not nations which fight against each other; rather the international disgrace, the profession which controls the world, not despite but because of its irresponsibility, deals out wounds, tortures prisoners, harasses foreigners, turns gentlemen into thugs [...]. There are numerous nations, but there is only one press (Kraus 1914:10).

It will be noted that Kraus is, in December 1914, launching the idea of the press as the provoker, through its lies, of future evil, corrupt actions and news events.

For Kraus, at the centre of this process of media provoking atrocities is linguistic corruption. This comprises his whole conception of the death of imagination and public disorientation through the commercialisation of language, and his detailed unpacking of *how* language is instrumentalised by the press for the purposes of deceit, control and profit. Thus, in another debate between The Optimist and The Grumbler, we have this exchange, where Kraus posits that the use of cliché to promote hypocrisy and double standards when referring to one's own and 'the enemy's' attributes, is an example of how misuse of language makes war possible:

The Optimist: Are you then in a position to make a connection between language and war?

The Grumbler: Try this one: that the language which has to the greatest extent been petrified into clichés and stock expressions also has the tendency and the readiness to find itself blameless, in a tone of complete conviction, of everything that in another it would find worthy of reproach.

The Optimist: And that is supposed to be a quality of the German language?

The Grumbler: Principally. It is today itself a commodity which is flogged off to its speakers and makes up the content of their lives [...] (Kraus 1919:96).

Later in the same discussion, commercialised journalistic language is linked crucially to a loss of clear thought and imagination:

The Grumbler: The imagination of the modern era has lagged impossibly far behind its technical achievements.

The Optimist: Yes, but does one fight wars with imagination?

The Grumbler: No, because if one still had any, one would never fight them again.

The Optimist: Why not?

The Grumbler: Because then the influence of a phraseology left over from a worn out ideal would no longer find space to confuse people's brains; because one could imagine even the most unimaginable atrocity, and would know in advance how quickly the distance is travelled from the colourful turn of phrase and from all the flag-waving and euphoria to the grey clothed misery of the front [...]. So if one had imagination, one would know that it is a crime to expose life itself to chance, it is a sin to reduce death itself to an accident [...]. If one had imagination instead of newspapers, technology would not be a means of making life harder, and science would not be heading for its own destruction (Kraus 1919:104).

It is in this sense that Kraus, the Grumbler, claimed that: 'Sheets of newspaper have been the kindling for the world conflagration' (Kraus 1926:196), and:

We were turned into invalids by the rotary presses before there were any sacrifices to the cannons. Had not all realms of the imagination been evacuated by the time of that written declaration of war on the earth's population? [...] It is not that the press set in motion the machinery of death, but that it hollowed out our heart, so that we could no longer imagine how it would be; that is its war guilt (Kraus 1919:593-94).

Returning to the opening scene of the drama, and the reporters under instructions to capture the atmosphere in Vienna as war is declared, Kraus presents us with an episode in which crowds are out on the *Ringstrasse*, some groups are excitedly shouting chauvinistic slogans and others are involved in xenophobic harassment of any foreigner they encounter. An aggressive cab driver refuses to accept a valuable piece of foreign currency as payment, but keeps it, giving no change, chasing the passenger away with a flood of crude abuse. This menacing atmosphere, observed and documented by Kraus, is treated by the reporters as follows:

The First Reporter: Not a hint of arrogance or weakness. They have today swept in their thousands and hundreds of thousands through the streets – arm in arm; rich and poor; old and young; exalted and lowly. The behaviour of each single one of them showed that he was fully aware of the gravity of the situation, but also proud to feel in his own body the pulse of the great era which is dawning.
A Voice from the Crowd: Bugger off!
The Reporter: Hear how again and again the *Prince Eugen March* rings out, then the National Anthem, and how naturally this is followed up by the *Watch on the Rhine*, a sign of loyalty to our ally (Kraus 1919:40).

The reporter creates an illusory image which corresponds in no respect to the reality around him. He is describing the scene in such a way that those reading his account will come to believe themselves to have participated in, or to have missed – exactly as their newspaper wants them to believe – a joyous and dignified celebration of the outbreak of war. The sordid reality will be replaced in the readers' minds by the glamour of the press report.

Kraus's portrayal of the act of corruption of language by reporters/propagandists ranges from cases of crude misrepresentation of facts and deception about the realities of war, to cases of linguistic 'decoration'. Here those realities are given an aura of romance, made attractive through humour, or presented as personal adventures of the journalists, who manipulate the sober language of the report by appropriating literary forms. They thus intentionally conceal or distract from facts and images which would turn publics against the hostilities, pursued for their own ends by power elites of which the media are a crucial, and in Kraus's view dominant, component.

For example, Kraus contrasts press descriptions of the front as being like a convalescent home, where soldiers enjoy close and friendly relations with their officers, with the reality of soldiers going to the lengths of infecting themselves with venereal disease in order to get away from the intolerable conditions, in such numbers that the 'friendly' officers were threatening daily beatings for venereal disease sufferers.

On other occasions, Kraus condemns warlike parodies of poems by, and quotations from, German literary masters such as Goethe as the desecration of authentic artistic expression for materialistic, journalistic ends, and as the ultimate negation of the German cultural tradition. An outcome of such cultural desecration is manifested in the acceptance by Christians in Catholic Austria of the melting of church bells for munitions, and their inability to see the grotesqueness of the converse, fabricating rosaries from pieces of shrapnel. Linguistic corruption is at the origin of the destruction of the moral order, and this in turn leads to barbaric actions and public participation or acquiescence in them.

Kraus reserves a significant space in *The Last Days of Humanity* for the mockery of star war reporters such as Roda Roda and Alice Schalek, for their self-importance, self-promotion and connivance in the creation of stories that mislead the public and suit the commercial and military elites. In Kraus's portrayal, Roda Roda's career has been made by the war. Previously an undistinguished hack, he has risen to fame and fortune through his reports from the front, and now struts from one battle scene to the next, not exposing himself to danger, but expecting VIP treatment from the officers in return for favourable mention in his reports, regardless of what is actually happening. In a significant phrase, during a scene in which Roda Roda interrupts the action with a song about himself, Kraus presents him as someone who is 'making up new world history':

To bring you tales
Of soldiers lives
That is for me no mystery
I boost our sales
From the front lines
And make up new world history.

Today I'm by
The Vistula
Tomorrow the Isonzo
I'll tell you why
I've missed no war –
Because I've got the know-how.

The Brigadier
Reports to me
The foe will get sent running.
So when it's here
Their victory,
I just write that *we're* winning (Kraus 1919:170).

Alice Schalek makes repeated appearances throughout the drama, haunting the battle zones in search of 'authentic insights' from the 'ordinary soldiers', yet constantly finding that they do not react in the way that she needs them to for her journalistic purposes. Her 'interviews' typically consist of a florid monologue by herself, vaunting her personal courage and her own intrepid insistence on gaining access to the real action, interspersed by a few terse phrases by the interviewee to whom she scarcely listens, merely picking out a usable word or phrase. In one scene, she arrives at a mountainous *Vorstellung* (= outpost) on the south-west front. Her careless intrusion into the observation point reveals its position, provoking an exchange of fire. Unaware of the consequences of her actions, she says as the firing starts: 'Thank God, we arrived just at the right moment. Now the *Vorstellung* (= performance) is beginning.' Then, a little later, interviewing the officer in charge, she says: 'Isn't it so, Lieutenant, you, who are right in the midst of war, admit it, many of you just don't want it to end.' He replies: 'No, that's what none of us wants, that is to say, everyone wants it to end.' As the shooting stops, she says: 'It seems that the show is over, what a shame! It was first-class' (Kraus 1919:223).

For Schalek, the journalist, the war is a self-publicising ego-trip in which soldiers are bit-players and the events a mere backdrop to her heroic adventure. While purporting to probe the psychology of the combatants, she is in fact imposing her *Vorstellungen* (= conceptions/prefabricated phrases/clichés) on to them, and these distortions are what reach the reading public on the home front.

Holding the scene together linguistically with the triple pun on the word *Vorstellung* is a typically Krausian technique which, with the three meanings, goes beyond wordplay in its revelation of the journalistic process of transforming reality into story or show and thence into false or misleading report.

The Last Days of Humanity is also populated with newspaper readers, and replete with scenes in which subscribers converse in terms determined by what they have read, and according to the standpoint of their newspaper. Foremost among these is the character Old Biach, his copy of the *Neue Freie Presse* under his arm, its contents in his head, and the words of owner/editor Moriz Benedikt in his mouth. In an early scene, Biach is sitting in a café where one of his cronies remarks that his style of speaking resembles that of Benedikt's editorials. Biach replies: 'So what? That's hardly a miracle. One falls involuntarily under his spell! [...] He talks like one of us, but even more clearly. One can't tell if he's talking like us, or we like him' (Kraus 1919:58). This confusion of Biach's words with those of Benedikt in the *Neue Freie Presse* is satirically pushed to the extreme in Act 4 Scene 27, in which Biach carries out a conversation where his speech is composed entirely of citations from the *Neue Freie Presse*, and resonant clichés from Benedikt's leading articles. In the final act, Biach collapses and dies, still muttering Benedikt's phrases. His last words are: 'That...is...the...end...of... the...editorial' (Kraus 1919:475).

Biach's death symbolises a broader death of the imagination, a spirit ultimately overcome by corrupted language. For Kraus, Benedikt is the embodiment of this manipulative process, or, as The Grumbler puts it:

> He is only a newspaper publisher, yet he triumphs over our spiritual and moral honour. His tune alone has caused more deaths than the war which he whipped up and fuelled. The screaming tones of the banker-slaughterer, who holds the world by its throat, is the elemental accompaniment of this bloody action. Even the reader who is distant in time and place will feel that we have here suffered something quite exceptional. I have an old subscriber die of this language [...]. It overpowers life, and then causes the release of the fatal stroke (Kraus 1919:514).

There is no doubt that for Kraus, as a result of his minute daily observations in wartime Vienna, the control of press discourse over ordinary readers' minds was pervasive. However, he also shows many people operating at two levels. Publicly they conformed to the rhetoric to the extent that it blinded them to the war's insanities and barbarisms, while privately they pursued personal advantage or survival, vociferously supporting the war in line with the propaganda while at the same time arranging exemption from military service for themselves or their family members, or investing for personal gain in companies profiting from the war.

In the epilogue of *The Last Days of Humanity*, entitled *The Last Night*, Kraus's demonisation of Moriz Benedikt reaches its climax, but it also transcends into far more than an attack on an individual. Benedikt is elevated here into the archetype of the evils of a corrupt journalism. Just as Kraus intended the play *The Last Days of Humanity* to lift his time and place bound World War materials out of their specific context, turning them into a commentary on modern warfare and commercialised, materialistic anti-culture of much broader significance, so the figure of Benedikt is transformed in the apocalyptic versified epilogue of the tragedy into the all-powerful 'Lord of the Ratpack'. Here, as the war approaches its end (the epilogue is dated 1917 and was published in 1918), its diabolical editor-in-chief steps forward victorious. He has achieved his aim of hell on earth while fulfilling his ambition of absolute power. We can forget the redeeming power of the crucified Christ, the supposed saviour, *he*, the Antichrist, has now taken over, thanks to the power of his pen, the black magic of printer's ink, and the mechanical printing press. As a result of this, the crucifiers now step out of the shadows, rejoicing in the rewards of their betrayal. The journalist king dominates the public and the money markets, and he replaces God, the cosmic emperor who, like Franz Josef, symbol of the dying Habsburg Empire, is obliterated. The last two stanzas of his apotheosis reiterate the means by which absolute power has been gained. He declaims:

> The secret trick we've found
> It is the loyal bond
> Of death, machine and ink.
> Your thanks you should express
> To the bloodied printing press.
> See black on red, and think!
>
> I hit with black inked dart
> My arch foe in the heart!
> Because it's done, now fear
> Your neighbour, hate is burning,
> Alone with Judas' earning
> The Antichrist is here (Kraus 1918b:29).

The Last Days of Humanity sees itself as unmasking how lies of instrumentalised nationalism, and concerning the reality of war were able to dupe national publics into readiness, even enthusiasm, to go to war, and thereafter to pursue it in the midst of the evident ruin it was causing. These were disseminated by the press in the interests of power elites ready to gamble with the lives, health and welfare of millions, following decades of prising apart language and meaning for commercial ends, and developing methods of thought control.

Conclusion

To return to John Pilger's story at the outset of this chapter, one is, in the light of Kraus's portrayal, provoked to envisage a scenario in which C.P. Scott had replied to Lloyd-George: 'I *will* tell the people the truth about the war', and had done so. To this can be added a further scenario in which *emancipated* majority publics on both sides of the conflict resisted war-mongering media propaganda. Neither premise is impossible. Both are totally consistent with what European culture likes to believe about itself. Yet, following them through, one would be forced to imagine a radically different twentieth century.

Although, after generations of subsequent media theory and analysis, some of his formulations appear antiquated and reductive, Kraus laid down in *The Last Days of Humanity* a fundamental challenge to the rest of the century, made continually pertinent by media behaviour in subsequent wars. The challenge is to react to his 'extreme' hypothesis, *either* by accepting it in principle (allowing for refinement and modification), and finding ways of resisting and neutralising the power of media discourse, *or* by demonstrating its falseness or basic inadequacy with convincing refutations and alternatives. From the perspective of a new century which wasted little time before deploying again the discourses and technology of destruction, it is all too evident that the Krausian challenge has yet to be answered.

Chapter 4

No Word that Fits.
Media Discourse and the Rise of Fascism

He showed how an 'inner' investigation of ways of speaking and writing, down to punctuation and even typographic errors, can lay bare an entire moral and political system (Herbert Marcuse on Kraus 1964).

Introduction

Karl Kraus had one fundamental insight in common with Hitler – that of the assignment of central importance to media discourse in controlling the mind of the public; but what Kraus set out to purify, Hitler poisoned beyond all previous intoxications. Hitler stated in 1923: 'Propaganda, propaganda, propaganda, all that matters is propaganda' (Curran and Seaton 1991:249). Two years earlier, Kraus wrote: 'In the beginning was the press, and then the world appeared' (Kraus 1967:56) (the opening of his much performed *Press Song*) expressing in lapidary fashion *his* knowledge that how we see the world depends on media discourse.

The state of physical and moral destruction in which Hitler left Europe in 1945 following world war and holocaust is described and debated in numerous well documented accounts in which interpretation of the role played by propaganda receives due attention, but we still seek a fully satisfying cultural explanation of how it all could have happened. Kraus's warnings of the 1920s and early 1930s based on his press discourse analyses, which do point to such a fuller explanation, are now seldom read. I am, however, going to resurrect them because, although a profoundly disturbed and tortured testimony, they bear crucial witness to moments of the deepest cultural betrayal, and add to our understanding of Kraus's seminal language-based interpretations of the course and causes of events in the German speaking world of the first third of the twentieth century.

The despair of *The Last Days of Humanity*, Kraus's critical interpretation of the 1914-18 war, with its concentrated mix of heightened documentary and absurd comedy-by-quotation in an apocalyptic framework, induced the kind of shell-shocked laughter that is born of disgust, contempt, helpless outrage and survivor's guilt. Here, the power of Kraus's portrayal is such that, generations on, cool critique is still inconceivable, and the sense of the grotesque which he creates leaves its permanent mark on the conscience. Like no other, Kraus, at that 'moment of untruth' had the ability to illuminate the palpable 'newstoriographical' lies woven into the everyday language and imagery which were inculcated into media consumers, including those in positions of power. He saw these same 'passivised' consumers to be enveloped in a fabric of untruth, and predisposed to conform, believe, and display their own subsequent thought and life patterns – and thence their actions – as ready-to-wear mental designer straitjackets, marketed, bought and worn as the latest discursive fashion item.

At least in his writings up to, including and following the 1914-18 war through to the mid 1920s, Kraus believed that some kind of residual covenant between language and meaning survived. Even if it was attacked and defeated, and the forces ranged against it were overpowering, they could be resisted and counter-attacked, whether by an embattled voice in the wilderness such as himself, or by collective social action. An ideal of true, meaningful expression, however distant, existed, and was worth defending. For Kraus, the writing and live performance of his works was emancipatory cultural action in the public sphere. In the new, drastically shrunken first Austrian democratic republic of the early 1920s, moreover, and in the brief flowering of socialist municipal culture that characterised 'Red Vienna', Kraus could perceive, on the one hand, a local setback in the military defeat of the old elites and the illusions they had succeeded in imposing on the people at such immense human cost, and, on the other, an opportunity for those on the left whose rhetoric could harmonise with his, to progress in the creation of a society in which the corrupting forces of commercialised journalistic language would not prevail.

It was not long, however, before, in the mid 1920s, Kraus was forced to conclude that the illusions were his, and that the new cultural menace was of a far more terrifying nature than the old one. Old elites recovered in fierce new guises, and old lies spawned monstrous offspring. The processes of declining democracy and rising Nazism led increasingly to glorification of brainless violence against both people and language, and to the trumpeting of shameless anti-culture which threatened, along with much else, simply to smash a dissident Jewish intellectual and burn his works.

One has to ask oneself what *could*, or *should*, be easy, readable, pleasant or consistent about the writings of someone trying to find a footing in the midst of this avalanche into the unspeakable, and Kraus certainly does not provide it. His mental processes at these moments are as convoluted as they are authentic, as horror-filled as they are sporadic and close to unreadable before being reduced to a self-acknowledged impotence and virtual silence between 1934 and 1936, just before he died. This may not sound like a promising basis for a cultural-linguistic understanding of the embracing of Nazism by Germans, Austrians and others, but Kraus's writings nevertheless pose the penetrating questions for all media criticism and analysis, and for any subsequent re-workings of history which foreground language and culture.

Kraus, Language, and Silence

For Kraus, the only appropriate response to Hitler's takeover of power in Germany was silence. He wrote because he felt he owed his shocked or disappointed readers an explanation of that silence, then he withdrew what he had written from publication, producing instead, in October 1933, a four-page issue of *Die Fackel* – number 888 – containing an obituary for his friend, the architect Adolf Loos, and a ten-line poem indicating his reason for silence:

> Let no one ask what all this time I did.
> My lips are sealed
> And no reason will yield.
> And silence rules us since our earth exploded.
> No word that fits.
> One speaks with deadened wits
> And dreams of the sun which happiness created.
> The worst was done;
> And after all was one.
> The word gave in when that dark world invaded (Kraus 1933:4).

Lines 5 and 10 make it clear: writing is useless in the face of the elemental brutish violence of Nazism.

Then, at the end of July 1934 (just before the assassination of the Austro-fascist chancellor Dollfuss, in whom Kraus had invested a much criticised remainder of desperately contorted and forlorn hope as the last bulwark against Hitler) he published a special edition of *Die Fackel*, the 315 pages of *Why 'Die Fackel' is not appearing*. This replaced what he had withdrawn from publication earlier (*Die Dritte Walpurgisnacht/The Third Night of St Walpurgis*, which, written in the summer of 1933, survived the war and eventually appeared only in 1952). Written in January and February 1934, *Why 'Die Fackel' is not appearing* integrates sections of what he had previously withdrawn and repeats the much misinterpreted words with which Kraus had opened *Die Dritte Walpurgisnacht*: 'On the subject of Hitler, I have no comment' (Kraus 1952:9 and 1934:2).

Far from being a sign of failure to grasp the significance of Hitler, this was an indication of Kraus's recognition of what his arrival in power really meant. If, *following* the Third Reich, Adorno could write of the impossibility of poetry *after* Auschwitz, Kraus, at its *outset*, recognised the mass-murder of language which *preceded* Auschwitz, and made it conceivable. In confronting this, Kraus realised the powerlessness of his own language, and, more than that, the failure of his whole life's mission: 'On the great theme of the outbreak of hell, he whose work was done in vain – that of imagining the worst – fails with passionate cowardice' (Kraus 1934:24). To comment on Hitler was now senseless, and it was only if people realised *why* it was senseless that they would understand the true gravity and tragedy of what was happening. While you are still capable of saying, 'this is the worst', Kraus was telling them, you have not yet experienced the worst.

Kraus had been aware from the earliest days after the 1918 defeat and subsequent founding of the first Austrian republic that the old elites, ghosts of the previous era, could and would reassert themselves, indeed he documented the process in *Die Fackel*, but it was from as early as 1925 that he started to express genuine and increasing fear that social democracy had failed, that the doors were opening up for the 'unconquerables' to return to dominance, and that, to use his metaphor, the bullets of the 1914-18 war had gone in one ear and out the other. One apocalypse had not been enough for lessons to be learnt, and a second was thus becoming inevitable.

Foremost among these 'unconquerables' – 'the invincible powers of the Austrian bourgeoisie between the swastika and the stock exchange listings' (Kraus 1928a:21) – was, inevitably, the press. Kraus wrote in January 1926:

> That the bourgeois press had the power to unleash the war was something we had to experience. But that it could also emerge from it unscathed and, more insolent than ever, raise its head, on which the cross of incorruptibility is drawn; that the revolution not only failed to cut off even one of the heads of the Hydra which has the body of the people in its clutches, but also that these heads are multiplying and causing offence in ever greater numbers – this is the terrible experience of these seven lean years, plentiful only for the ratpack, which was also able to make a profit from the battlefield of peace (Kraus 1926:10).

In placing the press, and its linguistic corruption at the centre of his socio-cultural analysis, Kraus was out on a limb relative to thinkers in the Marxist tradition who perceived him as making the error of giving a secondary superstructural phenomenon greater importance than primary economic considerations. Even as the tone of his writing darkened, and as, by 1929, he saw the Austro-Marxist Social Democratic Party, in which he had placed some hope, to have unforgivably sold out and compromised itself, Kraus stuck to his linguistic analysis convinced that it provided him with a clearer vision of what was taking place than that which was guiding his former allies. In early 1929, as he approached the 30th anniversary of the founding of *Die Fackel*, he wrote:

> It was my work to expose the press as the event-creating, death bringing organisation of moral and spiritual irresponsibility, as that greatest evil of human society which, by means of the fascination of the printed word was able to divert attention from the danger it represented; as the suicidal weapon by which all the cultural achievements were stripped away, which it purports to protect. To the flatness of the objection of those involved in class struggle that I only fought against one of the derivative manifestations or forms of expression of the capitalist world, I will make no response, because I am deeply convinced that journalism is also quite capable of corrupting the socialist world! And because I consider my battle against the press, which reveals the real face of the ruling class through the smallest report, to be more revolutionary than all the talk of development in bourgeois terminology that our revolutionaries have turned into a prolonged exchange of views with the agreement of both sides. Yes, indeed, I believe the derivative manifestation to be the root cause; the mirror creates the face (Kraus 1929:23).

From this, it was a small step to state, in 1933: 'National Socialism did not destroy the press, rather, the press created National Socialism' (Kraus 1952:280).

Kraus did not need to extend or develop his argument significantly from the position he had established before the 1914-18 war, and subsequently developed, to arrive at this standpoint. He merely had to apply it to the new historical context. His dilemma as a writer and thinker lay rather in his realisation of the superfluity of analytical argument and satirical expression when confronted by elemental barbarism.

The long explanation of the failure of language in the face of Nazism in his 1933 and 1934 writings is nevertheless also an extraordinary demonstration of *how* journalistic corruption of language opened the gates to Nazi barbarism, and of how Nazi barbarism took over this linguistic corruption, and brought about a further twist, the linguistic corruption of linguistic corruption. Whereas in the initial corruption 'word' is separated from 'world', in the secondary phase, that very separation is reversed in a grotesque reunion. When Nazis hear or use a clichéd image, metaphor, self-evident exaggeration or other manifestation of commercialised journalese, they are actually so primitive that they take the corrupted figure of speech literally, and act on it. 'Word' and 'world' become crassly congruent in the barbaric deed. Thus, for example, if lying clichés associated with German superiority and Jewish inferiority had in the Viennese context been part of the populist rhetoric and 'banal racism' that had for decades sold newspapers and pamphlets, polarised political campaigns, made political careers, underpinned nationalism, and provoked massive and equally lucrative counter-polemics in the liberal press, with its users not believing their, albeit despicable, words with any great seriousness, the Nazis took it literally, and turned the words into action. Worn out clichés like 'Jewish vermin' became believed *fact*, and led to the obvious conclusion that they had to be exterminated, and thence to actual extermination.

In an extraordinary early comment in 1923, Kraus showed that he had already recognised this. Far right and proto-Nazi groups were not considered as serious threats at this moment, but Kraus picked out an account in the *Schlesische Zeitung* of the September 1923 Nuremberg Rally in which Hitler stood side by side with the ageing First World War General, Ludendorff, and there were calls to take up the cudgel (to use an apt English metaphor) in the campaign to promote love of the fatherland. Within the report, Hitler is quoted as saying that: 'Each one of you should be decided to *force* onto others the law of love of the fatherland'. Kraus comments:

> It is only in Hitler that one finds something concrete, someone who knows how to get things done when he proposes to force the law of love of the fatherland onto others. He is referring of course to the use of the cudgel as a means of inducing love of the fatherland and as the one and only German reality [...]. In this fantasy world which seems to want to challenge its enemies [...] only with shouting and exuberance, he is concerned with weapons and reality (Kraus 1923:43-44).

Even in 1923, Kraus observes that, for Hitler, 'taking up the cudgel' meant precisely that.

A decade later, Kraus, faced with Hitler in power, perceived what had happened in similar vein. The German people was dealt a 'concussion of epidemic proportions' (Kraus 1952:11), when subjected to 'the cliché breaking out into action' (Kraus 1952:123):

This making real of the content of clichés is applied to all phrases in which an originally bloody or violent content has for a long time only been interpreted in terms of figurative aggression. None, not even those describing the most far-fetched procedures, could escape this, even the horrific: 'To rub salt in open wounds'. There must have been a time when this actually happened, but it had been forgotten to the extent that there was no more any conception of the actual deed, and to the extent that it was impossible to be conscious of the reality. The phrase was used to portray painful feelings on being reminded of a loss, or when someone brought back memories of inner suffering. Such things happen, but the action from which the image was drawn remained out of consideration. But here it is: 'When the old communist cut himself badly in the hand while peeling potatoes, a mocking group of Nazis forced him to put his heavily bleeding hand into a sack of salt. The old man's cries of agony were a great laugh for them'. It is quite inconceivable, yet since it happened, the phrase can no more be used (Kraus 1934:95-96).

To this Kraus adds with gruesome irony that a Nazi claim that they had 'not touched a single hair on a Jew's head' *could* still be used; this, he commented, was just about the only thing that Nazis had not done to Jews, since when they were shaving heads in order to brand them, they did it by pulling off the skin as well.

It was highlighting this perverse reuniting of 'word' and 'world' which was one of Kraus's emblematic ways of characterising the linguistic, cultural, and hence actual barbarities of Nazism in the opening months of the regime. Critical analysis of their very real 'use' of language as illustrated here revealed intensely for Kraus, as to few others at the time, the kind of lengths to which they would be prepared to go in action: 'The regime which says it will "brutally lay low anyone who opposes it" – does so', and 'for the first time in the history of politics the cliché has given birth to real meaning, and not the other way round' (Kraus 1934:95). One may reflect here on what Kraus would have thought of the attack on the twin towers of the World Trade Centre in New York on 11 September 2001, which took literally a scene from a computer game portraying exactly that event. Likewise we may imagine his thoughts on President George W. Bush's making literal of the cliché of countless Westerns, 'Wanted, Dead or Alive' when referring to terrorist leaders in his largely successful attempt to whip up war fever in the US public following the attack.

The taking of clichés and metaphors for facts was just one facet of Kraus's analysis of a much more comprehensive destruction of language by the Nazis – the 'irrational socialists' (Kraus 1952:159). Also central to his critique was the blatant and constant self-contradiction, and contradiction of fact in Nazi discourse, wrapped up in ungrammatical structures which turn what purports to be coherent speech into nonsense. This, for Kraus, was the 'dictatorship which masters everything, apart from language' (Kraus 1934:93), and he gives examples, both through parody and quotation. In the following extract, he perceives a cascade of words contradicting deeds which are then contradicted by further words until not just logic, but language itself collapses:

The world whose thoughts are still functioning looks on with shock and foreboding at this confrontation of words and deeds, full of suspense about the outcome. If it gives more credence to the words and their warlike tone, the answer is trotted out that they should judge the Reich more by its deeds; if it then makes reference to these, then they get Reichstag speeches quoted back at them. If the contradiction is then pointed out, then there is talk of marginal events which cannot be associated with the heart of the revolution, which took over the reins of government by legal means; moreover, an evolution is now on the agenda, for the revolution has been completed, and its major successes are worthy of respect, but it is still in its early days, and what has happened up to now is no more than child's play: first of all the commissars must be removed, and if irresponsible elements intervene, then you'd better get out of the way, otherwise we will sweep you out of our way and take full responsibility for doing so (Kraus 1952:156).

The gradual descent of this passage into incoherence is not parody for its own sake. It exposes, without hyperbole, the disintegrated thought processes that Kraus identified in Nazi discourse, and found to be symptomatic of its abandonment of language as the source and communicator of meaning. It demonstrates the Nazis' corrupt implementation of language for the purpose of manipulating already befuddled minds into total inability to discern the coherent from the contradictory, the imaginative from the unimaginable, that which exposes and illuminates from that which obfuscates, mystifies and demolishes. When, in the face of the Nazi onslaught on language, millions of Germans are swept along with the process, evidently without having their critical faculties alerted, then, Kraus argues, there is no defence left for humanity, and the way is wide open for unchecked barbarism. He provides an example of reality outstripping parody in quoting a sentence from a Hitler speech where he is supposedly answering (justified) accusations of incitement to anti-Semitic violence in the course of a speech in Essen:

> If now many are saying that in my Essen speech I incited the subsequent lack of discipline, indeed the plundering and the like, I refute that. But I have not been so cowardly as to repudiate what they did, indeed I approved it. And if in the heat of the moment they overdid it, then we leaders are to be blamed. For we preached it. We shall continue to clean things up, mercilessly! Exterminate (Kraus 1952:157).

Kraus simply comments that this came from those who claimed that they had not touched a single hair on the head of a Jew.

Integral to Kraus's analysis is that such treatment of language, and the possibility of its effectiveness, would have been impossible without the longer cultural process of previous journalistic corruption of language, and habituation of the reading public to such abuses. Thus his whole prior vision of cultural/linguistic decadence feeds into his explanation of the possibility of Nazism. Hitler's arch-propagandist, Goebbels, is named by Kraus as 'the thorough connoisseur of journalistic dialect' (Kraus 1934:91), that is, he who has appropriated the full range of corrupt manipulative practices of the press, and fashioned out of them the whole set of Nazi propaganda instruments, which he then applied to the brains of the German public, already anaesthetised by previous journalistic practice. Only those who had in the 1914-18 war, accepted that shrapnel could be turned into rosaries or church bells into shells, could now also acquiesce in an Oberammergau passion play in which a blond, blue-eyed Christ figure would wear a robe adorned with swastikas:

> There broke out there a tragic conflict between tourism and better judgement. Those renting out rooms, who were also dressing up as apostles, had apparently become converts to National Socialism, and were suffering pangs of conscience because they were having to act the part of Jews. Now, in order to overcome this embarrassing feeling of pretending to be someone else, they had already grown the long beards and side-locks which they needed for the passion play. And what happens? Compatriots from the north come along and tear at the real beards in the false belief that they are real. Following such physical participation in the Passion they were staging, they had to acknowledge that they were no longer passionate about doing so, and made the suggestion that their beards should be reduced to a minimum, and that, instead of the suffering of Christ, they should do a play *based on the life of Hitler*. This, however, was rejected, since *it was thought that this theme would not attract foreign visitors*. Finally, they came to a compromise solution – the golden mean; they would keep the play in its old form, only give it a face-lift through repeated singing of the *Horst-Wessel-Lied*. With reference to the actors, it was determined that 'the role of Christ should only be played by a blond man with blue eyes, with swastikas emblazoned on his robe', and that the loyal apostles should be of Aryan German type, while Judas should be played 'as an unmistakably Jewish type' (Kraus 1952:253).

Within this anecdote we see the same total cultural/linguistic breakdown and severance of link between original meaning and present action. This leads to the aggressive assertion and performance of a nonsense which outstrips satirical invention, and ushers in the reign of linguistic wonderland, abysmal ignorance, and complete ethical disorientation, leading to arbitrariness of action and removal of restraints on barbarism.

The passage from disintegrated discourse in the service of power elites to barbaric acts and public passivity, and acquiescence in the process and results emerges unmistakably from Kraus's writings on Nazism. Contrasting Nazi practices of blacklisting and burning literary works using racist criteria, with the literary output of writers favoured by the Nazis, Kraus performed a spoof literary critique on a poem that had been praised as an example of the re-awakening of German culture by the pro-Nazi critic Bernhard Diebold. The section quoted by Kraus runs (my translation tries to maintain the attributes of the original):

> This alien race, these leeches, which, strangers to our species
> So incredibly sucked Germanic blood from our people
> Now out with the Jew!...
> Everywhere in German lands they grovel
> Be it in city, village, palace or hovel
> Everywhere the hooked noses
>
> In business and commerce – everywhere the Jew
> Press, theatre, film, look where you will
> Everywhere the Jew, miming the leading role
> Every, everywhere, yes soon every lavatory
> Will be occupied by some Jew (Kraus 1952:46).

Starting his critique in pseudo-academic style, Kraus states: 'The free rhythm, with a certain informality in syntax and punctuation, is naturally adapted primarily for acoustic rendering' (Kraus 1952:46). Then, having treated each section of the doggerel to ironically serious commentary, he concludes:

> While we are certainly dealing here with an indigenous artistic phenomenon, the moulding of the folk will which is undoubtedly intended here in fact only achieves its effect through the voluntary renunciation of the highest spiritual formation, and the few bits of punctuation were added by the type-setter (Kraus 1952:48).

The bathos of the last eleven words spices the persiflage, and mocks the crass pretensions of the critic who had praised the poem; but most of all it indicates Kraus's placing of the piece, and by extension the rest of Nazi literary and critical output, beneath literate comment, and points to his dismissal of it as the mendacious prologue and discursive counterpart of the brutality it sanctions.

The progression from the social naturalisation of such material within publics with minds long infected by journalese, to the actual carrying out of the kind of deeds it incites, and the development by witnesses and readers of rationalisations and strategies permitting at least tacit acceptance of them is, for Kraus, an observable process which he records in later sections of *Die Dritte Walpurgisnacht*.

Unquestioning Nazi supporters such as those who joined Hitler's paramilitaries, could easily be incited through 'poems' such as that quoted above, among other means, to carry out anti-Semitic violence. Equally easily, Kraus showed, could media-besotted publics be persuaded to turn away from, accept, play down or disbelieve accounts of atrocities which were plainly taking place, once a dominating and increasingly intimidating expectance of such compliance had been discursively created.

Kraus's writings provide evidence that by 1933 there was already copious proof of what the Nazis were capable of perpetrating. He refers to accounts of concentration camps in which Jews were forced to kiss the feet and lick the boots of SA officers (more metaphors turned reality), and beaten up if they refused. Their hair was torn out with the skin attached and they were forced to hit each other in the face, or, if they refused, be beaten with cudgels until their blood spurted out. He also quotes the following report:

> An inconspicuous Jew feeds his five children through dealing in rags. SA people come to him and demand 500 Marks. He cannot give it to them because he does not have it; he has never in his life seen so much money all at once. They beat him up until he lies whimpering on the ground. He finally groans: 'In the chest of drawers are 30 Marks for the rent instalment.' They take the money. They then make him swallow a full litre of castor oil, tie him up by the neck in a cloth bag and drag him into the cellar. The oil has its effect, and the man crouches, literally covered in urine and excreta for four days. People hear his screams up in the street. A butcher sets him free. When the victim steps out of the bath, his flesh has been eaten away by the dirt, as if he had been lain, bound, for hours in an ant hill (Kraus 1952:98).

Kraus calls this just one of the thousand cases about which humanity of all races should shout out in protest, but where in fact most either just do not believe it, regard it as an isolated individual case, or accept the perpetrators' denials, and claims that the story is part of a smear campaign of 'atrocity propaganda':

> For worse than murder is murder accompanied by lies, and worst of all by the lies of those who are really aware of the full facts: the pretext of non-belief, which wants to believe the lie rather than the deed; compliance by making oneself as stupid as violence expects; cruel idiocy. No, there can be nothing more hypocritical and crass than this concept of 'atrocity propaganda' and, whenever it comes up, one can be sure that no atrocity could be so badly made up as this counter-attack of a guilty conscience which is only exceeded in its abuse by the urge to disbelieve what one knows, and by the resolve to believe that the inconceivable is also unreal (Kraus 1952:98).

The public's self-deception in the face of atrocity, its passivity and readiness to believe any construction of the story which will exonerate it from action or standing out from the majority, which Kraus refers to here, links back to the press-induced 'death of the imagination' which he identified prior to the 1914-18 war, and in *The Last Days of Humanity*, and at this moment too, Kraus links the public's asthenia to its manipulation by media discourse:

> This journalistic concept of humanity which prostitutes disaster as a sales slogan, and is even still lying when it tells the truth corresponds utterly to the disposition (Kraus uses the word *Habitus*, later to be adopted by Bourdieu. JT.) of a readership, which, even if it were to get really to feel a thousandth of that which it doesn't believe, would once again make contact with humanity (Kraus 1952:98-99).

Conclusion

It will be clear from this and the previous chapter that Kraus's writing, emerging out of, and overshadowed by, the two great human and cultural tragedies and climactic 'moments of untruth' of the first third of Europe's twentieth century, is a passionate and sustained assault on the processes of 'newstoriography' and 'passivication' identified in the introductory chapter. His use of media texts to track lies and processes of discursive deception through to their cumulative effects on their consumers' perceptions, and on subsequent events, sets him up as a provocative guiding spirit for all subsequent theorists and practitioners of radical media criticism. Although he was far from conceiving of himself as a theorist, researcher or distanced critic (he was in fact a university dropout), it is nevertheless against his central seminal insights and conclusions that subsequent debates and practice, as well as the reasoned arguments of their denigrators, have to be judged.

Kraus's passionate individual struggle to redeem a culture, which he rightly saw to be on the edge of self-destruction, failed. In January 1928, he used a quotation from Kierkegaard dating from 1849, which he may have come to think of as his epitaph: 'A single individual cannot help or save an era, he can only express that it is dying' (Kraus 1928b:16).

He died 21 months before Hitler's *Anschluss* of Austria, and thus actually lived through only a tiny proportion of what he had foreseen, but he saw enough to establish convincingly that, by 1933, the cultural prerequisites were in place for the savagery that was to follow. It would have been for him no more than the logical outcome of the rise to power of the anti-culture, rooted in journalistic manipulation of language, which Hitler and his supporters had always represented for him. If the subsequent development of Nazi power, through to world war and holocaust, is re-read in *this* sense, in the context of its many other established causes and facets, a refined working hypothesis for understanding the human capacity for unprecedented barbarism in the media age, which perplexes, and indeed continues to afflict, the post-1945 world, slips into place and demands detailed attention. Unfortunately, it also demands that we look at ourselves, rather than simply transferring the toxic potential and reality onto 'Nazis', 'Germans', or other 'embodiments of evil'. Viewed in isolation, there is an implausibility, even eccentricity, about identifying and highlighting linguistic corruption in media discourse as a neglected cultural root of the barbarisms of the first half of the twentieth century. Those who have followed the story this far will wish to maintain their scepticism, bearing in mind not just the insights, but also the lacunae and inadequacies in the multifarious range of hypotheses, and the heat of recent and ongoing historiographical controversies.

Those maintaining underlying scepticism about according a substantive role to mass media discourse in determining the direction of historical and current events may wish to consider the following internet appeal, by the organisation Search for Common Ground, emerging from Macedonia, apparently on the verge of civil war in early 2001, and ask what lies behind such behaviour by the international mass media:

> We in Macedonia are facing not an imminent civil war, but rather the possibility that irresponsible international media may incite more violence than the people with guns. The international press has been extremely provocative and irresponsible in this very sensitive situation. CNN has reported that Tetovo has 'been taken by the "rebels" who are advancing on Skopje'. The BBC has also been broadcasting alarmist and unconfirmed reports. This is utter nonsense, and incredibly dangerous […]. An urgent call must be made to all international media to stop escalating the situation by putting out inflammatory and unfounded reports that will provoke people here to believe that their only resort is to violence (Mango Website 2001).

The following chapters will seek to investigate and test the hypothesis further in relation to cognate events in the second half of the century. Given the increasing reach and presence in daily life of different forms of media discourse, it would certainly be expected that, if possibly exaggerated claims relating to its power and motives can be substantiated, then the evidence should be present.

Chapter 5

Comics and Communism.
Tintin Fights the Cold War

The more each side became convinced of its image of the other, the more they were locked into hostility (Martin Walker 1994).

I know of no leader of the Soviet Union since the revolution, and including the present leadership, that has not more than once repeated in the various Communist congresses they hold, their determination that their goal must be the promotion of world revolution and a one-world Socialist or Communist state (Ronald Reagan 1981).

Introduction

The years following 1945 in the 'mediatised' world saw an extraordinary discursive transformation in world mapping and in the ideological language with which power elites explained the world to the people. 'The East' and 'The West' – particularly 'Eastern Europe' and 'Western Europe' – were assigned new definitions. In the West, gallant Soviet allies, having played the major role in defeating Nazi Germany, and borne the brunt of the fighting and destruction on their territory, were transformed once again into menacing arch-enemies, as bad, if not worse, than the Nazis had been. Conversely, the German enemy, while still suspect, was, under this new set of perceptions, split into two implausible groups. There were *bad* suspect Germans in the East (sometimes associated with militaristic Prussian stereotypes), who hankered after continuing 'Eastern' totalitarian rule and a congenial transformation from one totalitarian dictatorship to the next. Then there were *good* suspect Germans in the West (stereotyped as more easygoing Rhinelanders), who could be educated into 'our' 'Western' ways of freedom and democracy. This was the simplistic new '(un)truth' which then justified a fortified barrier splitting Germany and Europe from north to south, and the amassing of an apocalyptic range of weapons of mass destruction on either side of it.

Appropriately enough, it was a Western *journalist* who invented the misleading name 'Cold War' to describe this situation. It was an inspired phrase, universally adopted by mass media, politicians and academics, and hence in everyday parlance, which justified keeping the economy on a profitable war footing, because there was an 'enemy' and a 'war', while convincing Western publics, the taxpayers for military budgets, that this was 'peace', since the war was 'cold'. It encapsulated and rendered plausible the insane 'Realpolitik' that the greater the capability for mass destruction, and related military spending, the more frozen the war and the greater the peace and security. Western 'Cold War' propaganda included a whole range of contorted discursive inventions such as the naming of a US nuclear missile 'Peacekeeper' (at least the French military more accurately called one of their affectionately nicknamed bombinettes 'Hades'). This was part of the broad creation of a majority public disposition which, in democratic societies, 'freely' accepted a policy of balance of terror, 'Mutually Assured Destruction', and a vast corresponding nuclear and biological arsenal, capable of destroying the world dozens of times over.

This could be seen as the greatest discursive coup, the most effective convincing of the largest number of 'free' individuals of the sanity of an insanity that world history has ever seen. The resonant term 'Cold War' was always a deceit, covering up a series of 'hot' wars in, for example, Korea and Vietnam, where millions were killed. However, even this newstoriographical distortion was grotesquely superseded in the 1960s, when the most important issue became not petulant East-West confrontation, but the threat to the entire planet of nuclear holocaust. One might argue that, from then on, the continued use of the misleading term 'Cold War' in the political and economic interests of those promoting and pursuing it, successfully imposed and reinforced the accompanying mindset, and criminally distracted media audiences from the really vital issues.

Bertrand Russell, who became in this period of his life one of the clear minds amid the predominant obfuscation and mendacity, expressed it thus in his book Has Man a Future? completed in July 1961, a month before the building of the Berlin Wall began, a year before the Cuban missile crisis, and thus at a moment of high danger 'Cold War' hostilities:

> I am writing at a dark moment, and it is impossible to know whether the human race will last long enough for what I write to be published, or, if published, to be read. But as yet hope is possible, and while hope is possible, despair is a coward's part.
> The most important question before the world at the present time is this: is it possible to achieve anything that anyone desires by means of war? Kennedy and Khruschchev say yes; sane men say no. On this supreme question, Kennedy and Khruschchev are at one [...]. If one could suppose them both capable of a rational estimate of probabilities, we should have to believe that both agree that the time has come for Man to become extinct [...]. Their own blindness is reinforced by a similar blindness on the part of powerful pressure groups, and by a popular hysteria generated by their own propaganda and that of their colleagues and subordinates (Russell 1961:120).

The passage may, with 'historical hindsight' (the 'correct' phrase for swallowing the self-justificatory historiographies of 'Cold War' victors) sound melodramatic, but we should not forget that, recalling 27 October 1962, during the Cuban missile crisis, Robert MacNamara, US Defence Secretary, said to former Khruschchev advisor Fyodor Burlatsky: 'I went up into the open air to look and to smell it, because I thought it was the last Saturday I would ever see' (Walker 1994:171), and Burlatsky responded: 'That was when I went and telephoned my wife and told her to drop everything and get out of Moscow. I thought your bombers were on the way' (ibid). This snatch of conversation demonstrates that 'Mutually Assured Destruction' was not just a phrase, it was *the* overarching issue of the last four decades of the twentieth century, deserving the foremost place in every healthy, well-fed citizen's mind, since it concerned the very survival of the planet and its inhabitants.

Yet if Russell and a significant, if relatively small, number of active citizens did understand and protest against the follies of the 'Cold War', the broad publics of Western Europe and the USA acquiesced in them over these four decades, in accordance with dominant media discourses. Russell was clear about the lies and half-truths fed to Western publics:

> There is in the West much more regimentation and much more misleading propaganda by the Establishment than is generally known. Nor is it admitted that all such restrictions diminish the difference between East and West, and make the claim of the West to be called 'The Free World' derisory (Russell 1961:40).

In support of his assertions, he quotes, among others, the story of Claude Eatherly, which demonstrates the lengths to which the US authorities were prepared to go to suppress truths about the effects of nuclear weapons:

> An extraordinarily interesting case which illustrates the power of the Establishment, at any rate in America, is that of Claude Eatherly, who gave the signal for the dropping of the bomb at Hiroshima. His case also illustrates that in the modern world it often happens that only by breaking the law can a man escape from committing atrocious crimes. He was not told what the bomb would do and was utterly horrified when he discovered the consequences of his act. He devoted himself throughout many years to various kinds of civil disobedience with a view to calling attention to the atrocity of nuclear weapons and to expiating the sense of guilt, which, if he did not act, would weigh him down. The authorities decided that he was to be considered mad, and a board of remarkably conformist psychiatrists endorsed that official view. Eatherly was repentant and certified; Truman was unrepentant and uncertified. I have seen a number of Eatherly's statements explaining his motives. These statements are entirely sane. But such is the power of mendacious publicity that almost everyone, including myself, believed that he had become a lunatic (Russell 1961:41).

The foregoing examples indicate how the 'Cold War' came to be both physically overshadowed by the threat of 'Mutually Assured Destruction' and culturally dominated by the largely successful operation of 'Mutually Assured Deception'.

The rest of this chapter focuses on an individual emblematic example of such mendacious publicity, a piece of spray thrown up by the 'tidal mendacity' of media discourse referred to by Steiner. It is indicative, picked from many possibilities and not meant to stand out as a 'special case'. As such, it may demonstrate along Krausian lines, how investigation of a small piece of widely available discourse, in this case a few pages of a children's comic strip, can suffice to expose the corruption of an entire moral and political system.

Tintin in Context

Hergé's Tintin is one of the legends of mainstream francophone popular culture, whose popularity grew from the first serialised newspaper comic strips, in 1929, to an iconic status in the post-1945 period, leading to translations of the comic books into 58 languages and global sales of over 200 million books (about half in French speaking countries) by the end of the century. The Tintin books continued to grow in popularity after Hergé's death in 1983; they are remembered with great affection by successive generations and are still widely available and read today. The publishers, Casterman, estimate that 44 per cent of French households possess at least one Tintin volume. Although Belgian in origin, Tintin was adopted in France, so much so that General de Gaulle is reported to have commented to André Malraux: 'Basically, my only rival on the international front is Tintin. We are the little people who don't allow ourselves to be walked over by the big ones' (Tintin website).

In February 1999, the French parliament showed its members' desire to be associated with the character as the Assemblée Nationale debated the issue: 'Tintin. Is he from the left or from the right?' in the wake of disclosures about Hergé's collaboration with the Nazis, and criticisms of racism and anti-Semitism levelled at the Tintin books. Fearing the appropriation of Tintin by the far right, speakers from the Gaullists, socialists and Greens all claimed Tintin as their own, with only marginal reservations being expressed. The long-term popularity of Tintin in Belgium, France, and elsewhere does not need to be further underlined. The stories remain an accepted – indeed vaunted – part of mainstream popular culture, and it is indeed because of this that the texts can be taken as both indicative and generative of a naturalised cultural climate. Even if, across the decades, not unlike early Disney cartoons, aspects of the drawings and texts have dated, and some stereotypes portrayed do not correspond to later historiographical judgements and standards of political correctness, it is argued, this should not prevent successive generations of children and parents from enjoying and re-enjoying the adventures.

The first Tintin story was *Tintin au Pays des Soviets* (1930) (English version *Tintin in the Land of the Soviets*, 1989). Some aspects of the publication history are of interest here. After its initial serialisation in *Le Petit Vingtième*, the weekly children's supplement of the Brussels right-wing Catholic paper *Le XXme Siècle*, in 1929, and its appearance in the French conservative Catholic young people's weekly *Coeurs Vaillants*, the first complete version was published in 1930, and went to nine editions. Hergé (Georges Rémi, 1907-1983) had been put in charge of the new supplement in 1928 as a protégé of its editor, Father Norbert Wallez, who presided over *Le XXme Siècle* and its distinctly nationalist, anti-communist and doctrinally traditionalist alignment. It was here that Hergé was to meet Leon Degrelle, later the founder of Belgium's fascist party, Rex, and leader of its wartime SS division. Hergé drew the cover for a political pamphlet written by Degrelle in1932, and Degrelle, without Hergé's approval, was to claim: 'Tintin, c'est moi!' (Indian Express website).

After the war, which Hergé spent working and producing further comic strips for the Brussels Nazi collaborationist newspaper *Le Soir*, including in his work gratuitous racist and anti-Semitic caricatures, Hergé came to regard *Tintin in the Land of the Soviets* as a 'sin of his youth' and was unwilling to let it be republished. Despite this, Casterman released a facsimile edition in 1981, leading to translations in nine different languages in the following decade, and further French editions in 1988, an appropriate accompaniment to the final crisis of the Soviet system, and 2000, when it was to be found on hypermarket shelves as suitable children's literature for the new millennium. Thus, however much the author moderated his views, there were, before and after his death, decisions to publish and re-publish, and significant demand for, his quasi-fascist anti-Soviet juvenilia of the late 1920s and early 1930s, which coincided with, and were rendered socially and politically acceptable in, the climate of the Reaganite re-polarisation of the 'Cold War' and the final push towards the demise of the Soviet Union in the 1980s. If the original work emerged from the kind of reactionary Catholic environment which saw fascism as the preferable option to atheistic Soviet communism, it found a congenial atmosphere for its re-emergence as the West escalated its nuclear overkill capability, in what turned out to be its final campaign against the collapsing Soviet 'evil empire'.

At the time of the first edition, for someone moving in the circles that Hergé did, as for a broader sector of mainstream Catholic and right-of-centre media and public opinion, the political position promoted by *Tintin in the Land of the Soviets* would have been seen as a healthy and desirable one to propagate to young people. In the political and economic confusion of the period, as, towards the end of 1929, the consequences of the Wall Street Crash (October 1929) started to open up popular support for the Nazis in Germany, it would still not have been unusual that Hergé's concentration remained on his anti-Soviet polemic, completed in May 1930. He had never visited the Soviet Union, and there are curious details in the story, such as the availability of Shell petrol, Huntley and Palmer's biscuits, and bananas, which reveal his ignorance of it. As the main source for the particular image of the Soviet Union which he created, he relied heavily on an anti-Soviet diatribe entitled *Moscou sans Voiles* by former diplomat Joseph Douillet, a book which, written out of a visceral *a priori* anti-communism, could only be ranked as a work of propaganda rather than a serious critique of Stalin's regime.

The fact that Hergé's work drew on such distorted material qualified it admirably for its 'Cold War' reprise in the 1980s. The book's acceptability, appropriateness and reinforcing role amid the insane Western dominant elite assumptions and media imagery of the 'Cold War' in the 1980s makes it an appropriate subject for analysis here. Five main anti-Soviet themes in *Tintin in the Land of the Soviets* help to show that the genealogy of Western, anti-Soviet discourse – like all effective propaganda, a tangled confusion of fact and fiction – maintained a blithe continuity in its earliest and later manifestations from the very different first decade of the Soviet Union to its last. They provided the rationale, aspects of which were also used by the Nazis to justify *their* anti-communism and invasion of the USSR, for the hostile public image of the Soviet Union in the West (temporarily reversed during the years when the West concluded that it had a worse enemy in Hitler's Germany) which was integral to the construction of the 'Cold War', and was successfully used to justify the demented conduct of the nuclear arms race.

Tintin and Anti-Soviet Propaganda

The five main themes, reinforced by the front cover which depicts boy hero, investigative reporter Tintin, and his dog Milou (Snowy), posed in front of a silhouette of Russian church domes, signifying his identification with a non-communist, Christian Russia, are, first, the ubiquity and deviousness of the Soviet secret police; second, the Soviet construction of fake factories to deceive gullible Western visitors; third, the holding of phoney elections; fourth, economic disaster – ruined buildings, bread queues, and famine as a result of the Soviet system; fifth, secret stores of luxury goods, used for propaganda purposes.

Ubiquity of Soviet Secret Police

About two thirds of the story's 138 pages are devoted to Tintin's pursuit, capture by, or escape from Soviet agents or authorities. Even as he sets out from Brussels by train on his reporting mission to the Soviet Union, he is shadowed by a black-bearded Soviet agent, who characterises Tintin as a 'dirty petit-bourgeois' (Hergé 1981:1), and attempts to assassinate him with a bomb. The bomb, described by the agent as 'one of the best cures for curiosity known to our times' (ibid), demolishes two train carriages, but Tintin and Milou naturally emerge unhurt, if bedraggled. The initial message is, however, of the constant presence and brutality of Soviet agents, and of the terroristic lengths they are prepared to go to in order to thwart a 'free' journalist from trying to find out 'the truth about the Soviet Union'.

On arrival at the Soviet frontier, Tintin is immediately marched off to the 'people's commissar', a clearly corrupt, uniformed state official, sitting behind a broken table, cigarette in mouth, drink and revolver on the table. Although Tintin's entry papers are in order, the agent who had already tried to blow him up objects, describing him as a journalist who needs 'suppressing'. The commissar is about to shoot Tintin without further ado, but the agent stops him, suggesting that it will be better to have Tintin 'disappear' by accident (Hergé 1981:11). From this point on, Tintin is constantly followed, and repeatedly escapes attempts to do away with him. On one such occasion, while in captivity, he is sent off to the torture chamber by his interrogator, who bears a passing resemblance to Lenin, to 'help' him reveal the aim of his journey. Hergé accords the torture chamber a double sized picture (Hergé 1981:66). It is filled with mediaeval torture instruments – a rack, with a bloody hand print on the wall beside it, and buckets beneath it; a board with long nails sticking out of it on the blood-stained floor; a red-hot iron heating over a fire; a selection of variously shaped pincers and hammers hung on the wall, and what looks like a severed head preserved in a jar. The two torturers are portrayed as Tartar automatons with identical Asiatic faces. They are, of course, following a heroic show of Tintin's martial prowess, subjected by him and Milou to the very tortures which they would have inflicted. The first one is impaled on the nails, the other branded with the red-hot iron. The enemy is demonised. Enemy deaths are of no importance, and deserved.

The final brush with Soviet agents takes place when Tintin and Milou have escaped to Berlin. Disguised as a hotel porter, Soviet agent Boustringovitch disables them with chloroform in their hotel room, intending to transport them back to the Soviet Union. He rejoices prematurely that Moscow will be pleased with his success. Tintin, however, who has only been pretending to be drugged, soon overcomes the agent, and while tying him up, discovers a coded message concealed on him. He alerts the German police, who lock up the agent, and tell Tintin that the secret document contained plans to blow up all the capitals of Europe with dynamite (as terrorists do). Tintin has thus saved Europe from destruction by Soviet terrorism, and receives a large reward in German money, with which he immediately purchases an expensive sports car. It is perhaps due to Hergé's political blinkers at the time that there is no hint of the situation in Germany as he was producing the final pictures of his story. He indicates no concern or awareness that democratic rule was crumbling, that millions were unemployed in the Depression, and that the Nazi party was on its rapid rise to become, in September 1930, Germany's second largest party. In this highly politicised story, Germany is a friend and ally against the evil and aggressive Soviet Union, which is out to destroy the West.

As long as we construe Hergé's 1930 Germany as post-war West Germany, the geopolitical portrayal fits remarkably well with the Reagan world vision of the early 1980s. It is not surprising that this diatribe should have been resurrected and translated into nine languages during that decade of nuclear escalation, when Cruise and Pershing 2 missiles were stationed in Western Europe amid much public protest, and Reagan's implausible Strategic Defence Initiative ('Star Wars') was in need of an evil, aggressive enemy to frighten Western publics into compliance. It may be recalled that François Mitterrand became France's president in 1981, and that he, unlike his predecessors, steered France with some stealth into US-friendly policies and pro-NATO positions. *Tintin in the Land of the Soviets* fitted well with the *zeitgeist*.

Soviet Construction of Fake Factories

During his escapades, Tintin comes across a group of English communists who are being shown the achievements of Soviet industry. We are shown the silhouette of an industrial skyline of smoking chimneys as their guide mocks myths of Soviet industrial failure, disseminated in the bourgeois countries, and points to the factories working to full capacity. The gullible, pipe-smoking English communists take photographs and comment 'Beautiful' and 'Very Nice' (Hergé 1981:25). Unlike them, Tintin does not take the scene at face value, and strides off to take a look inside the 'factory', discovering that it is a canvas façade behind which hay is being burned to simulate factory smoke, and pieces of sheet metal and corrugated iron are being banged with hammers to simulate the sound of working machines. Tintin comments: 'And that is how the Soviets cheat these poor people who still believe in the "red paradise"' (Hergé 1981:26). The episode serves a double purpose. On the one hand, it brands Western communists as naïve dupes of Soviet propaganda, and encourages others to see themselves as more sophisticated by not believing anything less than damning eyewitness accounts of Soviet life. On the other hand, it 'unmasks' the devious lengths to which communists were supposedly prepared to go to deceive the rest of the world into believing that communism was a functioning, viable system.

Both of these Western propaganda devices were alive, well and no more evolved in the 1980s, such that *Tintin in the Land of the Soviets* complemented admirably the dominant propaganda of the time. It was, after all, in addressing those whom he saw as dupes of the Soviet Union – the peace movement, habitually portrayed as communists or gullible fellow travellers – that Ronald Reagan made his notorious statement about the evil empire:

> In your discussions of the nuclear freeze proposals, I urge you to beware the temptation of pride – the temptation of blithely declaring yourself above it all and label both sides equally at fault, to ignore the facts of history and the aggressive impulses of an evil empire, to simply call the arms race a giant misunderstanding and thereby remove yourself from the struggle between right and wrong and good and evil (Reagan 1984: 8.3.83).

He had already, in his first press conference as President expressed his total mistrust of the Soviets and his belief that they would go to any lengths to further their cause of world revolution:

> The only morality they recognise is what will further their cause, meaning they reserve unto themselves the right to commit any crime, to lie, to cheat, in order to attain that' (Reagan 1981:29.1.81).

Phoney Elections

In another episode, depicted in three double frames, designed to hold the eye, Tintin comes across a crowd being addressed by a Party official, flanked by two armed and uniformed bodyguards, and realises that it is an election meeting. The official explains to the comrades in the crowd that there are three lists for which they can vote, one of them being that of the Communist Party. The people watch and listen, some of them smiling, although one of the bodyguards has a revolver in each hand. In the next frame, the other bodyguard has also picked up two revolvers, and the speaker has taken one from his holster; all three are pointing their guns at the crowd. The speaker announces that all who are against the Communist list should raise their hands and declare their opposition to it. The crowd is now depicted with bowed heads and gloomy faces, as Tintin and Milou peer over a fence, astonished at the proceedings. In the third frame, it is clear that no one has raised their hand in opposition, as the heads in the crowd remain bowed. Revolvers lowered, the official declares with evident satisfaction that the Communist list has been unanimously elected. Tintin's presence is then noticed, and one of the guards threatens him with a gun, accusing him of being a spy, but Milou knocks him over, saving the day.

Tintin is thus eyewitness to sham elections and coercive practices in what is revealed as a totalitarian regime which holds the people down by violent means, but wishes to give the impression of popular support to the outside world. Such a portrayal transferred seamlessly to early 1980s Western images of a totalitarian Eastern Bloc which held non-elections, persecuted opposition, and ruled by coercion and intimidation while simultaneously claiming to represent the will of the people democratically. Images from the Soviet Union's turbulent and brutal Stalinist past became particularly useful to Western reactionaries whose Manichean views required them to blacken the Soviet Union which, as the 1980s proceeded, first under Andropov, then under Gorbachev, was starting to throw off the authoritarianism of the Khruschchev and Brezhnev eras – in themselves steps forward from the previous bloody and barbaric decades. The Eastern Bloc concept and practice of democracy, and its corresponding electoral processes were wide open to criticism, which Western analysts and media did not cease to propagate. However, the double standards involved in making such criticisms when the USA and the UK were electing leaders who gained the votes of under 40 per cent, and even under 30 per cent of their electorates, were moving to ever higher degrees of concentration of mass media ownership and control, and were supporting dictatorships from Latin America to Indonesia via the Middle East, did, from a neutral standpoint, undermine their credibility and moral superiority. In this context, the reappearance of Hergé's crude 1929 view of Soviet elections could only serve as grist to the mill for those promoting outright Western victory in the 'Cold War', rather than its dissolution through reform and disarmament, and those who likewise, from the mid 1980s, spread mistrust of *glasnost*, described here by Gorbachev in 1984:

> *Glasnost* is an integral part of a socialist democracy. Wide, prompt and frank information is evidence of confidence in the people and respect for their intelligence and feelings, and for their ability to understand events for themselves. It enhances the resourcefulness of the working people. *Glasnost* in the work of the party and state organs is an effective means of combating bureaucratic distortions, and obliges us to be more thoughtful in our approach to the adoption of decisions (Walker 1994:283-84).

Economic Disaster

Tintin eventually arrives in Moscow, and, confronted with a scene of dereliction, harking back to a better world (feudal, imperial Russia) before the communist take-over, comments: 'This is what the Soviets have made of this magnificent city that Moscow used to be: a filthy mess' (Hergé 1981:74). The double frame shows a street with smashed windows and barricaded doors. A lamppost is bent and broken, and the street is littered with piles of rubbish and overflowing or upturned dustbins. Tintin observes one huddled figure hurrying across the otherwise desolate scene.

In the following double frame, Tintin encounters a queue of ragged, starving children, awaiting distribution of free bread by a uniformed official. Lest we should be taken in by this benevolence, Tintin approaches to find out exactly what is happening, and identifies those in the queue as one of the groups of abandoned children who roam the cities and countryside, living from theft and begging – typical of Soviet Russia. Even Milou the dog comments: 'Poor kids' (Hergé 1981:74) – the simple emotional reaction to Tintin's rather long-winded information which takes up a quarter of the double frame. The smiling official in each picture asks the children one by one if they are communists, and gives out the bread on receiving a positive answer. When one child replies 'no', the official pushes him to the ground, kicking and yelling at him, angering Tintin and Milou. Milou then steals a loaf of bread from the pile, and, chased by the enraged official, gives it to the crying and injured non-communist boy. Even a dog has more humanity than a communist.

The failure of the communist economies, characterised by images of queues for basic food items, was another long running feature of anti-communist discourse which was impregnated into the minds of Western media audiences in the 'Cold War'. Hergé's early portrayal was based on an account of actual famine in Russia in the early and mid 1920s, but his attribution of the blame for it on the scarcely established Soviet system in post-revolutionary Russia creates the propagandistic link between poverty, economic breakdown, and communism, and underpins the corresponding counter-argument for the inherent superiority of capitalism. Again, it could certainly not be asserted that by the 1980s the Soviet and Eastern Bloc economies had developed to the same pitch as the richest Western economies, but it was false to represent them as typically unable to provide their peoples with essentials, or to suggest that there was greater systemic destitution in the East than there was in the West. The 1980s resurrection of images of bread queues, starving children, and social breakdown in this Tintin story was symptomatic of the persistence of the myth which associated the communist system with inbuilt inferiority, chronic backwardness and economic failure. In 1981, the year that *Tintin in the Land of the Soviets* was reprinted, figures published by the West German Government comparing the most successful West European economy (The Federal Republic of Germany) with the most successful East European economy (The German Democratic Republic) indicate that, while the West was clearly more prosperous on most indicators, the difference was much less dramatic than Western propaganda suggested. Thus, for example, under the heading 'Per capita consumption of food and semi-luxuries, 1978', we can note that, while the West consumed notably more fresh and citrus fruit, wine, coffee, and red meat, the East consumed more flour (bread), butter, milk, and potatoes. The figures for sugar, egg products, pork, poultry, beer, and spirits were so close to each other as not to represent a significant difference. Under the heading 'Ownership of durable consumer goods, 1978', the West was well ahead on cars, freezers and telephones, but the East was ahead on motorcycles. The figures were again not significantly different on radios, TVs, refrigerators, washing machines and vacuum cleaners (Federal Ministry for Intra-German Relations 1981:46-47). It was up to economists to carry out their comparative economic analyses according to the criteria of their discipline. It was, however, also plain to the non-economist travelling from a 1980s Britain, with its over three million unemployed and tens of thousands of homeless living on the streets of major cities, to visit a GDR with no unemployed and some shortages of bananas, citrus fruit and coffee in East Berlin supermarkets, that there were anomalies and distortions in dominant Western, as well as Eastern, representations of attributes of the two economic models.

Secret Stores of Luxury Goods

Still on the run from Soviet agents trying to prevent him from discovering the reality of Soviet life and society, Tintin comes across a vast, heavily guarded, underground complex of stored goods. The illustrations show a system of corridors, and locked metal doors, each with a sign. One is labelled 'Wheat Store – Soviet Propaganda Exports', the next, 'Caviar, Vodka – Soviet Propaganda Exports', a third, 'Dynamite Store – Soviet Propaganda – Assassinations' (Hergé 1981:103-104). Tintin reflects: 'So while the Russian people are dying of starvation, vast quantities of wheat are sent abroad to provide evidence of the so-called wealth of the Soviet paradise' (ibid).

This episode illustrates how readers are presented with a closed circuit of discourse and imagery about the Soviet Union which, once entered, can only lead to a negative conclusion. That which is bad is clearly bad, but that which might appear good is also bad since it is always a devious illusion set up by an inhuman regime to deceive the naïve. The text thus warns the reader against anything which might moderate an unmitigated black image of the Soviet Union and its regime. If you view *everything* negatively, then you are smart because you have not let yourself be taken in; if you view *anything* positively, then you are naïve because you have let yourself be duped by Soviet propaganda. There may or may not be positive sides to this society, but once caught in this hermetic discursive mechanism, readers could not know if there were; they were prevented from making an independent, reasoned judgement.

At no time was the effectiveness of such discursive blockages more crucial than in the 1980s. The arrival of the genuine reformers – briefly Andropov, then Gorbachev – as leaders of the Soviet Union (with the short interlude of the ailing, old-school Chernenko), brought dramatic opportunities for nuclear disarmament, and major new energies for internal reform. It was met at Western power elite level with media-backed mistrust, the fear of being duped, and the desire for a one-sided 'Cold War' 'victory', rather than co-operation and conflict resolution.

Conclusion

Tintin in the Land of the Soviets was, very obviously, not in itself a cause. I have been at pains here to show that it was a microscopic atom of energy among many thousands which helped to compose the cancerous cellular structure of the 'Cold War' mentality. But the comic book was also symptomatic in that it contained within itself key characteristics of the larger propaganda system, and instructive, in that it demonstrated how lies, distortions and misleading images, served up for one audience in an earlier context, could take on their own continuing existence. It may not even have been within the direct, conscious intention of the publishers to be participating in this process.   It did, however, certainly belong to what was acceptable, and was part of the momentum and climate of the times, that, two generations later, such material could be served up again, re-appropriated for a new context, ready to underpin the new 'moment of untruth' as it had underpinned the old one. As such, it added texture, depth and credibility (and perhaps elements of ironic, but conniving amusement) for contemporary audiences, to the primal anti-communist message. The promotion of this was in the perceived interests of dominant, neo-liberal power elites in that it helped to strengthen support for huge real increases in nuclear, conventional and experimental military and military-related expenditure, and for a massive, ultimately successful, effort to destroy the Soviet Union and its dependencies by economic attrition.

Chapter 6

Consuming Reality.
Mutually Assured Destruction and
Routines of Embedded Deception

Reykjavik marked a turning point in world history. It tangibly demonstrated that the world could be improved. A qualitatively new situation had emerged. Now no one can act in the way he acted before. The East-West dialogue has now broken free of the confusion of technicalities, of data comparisons and political arithmetic... Reykjavik mapped out a route by which humankind can regain the immortality it lost when nuclear arms incinerated Hiroshima and Nagasaki (Mikhail Gorbachev 1987, on his Reykjavik meeting with Ronald Reagan).

It is time they [the US government] stopped devising one option after another in search of the best ways of unleashing nuclear war in the hope of winning it. Engaging in this is not just irresponsible. It is insane (Yuri Andropov 1983).

Introduction

It was one of the more awesome ironies of the later twentieth century that the final arrival in power of more enlightened leadership in the 1980s Soviet Union came too late, and came up against Western leaders who chose to go for ideological and economic victory rather than conflict resolution. The additional irony was that, in the East, the reforming hegemonic discourse of a discredited authoritarian system, finally talking good sense on the major issues, was democratically rejected on account of the pent-up frustrations of the people, while in the West, effective, controlling, but insane world-threatening hegemonic discourses held sway among peoples who believed themselves to be free and the bearers of liberation. The study of dominant discourses and public attitudes in the 1980s is indeed a fascinating and alarming one. This chapter, like the previous one, poses and contextualises the issue, then seeks to throw useful light on the subject through examination of specific symptomatic discursive materials.

When, in 'democratic' societies of the media age, one speaks of dominant, or hegemonic, discourses, and the control they exercise, such as those which during the 'Cold War' told publics in the West that the Soviet Union was so evil that they should support policies which took the world to the edge of total destruction, one is speaking neither of a monolith, nor of a simple process. Western power elites had long since learnt that people react against monoliths, and are by definition not taken in by what they can easily see through.

The effective dominant discourse (Goebbels already knew this) is one which we, the public, choose, or believe we choose. Its adoption makes us feel intelligent, it stimulates us, tells us good stories, makes us laugh, contains colour and texture, makes us feel better, and better off, than those elsewhere or excluded. Above all, it makes us feel *normal*, and that we are freely representing the natural order of things against alien attempts to deprive us of our birthright. If this is how we all feel about the stories being spun to us, it is easy to get on with our personal lives, to find our presuppositions comfortably confirmed at every turn, to feel safe, culturally integrated and accepted in our social environment, and collectively to forget or ignore what power elites (and ultimately the manipulated versions of ourselves) do not wish us to remember.

For mass media consumers, acceptance, especially intelligent but mildly critical acceptance which remains within a limited but apparently plural range of opinion and conviction options, is (consciously or unconsciously) the most usually favoured and congenial position to adopt *vis-à-vis* dominant discourse. Mild criticism shows independence, subtlety of mind and freedom of spirit, while ultimately endorsing the hegemonic line. Being, or at least successfully playing at being, 'onside' within the 'correct' spectrum of dominant *idées reçues*, going with the broad flow of the consistent and persistent pressure of perceived elite and peer expectations, these are the open secrets of survival, success and happiness for the conforming majority within a 'mediocracy'. There is much to be said for it. Noelle-Neumann (1984) made comparable points with her hypothesis of the 'spiral of silence'. As Swift observed, happiness is successful self-deception.

Such positions are frequently neither arrogant nor pretentious, neither lazy nor thoughtless, just resplendently *normal*. To use Voltaire's metaphor from the end of *Candide*, those thinking and living in this way 'cultivate their gardens', seemingly arriving at a version of Candide's exhausted conclusion but already too canny or cautious to undergo the tumultuous processes which brought him there. This may be a kind of wisdom, if wisdom can be described as a substitute for hope. Many in stable, prosperous Western societies have seen out fulfilled, or at least tolerable, lives within this apparently robust and balanced lifeworld.

To borrow a very strange cliché from normative hegemonic discourse, conventional, socially integrated citizen-consumers will habitually consider themselves to be 'middle of the road' kind of people. They may or may not fully appreciate that hegemonic discourse determines and expresses what 'middle of the road-ness' involves and excludes, but the majority seek it out, mainly in the media and with peer groups of fellow media consumers, and aspire to become or locate themselves within it, assuming it to be a desirable, safe or necessary position. The enlightening irony of this particular metaphor is its contradiction of reality, for we all know that the middle of any road is in fact a suicidal place to be. Certainly, returning to the 1980s 'Cold War' context, the irony is particularly apt, since 'middle-of-the-road' conformism to dominant discourse was indeed a suicidal position for the human species and the world environment, and one had to have been deprived of one's better judgement not to realise that. Yet substantial majorities in the USA and Western Europe were consistently disposed to accept this position, supporting, or at least passively condoning the hegemonic line, or just preferring to ignore or repress the insanity of what they were doing. One might add that ordinary West Europeans and US Americans going along with dominant discourse and getting on with their lives in such a context was comparable with, and as shockingly normal (if not more so in 'free', 'democratic' and 'informed' societies) as the frequently condemned 'ordinary Germans' and others getting on with *their* lives, and finding it preferable not to notice the persecution, expropriation and transportation of Jews, communists, gypsies and others to labour and extermination camps during Nazi rule. The fact that full scale *nuclear* holocaust has not yet happened, and 'limited' wartime use of nuclear weapons has not reoccurred since the US bombs dropped on Hiroshima and Nagasaki in 1945, does not transform the insanity into sanity; it merely shows that the longer insanity lasts, the more 'normal' it becomes, and the less we concern ourselves with its consequences.

Although the 'Cold War' is now 'history', the stockpiles of weapons of mass destruction are still there, being replenished and further developed; most of its follies, myths and sophistries continue, often re-emerging in new guises. These are matters which most citizens are far from confronting or dealing with; they are so important and so often misunderstood or circumvented that re-examination is appropriate.

The big questions which come to the forefront about the 'Cold War', especially the determining decade of the 1980s are: Was it actually possible to take people in to such an extent that they could be made to forget their humanity and believe that building up a capability to destroy the world many times over was sane? Further, was it possible for publics to accept declarations from their elected leaders that they were ready and willing to unleash world destruction, and that such readiness could be equated with peace and peace making? To the extent that this was so, how could this ultimate deception be achieved? What happened, or failed to happen in people's minds to make this possible? What was the role of public discourse, particularly media discourse, in these processes, as compared to other discursive channels of information, education and persuasion?

The answers to these questions may seem simple, especially in the flow of the current narrative. The large facts need not be disputed. Particularly during the most advanced phase of the 'Cold War', the 1980s, millions of responsible individuals in the USA and in Western Europe, acting within the constraints of their electoral systems, invariably voted for, or at least failed to vote in sufficient numbers against, insane, suicidal policies and leaders who represented them. Reagan, Kohl, Mitterrand and Thatcher were elected and re-elected. In 1983, Thatcher was returned to power with a huge parliamentary majority of 188, when opposed by a Labour Party clearly committed to radical nuclear disarmament policies, in particular the cancellation of the Trident submarine-based weapons system which, purchased from the USA, represented a dramatic escalation of Britain's nuclear destruction capability. Logically, there could be nothing more important to be voting about than policies which would take the world closer to, or back from, the edge of annihilation. Yet voters, perhaps suffering from the kind of 'death of the imagination' of which Kraus wrote, were distracted away from this. Election campaigners and media debates, operating with distorted priorities, were focused elsewhere.

Thereafter, the truly extraordinary notion that increasing nuclear lethality and *overkill* capacity, and deploying new classes of nuclear weapons which escaped enemy radar detection (Cruise), or which could reach and destroy the major Soviet cities in less than ten minutes (Pershing 2), could only be a contribution to world *security* and *peace making*, remained dominant through the 1980s, bolstered by grotesque discourses of 'deterrence' and 'balance of terror'. That such discourses could achieve credibility can be seen as further evidence of the separation of 'word from world', 'language from meaning', 'rhetoric from fact' (Chomsky 1999b:56), and the self-perpetuating dominance of 'untruth' which is the central motif of this book.

From this perspective, it is easy to surmise that the elite-promoted media demonisation of the Soviet Union left a strong trace of fear in consumers' minds. The dominant message that nuclear war would either be *won* through superior firepower and technology, or, more likely, not take place because the enemy's fear of that superiority (that is to say that it would never be *lost*), added a demented sense of security. Together, these two factors combined to achieve actual public support for, or acquiescence in, the apocalyptic power games that world leaders were playing, and the extremely profitable high wire act that the military-industrial complex was performing with the planet and millions of lives on it. In the 1914-18 war and its reprise in 1939-45, populations were successfully convinced against their true human interests that their country's aggressions were really acts of pre-emptive self-protection. Likewise, the 'Cold War' propagandists succeeded in recycling the same old lies and deceits in the nuclear context, now playing for stakes which were so high that, whatever the arguments about the 'justness' of previous wars, *this* time there could be no possible doubt that they were acting *against* the interests of the people, the species and the planet. In this context, security was eating its own tail, for the more each superpower pursued it, the greater the *in*security. Yet the West's publics were conned into accepting that a future world war, like the previous ones, would be survivable. Films like Peter Watkins's *The War Game* which tried to tell a different story, were banned. It was totally atavistic slogans such as 'Those who beat their guns into ploughs will plough for those who don't', which expressed 'normal' opinion.

Such answers, however, do not suffice on their own. They fit into the hypothetical framework which this narrative is developing, but they do not delve far enough into what was going on in the 1980s between the purveyors of hegemonic discourses and the collective and individual minds of their consumers.

Attitude Formation at Work

To investigate these processes further, we shall turn to a set of materials which I gathered in survey form in 1984-85, and followed up with a set of interviews. While representing the opening phase of what would have been a larger project had the events of 1989 not intervened, they can provide a revealing testimony from that crucial historical moment, as it emerges both in the questions and in the attitudes found in the responses of the particular group of individuals in the sample.

The survey arose from my experience, as a German Studies specialist in British Higher Education, of trying to bring to students a fair image of the two German states, societies and cultures in the polarised atmosphere of the 1980s. The 1970s, the decade of so-called *'détente'* which had seen ongoing development of the technologies of mass destruction and continued rapid increases in nuclear weapons stockpiles, *had* at least brought the German Democratic Republic (East Germany) into existence in the perceptions of Western diplomacy. Willy Brandt, with his historic visit as West German Chancellor to the Eastern town of Erfurt in March 1970, and Egon Bahr, with his realisation of the Social Democrats' (SPD) policy of small steps towards *rapprochement* and recognition of the GDR by the Federal Republic, had brought about easier access, some circumscribed contacts at official and personal levels, and a series of agreements and treaties which signalled the beginnings of a pragmatic thaw and a sort of cautious trust and co-operation between the two states. Accompanying this had come the publication of some materials which started to reflect an incipient process of normalisation and tentative neighbourliness in German-German relations.

However, the ongoing rigidities of East-West ideological and physical division and military confrontation, the momentum of hostile propaganda, revived and intensified in the early 1980s by the Reagan and Thatcher regimes, meant that there were continuing problems over the concept of fairness, and the possibility of conveying it to students, for academics in this field. Sources were not neutral. The rosy self-image propagated by the GDR was contradicted by its Western depiction as dour and grey. Both were different from what one saw independently, or what one was shown when one travelled there. Most UK academics in the field placed themselves somewhere between the strongly politicised extremes, since both were manifestly exaggerated and ideologically predetermined. Many also combined their analysis with a critique of the distorted hostile images manifest in hegemonic Western and Eastern material, and addressed the assumptions, stereotypes and prejudices which they expected dominant discourses to have instilled into their student audiences.

BBC German language courses of the time provide symptomatic evidence of what one was confronting and reacting against. These were then probably the most popular and widespread ways in which an interested, but non-specialist British adult public was brought into contact with German language and culture. They also had the cachet of the BBC's international reputation for fairness and balance. In the late 1970s and early 1980s, what one found in these courses about the GDR, apart from the rare passing reference, was nothing. The courses' multi-media materials took us from Schleswig Holstein to Bavaria, and into Austria, but the GDR did not exist. The 17.5 million Germans in the GDR, and information about their country, were not considered worth a mention over the three years and levels that the then current courses ran. Not, that is, until 1986, when *Deutsch Express*, a new second year course, broke the taboo, ending with three chapters and broadcasts on Berlin and on 'The Other Side'.

This seemed like progress until one looked at the kind of material that was included. One typical example, a follow up exercise to one of the dialogues, caught the perspective. It consisted of an illustration of a toddler in nappies firing an army rifle and blowing the head off his teddy bear. The exercise was to put the following words in the correct order:

KINDER - AUF - DIE - IN - DER - KLEIN - VON - LERNEN - SCHIESSEN - MÜSSEN - DDR
CHILDREN - ON - - HAVE TO – GDR THE - IN - THE - EARLY - FROM - LEARN - TO SHOOT

The correct answer being:

IN DER DDR MÜSSEN DIE KINDER VON KLEIN AUF SCHIESSEN LERNEN
IN THE GDR CHILDREN FROM EARLY ON HAVE TO LEARN TO SHOOT

In the illustration, one can observe such details as the teddy bear's eyeball springing out of its socket, and the look of sadistic pleasure on the face of the GDR infant.

Militaristic elements of school education are abhorrent wherever they occur, and they did occur also in the GDR, but for this kind of deformed message to be put across in a supposedly humorous way as a significant part of the very small amount of information about the GDR provided to those on this course, was simply hostile propaganda of a crude variety.

The idea of *détente* in the 1970s had been a powerful and positive one, however limited its achievements. To pursue it in the 1980s, despite the renewed grotesque discourses of 'Cold War' at all levels, with their evident exaggerations and inaccuracies, seemed at the time to be academically sound as well as humanly necessary and morally justified. In the atmosphere of the period, however, the search for accuracy in reporting, portrayal and analysis, and the desire to correct misrepresentations in this field, had its controversial aspects, and inevitably led to self-questioning. To take up a position *vis-à-vis* the GDR, or the Eastern Bloc in general, which was less than relentlessly negative and automatically dismissive was, after all, to soften the certainties underpinning the hardening Western orthodoxy which, in turn, justified the spiralling military budgets. The academic inevitably became mingled with the ideological, and found itself at odds with establishment interests and media-propagated normality. It became necessary to define one's position and aims and to be able to uphold them against criticism and pressure when involved in the education of future elites, middle-range managers, educators and functionaries, and in receipt of public funding for doing so. At this point, the limits of academic freedom were clearly discernable. My survey project was conducted in the context of such tensions.

One of the main aims of the survey was to arrive at a profile of student attitudes to the GDR. The particular student sample consisted of those undertaking courses in which there was a significant element of GDR studies. It was thus *a priori* a sample with interests in and some previous understanding of German affairs, and this would affect the responses. The choice of such a group was, however, important to enable the gathering of information on the effects on attitudes of attending a course on the GDR, a further aim of the survey. It was thus hoped that the survey would provide useful insights both into the power of hegemonic discourse, as reflected in survey forms filled in by students *before* attending their course on the GDR, and into the power of educational courses to modify the effects of hegemonic discourse, as reflected in the same survey forms filled in at the end of the course. Whatever the inherent variables and possible methodological loopholes, there seemed to be significant questions here, and a framework for eliciting answers to them which would be worth debating. 345 students and 20 lecturers from 17 British universities took part.

The survey took the form of 50 statements expressing a range of common prejudices and attitudes to the GDR to which the student sample was asked to react positively or negatively on a scale of five. The statements were not designed to test knowledge of the country, but attitudes to it. Thus, respondents were encouraged to react viscerally to the prompts, even if they did not feel sufficiently informed on the particular subject. The statements used were not intended to be objective, rather they were a selection of 'hearsay' which tried to encapsulate the range of current, largely negative, ways in which discourses about the GDR filtered through to individuals. It was made clear to respondents that there was no expected or correct reply, that they should react as they felt, and that their anonymity was guaranteed. The fifty statements were divided into six sections. The first contained statements of a broad nature concerning the GDR as an Eastern communist state; the second involved statements covering the GDR as a 'big brother' or 'police' state; the third consisted of statements about the political system in the GDR; the fourth addressed attitudes to the economic situation; the fifth covered a number of cultural aspects, including history, religion, artistic and journalistic expression, and sport; and the sixth asked for overall reactions to the GDR *per se*, and in relation to the Soviet Union and the rest of Eastern Europe.

At the same time, the lecturers delivering the course were asked to respond to the questionnaire, stating at the outset, first, how they thought the majority of their students would react at the beginning, then how they thought they would react at the end of the course. Once the course was completed, lecturers responded a third time, stating how they thought most of their students actually reacted at the end of the course. Lecturers would, as a result, be able to compare and reflect further on their assumptions about the student mentalities they were addressing, and on the *effects* of what they were delivering relative to what they delivered.

Here, to provide a snapshot of what emerged from the project, responses to three of the statements will be looked at. Following this, analysis of salient extracts from the follow-up interviews add a qualitative perspective to the reductive percentages emerging from the survey.

It should be re-emphasised here that the student participants cannot be represented as a typical cross-section of society. They were special insofar as they were almost all around 20 years of age or in their early twenties, and were thus coming to social awareness and political consciousness at a moment when 1970s *détente* discourse was being transformed into the extreme 'Cold War' ideological revival of the Reagan/Thatcher era, in the early 1980s. But they were also part of the young British intelligentsia, mostly thoughtful, open-minded and curious, who had chosen to specialise in German affairs, and were thus, through their experience in higher education, becoming exceptionally aware of the German situation, dominated as it was by the East-West divide. They were thus untypical insofar as one would, on the one hand, expect them, at least at the end of their course, to be unusually well-informed on, and sensitised to, East-West issues, and thus more resistant to propagandistic material and images than the average citizen, but, on the other hand, expect them to be on a steep learning curve, less set in their views, and more critically open to the range of perspectives and materials confronting them than those in other age groups and social categories.

The first set of responses we shall look at are those to the statement: 'We in the West are free; in the communist GDR, they are oppressed.' This was a classic 'Cold War' statement of a type that was frequently used by right-of-centre, centre, and some centre-left political leaders, journals and broadcast media all over the Western world. They may not have always put it as bluntly as this, but it was the underlying message, used again and again to justify East-West confrontation and further increases in nuclear weapons. It was graphically illustrated by regular news stories about Soviet labour camps, dissidents in psychiatric hospitals, 'escape' stories across the East-West divide, and, as seen in the previous chapter, through popular culture products such as the Tintin comics. The particular GDR variants were the Berlin Wall stories of escapes and/or shootings, reinforced by such institutions as the Checkpoint Charlie museum in West Berlin (then a *sine qua non* of the tourist circuit), and TV pictures of goose-stepping GDR soldiers (included without historical explanation, or reference to the fact that they were changing guard outside the East Berlin anti-fascist memorial) to encourage viewers to make the crude association between the expansionist, racist and barbaric Nazi regime, and the GDR regime which could be criticised for many things, but which was a quantum leap away from Nazi ideology and atrocities.

Student reactions to the statement, expressed in percentages and ranging from strong agreement (++) to strong disagreement (--), were as follows. S1 denotes their reaction before their course, and S2 their reaction at the end of it:

'We in the West are free; in the communist GDR, they are oppressed.'

%	++	+	0	-	--	no response
S1	15	39	18	19	8	1
S2	9	34	15	28	14	0

The set of initial reactions (S1) shows just over a quarter of the sample reacting negatively to the statement, with twice as many, an absolute majority at 54 per cent, reacting positively to it. Within a 'free' system relying on methods of mass persuasion to achieve its majority, this is a solid result in favour of the dominant discourse, the more so since it is taken from the age group most likely to question it. It also shows almost twice as many (15 per cent) with a strong positive reaction than with a strong negative reaction (8 per cent), indicating a greater degree of certainty and solidity in the positive reactions. However, the responses show that a significant 27 per cent of the sample decided to contradict the hegemonic position, and that 45 per cent were not prepared to endorse the view propagated by the overwhelming majority of the media. This lends credibility to the view that media persuasion is not an automatic or definitive event, more a process which requires constant feeding and continuous effort to be as satisfactory to the elites as this result ultimately was.

The post-course responses show significant change. The percentage of those reacting negatively to the statement increased from 27 per cent to 42 per cent, with those reacting positively decreasing from 54 per cent to 43 per cent. Confirming the swing, the percentage with strong positive reactions decreased by 6 per cent, and the percentage with strong negative reactions increased by a corresponding 6 per cent. The trend in student reactions corresponds to their lecturers' expectations and efforts insofar as 88 per cent of lecturers expected the positive majority student reaction to the statement before their courses, 70 per cent of them hoped that they would change the majority positive reaction into a majority negative one by the end of the course, and, at the end of the course, 40 per cent of them thought that they had actually achieved this. The S2 results again provide evidence of a real struggle taking place, since the lecturers clearly did not have a simple task; if they wished to bring about a change in their students' attitudes, they clearly met with resistance from deeply engrained attitudes or competition from other influences, and did not succeed to the degree that they would have wished.

The second set of responses for consideration here was to the far more extreme statement: 'It would be worth fighting a war not to have to live in a communist society such as the GDR.' It was a statement designed to isolate the most adamantly anti-communist from the rest, those who would be 'better dead than red'. In the early to mid 1980s, information about the state of the nuclear arms race was easily obtainable and widely known. There would have been no doubt in anyone's mind that war with the Eastern Bloc would mean nuclear war and consequent world destruction. This statement was thus the acid test of the penetration of hard-line anti-communist ideology into this generation of educated and intelligent young people in the UK. Only 5.5 per cent of lecturers expected a positive response from most students at the beginning of their courses, and none of them expected this at the end. Indeed 73 per cent of lecturers expected a strongly negative reaction from the majority of their students at the end of their courses on the GDR.

The student responses were as follows:

'It would be worth fighting a war not to have to live in a communist society such as the GDR'

%	++	+	0	-	--	no response
S1	11	15	17	24	33	0
S2	7	18	14	25	36	0

There is a clear majority negative reaction to the statement from the outset – 57 per cent before the courses compared to 61 per cent after them, and this was one of the few occasions when the strong (double minus) reaction (33 per cent and 36 per cent) outnumbered the moderate (single minus) one (24 per cent and 25 per cent) indicating a healthy survival instinct among the respondents, as well as a view that, if forced to, living in a society such as the GDR would not be intolerable.

However, two other significant points arise from these sets of responses. The first is that there is only minor movement between the pre- and post-course results; the second is that the percentage ready for war is so high. 26 per cent would have fought at the beginning, 25 per cent at the end, if less enthusiastically; 57 per cent would not have fought at the beginning, 61 per cent at the end. These extrapolations would appear to lead to the conclusion that among the sample there was about a quarter whose immutable gut feeling was that the Eastern Bloc was indeed Reagan's 'evil empire'. If one then includes the neutral responses, one arrives at the alarming conclusion that about 40 per cent of the sample were not categorically opposed to risking world destruction as an alternative to living in a society such as the GDR, even after having attended courses in which the lecturers all hoped and believed that they had convinced them otherwise. The lecturers' responses were correct in that the *majority* of the students *did* record negative responses, but the figures imply that most would nevertheless have been disturbed that such a large minority did not reply on the negative side. It is possible that when it was a case of responses invoking *knowledge*, students' responses changed as their acquaintance with the country via their courses grew, but where responses were based on visceral feelings, it was other, more engrained influences which dominated. We shall return to this when looking at samples of the student interviews.

The final set of responses to be looked at here was in response to a summative request at the end of the survey. Participants were asked to: 'Rate your overall feeling about the GDR from "very positive" (++) to "very negative" (--), using the same scale as that for the rest of the survey.' In isolation, such a request would have been too generalised to have much value, but in its context at the end of quite a long survey, it served two valuable purposes.

First, it put respondents on the spot by demanding an overall view, a real complex attitude or composite gut feeling. It was understood that such feelings would, in part, be irrational (fear, wishful thinking), in part *a priori*, that is based on considerations preceding the cool processes of data gathering and analysis (ideology, and first or second hand assumptions based thereon), and in part rationally drawn from experience and learning (perhaps in themselves contradictory or ambivalent). Just as such an amalgam of influences and incomplete knowledge does not prevent us from voting in elections (often for a party that we only partly agree with), it did not need at that moment to prevent the respondents from making an overall judgement about issues such as the Eastern/Western ways of life, the 'communist threat', the nuclear arms race, freedom and democracy, or East-West *détente*, all of which, among others, played a role in determining underlying attitudes to the GDR as a whole.

Second, responses to this statement served to put responses to the rest of the survey in perspective. They showed, for example, how some respondents were hostile and angry about certain aspects of what they perceived to be going on in the GDR, while retaining an overall positive attitude to the country. Conversely, they revealed others who were full of praise for certain GDR achievements while remaining fundamentally negative, or deeply unable to be positive about the place as a whole. Equally, they showed many to be agnostic or balanced between overall positive and negative, while nevertheless having clear attitudes on specific aspects of what was, or was reported to be, going on there.

The student responses to the request to make this global assessment were as follows:

'Rate your overall feeling about the GDR from "very positive" to "very negative" using the same scale as that for the rest of the survey.'

%	++	+	0	-	--	no response
S1	1.5	22	32	39	5	0.5
S2	2	40	27	26.5	4	0.5

These results enable us to think more carefully about the relative impacts of different, conflicting influences on the consciousness of the participants, and about the different levels at which persuasion or control takes place.

Given that the overwhelming majority of lecturers involved in the survey were in favour of promoting *détente* attitudes and a more open, if critical, perspective on the GDR, resulting in an image of it which would be more positive than that propagated by the Reagan/Thatcher coloured dominant media, a certain success for them can be noted. While around 30 per cent of the students placed themselves on the fence both before and after their courses (not the same 30 per cent, it should be noted), a 44 per cent negative judgement at the beginning was changed to a 42 per cent positive judgement at the end.

Yet any propagator of the hegemonic view would not have been much disturbed by this outcome, and would indeed have felt a degree of satisfaction. Such a person might have felt some distaste or disdain for the lecturers' perspectives, might have preferred a more robust, pro-Western line, but (s)he could sleep well at night, confident that, despite significant periods of face-to-face tuition and discussion, 58 per cent of this student sample declined to pass an overall positive judgement on the GDR. Even following the special, *relatively* positive influences with regard to the GDR which they had been subject to on their academic courses, other influences – primarily the media – had proved stronger for most of them; the propaganda battle was clearly being won. Opposition to hegemonic discourse was evidently containable. It could be safely assumed that only a minority of the minority would actually take any kind of action, and that such a level of action could be controlled, negatively exploited and dismissed.

Within this global picture, however, fascinating and instructive processes took place. These were revealed particularly in a set of follow-up interviews which took place towards the end of the final academic year of the students concerned, 1987.

For present purposes, transcripts of salient extracts from just one of these will be used, following a summary of the tone and range of the five others. While these six interviews make no claim to be representative, they do provide a revealing snapshot of the moment.

Each of the interviewees had followed up the second year course which had formed the context of their survey responses with a final year option on GDR society. They were thus, by the time the interview took place, better informed about the GDR than when they had done the survey, and had had further opportunities to reflect on their attitudes. Only two of them had made brief visits to the GDR. Their lecturer, who was present at the interviews, was an established authority on the GDR who sought to give students a rounded critical view of the country, without political or ideological bias, believing in the goal of objectivity and balance.

All but one of the interviewees felt that they had a generally more positive or slightly more positive view of the GDR than they had had at the beginning of their courses; the final one retained the same negative attitude that he had started with, despite having been made conscious of some positive aspects. All felt that, on the whole, they were now seeing the GDR in a more informed way, and that their course had enabled them to gain insights into how people actually lived, in terms of education, social welfare, health, job security, housing and the family. Such knowledge had replaced *a priori* judgements based on – again for all but one – what they had picked up in general about the Eastern Bloc from the Western media. One pointed out that since there was next to nothing in the UK media about the GDR, his view of the GDR could not be influenced from that direction.

All the interviews contained contradictions, and expressions of the view that they still really knew too little about the GDR to make definitive judgements. They did, however, now feel more knowledgeable about it than most of their peers, and their parents. Where the survey forms had explicitly asked for categorised instant reactions, and had received them, the interviews elicited a far more confused state of mind in which their new knowledge did not lie comfortably with persistent, more visceral prejudices. While they were not highly politicised, they had clearly been on the receiving end of anti-Eastern Bloc, anti-socialist ideology, and were to varying extents aware of this and critical of it. Thus one of the students, in the very course of the interview, changed an overall positive judgement of the GDR to an overall negative one while still claiming to see it more positively than before, and saying that she would defend it against standard 'Cold War' attitudes among other students, whom she now saw as 'bigoted'. The students had now, on the one hand, the ability and knowledge to balance genuine positive and negative factors about GDR society, but on the other, they were suspended between relatively negative ideological reactions, and selectively positive knowledge-based judgements.

The case of Diana illustrates this clearly. The following section of her interview is quoted at length to demonstrate the thought processes which were taking place. In the text, (-) denotes a pause, [...] denotes that both participants are speaking at the same time, and italics denote the speaker's emphasis.

Interviewer: What do you reckon was your initial attitude to the GDR when you first arrived on your course?
Diana: Reasonably negative, I think in most senses (-). I didn't really know anything about it (-) only what I actually heard (-) *(clears throat)* uh (-) through the media, which was obviously very negative.
Interviewer: Yes...
Diana: I think my answers to *that (indicating the survey)* sort of prove that.
Interviewer: Do you feel that there was a, yes, fairly strong negative influence from the media?
Diana: Yeah, certainly.
Interviewer: [Uhh]
Diana: [I actually] can't think of anything positive I had heard about it before at all.
Interviewer: Right, um, and do you, did you feel that, in the first two years of study, your attitude *changed* an awful lot to the GDR?
Diana: Yeah, definitely.
Interviewer: Uhuh. Can you tell me some sort of ways in which you think it did?
Diana: Well I only really knew about the socialist state type of thing.
Interviewer: Yeah.
Diana: Um (-) no feeling for the individual, which is totally *(clears throat)* totally different now. I've changed my attitude on that.
Interviewer: Yes.
Diana: The individual, you know (-) is looked after, the individual is, you know, promoted to do whatever he wants to do to the best of his ability.
Interviewer: Yeah.
Diana: I only thought that the individual was, y'know, restricted in what he could do.
Interviewer: There seem to be quite a lot of dramatic changes that took place in that second year of studies.
Diana: Really?
Interviewer: Well, at the *beginning*: 'It would be worth fighting a war not to have to live in a communist society like that in the GDR' (-) Double *minus*, and at the *end*, a *plus*.
Diana: So I actually, at the end of it was saying that I *would*?
Interviewer: You were saying that you would, yeah.
Diana: But I wouldn't to start with.
Interviewer: Mmm.

Diana: Oh goodness, I don't know why this (-) mmm, maybe (-) maybe at the beginning, I mean maybe, I mean I still wouldn't like to *live* in that sort of society, but, but that I should have changed from *that* to *that* (-) um (-) I suppose it's because I wasn't, I mean I never have been living in that sort of society so (-) at the beginning of the course, well, it wouldn't be worth fighting for it because most of the East German people were reasonably contented, if they are, so that would be that part. (-) Why should I suddenly decide that's not for me and that I would fight it? I really don't know. There's nothing in that from what I've learnt, from what I've read.

Interviewer: No, no. What would you say now?

Diana: Um (-) Goodness (-) I wouldn't *like* to live in their sort of society, but I've never actually witnessed it, so ... (-)

Interviewer: Would you think it worth fighting a war not to, not to have to live in that sort of society?

Diana: Yes, I think so.

Interviewer: You think you would, um (-) And would you *now* characterise the GDR as a totalitarian state?

Diana: Now, um (-) maybe *one* 'plus', not *two*. [referring to her survey answer]

Interviewer: Uhuh, but nevertheless totalitarian, you react positively to that statement still, yeah? OK. And so you, I mean you seemed to be saying at the *beginning* that there is a very strong or strongish negative attitude at the beginning, influenced by the media, but you seem to be saying some *still* quite negative things about the GDR, I mean, being prepared to fight a war, calling it a totalitarian state, that's still quite strongly *negative*.

Diana: Um, I think it's negative towards the actual *political* um framework of the state.

Interviewer: Um...

Diana: I was negative about the individual having absolutely no freedom whatsoever to do anything, that everything was watched over. You couldn't do this. You couldn't do that. I *don't* believe that any more. I still think that the framework of the state, you know, is, you know, along those lines, but I think, y'know, the individual *isn't* as restricted as I thought he was.

Interviewer: Uhuh

Diana: I mean, he's looked after. He can do things, he can join groups and things, and obviously they have *more* of that kind of thing than *we've* got.

Interviewer: Mmm. So there are a certain number of, kind of, positive elements that come into your view of the GDR. Can you mention a few more?

Diana: Um (-) well basically the fact that the worker, if you look at, for instance, the factories, the worker is integrated into the hierarchy, you know, there *is* this feedback; they can express their feelings, difficulties or whatever.

Interviewer: Yeah.

Diana: And the links with the society, and (-) old peoples' homes and police and that sort of thing. I think that's all very positive.

Interviewer: Um, yes, er, and, but you'd still feel, er, that *overall*, that your view of the GDR would be a *negative* one. Not from the point of view of wanting to live there, or anything like that, but just from the point of view of (-) comparing it with what you thought before.

Diana: Um, I don't know if I say it's negative. I mean, having said that I think its reasonably authoritarian and that I'd fight a war over it, I don't think it's really that negative, and it's just, just different, and I'm not used to living like that, in that sort of state, but then I haven't ever been to East Germany. So it's very difficult to know how I'd actually find it.

Interviewer: Yeah, um, yeah. I'm still finding your view very contradictory. Er, maybe it *is* very contradictory. I mean there's nothing necessarily *wrong* in that, I mean you're still in the process of learning about the place, er, because it's, as I say, very extreme to say that you'd fight a war not to live in a country like the GDR, and especially the kind of war it would be, in reality. And yet you *are* saying quite a number of positive things about it, yeah? Er, what's the sticking point? What's the actual thing that…

Diana: I suppose I could just say 'socialism', I won't say 'communism', but 'socialism'. I wouldn't like to live in a socialist state, um…

Interviewer: East European model socialist state…

Diana: But I am, obviously, living in the West and a capitalist society.

Interviewer: Yeah.

Diana: And that's how I have been conditioned.

Interviewer: Yeah.

Diana: And maybe if I had an insight into what it's like, I could judge better.

Interviewer: Yeah, and this is a conditioning to what, to be in favour of the competitive society?

Diana: Mmm, and to despise the socialist society. Really. It's the enemy, and [if you see it that way]

Interviewer: [You do see it as, you do see…]

Diana: You're conditioned; not that I *do* see it as the enemy, but I think that's how we're conditioned – to oppose without thinking, as I was when I first came here.

Interviewer: That's right. But you *still* feel conditioned like that?

Diana: To some extent.

Interviewer: Yeah.

Diana: Maybe it would be broken if I actually went to East Germany.

Interviewer: Maybe, maybe not [laughter]. But clearly not a view of the GDR that [lecturer's name] has been giving you in lectures and tutorials and so on.

Diana: We've been getting a very fair view of it.

Interviewer: Right.

Diana: A very balanced view of the society.

Interviewer: But you feel that there are other influences on you.

Diana: Mm. Definitely.

Interviewer: Which come from?

Diana: Well (-) from the media, from a lot of things.

Interviewer: And you feel that those influences are quite strong?

Diana: I know a lot more about the country, so I would dispel most of them. They're weaker now. But there's still a lot of things which make me feel, well, you don't really know what your opinions are.

Interviewer: Well Emma [another student] was saying before that she gets into discussions and finds herself *defending* the GDR. Does that happen to you at all?

Diana: Yes, it does. Only last week actually, I was talking to my father. And he just said: 'Well it's a socialist state.' And I had to sort of say, well I, I've been learning certain things, and I think it's good, what they do with the individual in society as an integrated whole. And he really didn't know because he hasn't studied anything about it; he just got the opinion that 'socialist state' – 'no freedom', you know…

Interviewer: Uhuh.

Diana: No liberty.

Interviewer: And how did he react to what you were saying?

Diana: Oh, I did defend it. I said I wouldn't fight a war not to live there [laughs], but I was saying [clears throat] I've learnt certain things about the society which I think would be beneficial to *this* sort of state.

Interviewer: Yes, and how did he react to *that*?

Diana: He didn't really say a lot, actually […] I don't think he particularly wanted to listen, which is what most people do. They just dispel 'socialist state' without any reason, I think.

Interviewer: So you still reckon that your course here has actually taken you away from that simplistic attitude?

Diana: Yeah, definitely. And that's led me to make my *own* mind up anyway.

This remarkable dialogue catches Diana quite graphically in two minds. Her zig-zag progress through the interview seems to take her by surprise as she at various moments realises the contradictions in what she is saying. Having initially indicated a positive trend in her attitudes to the GDR, and then at one moment showing apparent shock at one of her survey responses (in relation to war), she very soon confirms the view that she had just appeared shocked about, before, towards the end, saying that she had actually told the opposite to her father.

There are clearly complicated processes taking place here, but a strong strand of the story must be that she is expressing a real conflict between what she has learnt on her course – identified by her as objective, and 'balanced', and what she has absorbed from the media (directly, or indirectly via parents, etc.), identified as prejudice, and recognised as 'simplistic' and something which has 'conditioned' her. At the moment, she seems at a loss to decide which version to accept. Thus, in one sense, she has, in terms of what is going on in her head, gone from being part of a passive media audience at the beginning of her course, to being part of a critical, or relatively active one at the end; in another sense, however, she is still objectively passive, since the higher quality of information and debate to which she has been exposed on her course is cancelled out by the power and pressure of hegemonic discourse, which has set up a large, deeply embedded irrational barrier in her consciousness against any positive evaluation of 'socialism'. In this sense, she is still a media dope (thinking and acting the dominant discourse and complying with the desired effect) albeit a conscious one who is becoming uneasily aware of her position, and the possibility and risks of self-emancipation.

Diana's case takes us to the centre of active/passive audience debates in the 'Cold War' context. We do not know how she developed from this point on, but the evidence of this particular interview is that engrained hegemonic discourse is the stronger force when faced by a challenge from an alternative discourse. It may not be impregnable, nor could it afford to cease its work, but if it remains alert and active, it has the power to maintain sufficiently its hegemonic position in Diana's mind.

This is particularly illustrated by two sections of the interview. The first occasion is when she is initially questioned about how her view, as expressed in the survey, had changed from 'very negative' to 'positive' in response to the statement that it would be worth fighting a war in order not to have to live in a society such as that in the GDR. While at the beginning of the interview she seemed confident that her attitudes had developed in a positive direction, she is here confronted with evidence that the opposite had been the case, or that, despite her greater understanding of GDR society, her sympathy for aspects of it, and her move away from stereotypical, media-based ideological judgements, she had expressed a more hostile attitude at the end of her course than at the outset. She initially seems quite baffled by this, and one is led to think that, since she could not believe that this is how she had reacted, she is about to retract or deny that hostile judgement. There is a moment of genuine confusion, characterised by hesitations and repetitions, but then she tries to think back over the two years and explain how she must have felt. She can reconstruct her original negative reaction to the statement, based on a tolerance of the way other people choose to live, but still cannot explain her positive reaction to the 'war' question at the end of her course, attributing it specifically to something – undefined – outside the course she had followed or anything she had read in connection with it. The implication is that it cannot have been an intellectual response that could be explained rationally.

All this would seem to prepare us for a retraction of that hostile reaction when asked what her reaction would *now* be – two years later and after having followed a further course on the GDR with the same lecturer. But her response is not as expected. She seems once again plunged into an irresolvable conflict, leading to hesitations and an initial attempt to avoid the question – pleading insufficient experience, and returning to the statement that she would not want to live there. When pressed on the more strongly expressed 'war' question, however, she seems ultimately unable to say 'no'; despite all her learning and more rational analysis, she comes out with: 'Yes, I think so' – it *would* be worth going to war.

We are not here simply confronted with someone becoming more hostile to the GDR following a course which made her realise, on reflection, what an intolerable place it was. She specifically denies this herself, and it is confirmed by other student comments. Her lecturer also emphasised in a separate interview that the aim of the course was to provide a rounded, balanced picture of GDR society. Further clues to what was actually going on can be found in a later section of the interview. The interview returns to the 'war' question, and asks Diana to try to put her finger on the real reason for her contradictory answers. The answer is revealing in that, when pressed in this way, she, first, does not change her mind, which she could have done, indeed, it would not have been surprising, given the tone of the rest of the interview, and second, she actually falls back on the kind of crude 'Cold War' ideological answer which she has repeatedly claimed to have superseded in her thinking elsewhere in the interview. Despite the fact that the predominantly positive features of the GDR that she has identified are *inherent* to socialism, the strongly negative connotations in her mind of the word 'socialism' cannot seemingly be connected with this. 'Socialism' in the form of specific social structures, policies, and benefits to individuals, as long as the *word* is not mentioned, is good; but 'socialism' as an ideology, a political system operating in the Soviet Union and the Eastern Bloc, is a generalised, threatening evil. That the former might be a concrete manifestation of the latter is hard to confront. Thus Diana's reaction is either that more experience is necessary, perhaps in the form of a visit to the GDR, which she would welcome and which could clearly clarify the issue, or that her university knowledge comes up against her media preconditioning, and that, despite her consciousness of the conditioning process, and her confidence in her GDR knowledge, the conditioning is stronger and wins out. Interestingly, she sees the conditioning as something which would need to be 'broken', like a spell. It is something imposed from the outside, controlling the mind, holding it in a more primitive state despite higher quality knowledge and influences. This, she says, comes 'from the media, from a lot of things'; it is what we would define here as the power of hegemonic discourse.

Conclusion

The splinter of data in this chapter clearly does not provide a basis for generalisation. It can, however, in the flow of the current narrative, be taken as a further piece of circumstantial evidence, testing a hypothesis and inviting reflection on persistent questions within media effects debates.

There can ultimately be no doubt that Western 'Cold War' propaganda, its historiography and newstoriography, was successful. All of the time, greater or smaller majorities of Western citizens and media consumers were sufficiently convinced by the constantly repeated hegemonic story to either agree with or at least consent to it – and to remain passive. The story was ever present, told most frequently in indirect ways, penetrating the small details of life with pro-USA and anti-Soviet messages within an illusion of genuine pluralistic discussion, and creating the predominant pro-Western assumptions which emerged in the survey, along with the black and white polarisations which led away from conciliatory or neighbourly relations, and justified insane military escalation.

But this was not a straightforward process, for there was plenty of movement and activity, plenty of intelligence and independent thinking beneath the crust of passivity and successful passivication. The control could thus never be taken for granted. To this extent, models proclaiming weak or minimal media effects dent, but do not demolish those hypothesising stronger ones. One can see that strong media effects were not a system-inherent *a priori* principle – the legendary hypodermic syringe – merely a historically demonstrable series of more or less hard fought victories, which were perhaps less a question of effective mind control than a successful holding down of the lid of a pressure cooker within which energies were manipulated to be in conflict with each other rather than combining to raise the lid. Thus, in the 'Cold War', citizens and audiences could be subjectively active while remaining objectively passive, and objective passivity could cover a range of subjective states of mind, mental processes and courses of action.

The fundamental characteristic of passivity, of having been passivised, and thus making decisions *not* to utilise citizens' rights and fulfil social responsibilities in the face of insane government and elite positions, was failure to *act publicly* against them, and thus to conform to hegemonic discourse. There was in the 'Cold War' a huge variety of pretexts and excuses for inactivity, all of which were understandable, but none of which were ultimately valid in the face of evident urgent threat. If mass media propagation of hegemonic discourse had been *overpoweringly* strong and effective, then the story would be simple: powerful media control minds and actions of passive, manipulated citizen-consumers who are *ipso facto* no longer responsible. If, however, the top-down flow of information and control was *not* so all-powerful, then a proportion of the onus for decision making and action returned to members of society, and some blame for failure to act fell back onto them. While the main guilty party remained the power elites of which the mass media formed a part, responsibility falls on citizens in inverse proportion to the strength of hegemonic discourse and media effects.

So if the system of mind control *was* porous, why did most citizens exploit the porosity so little? A simple explanation is that it was just not very porous, but this again is unsatisfactory. That citizens felt powerless, intimidated, or unwilling to stick their heads above the parapet, or that they felt unable to make definitive judgements on an issue due to its complexity and a lack of full or precise information, or just that they felt that they had too much else to do, may be seen as the result of deliberate obfuscations and techniques of the passivication process. However, such techniques did not *have* to succeed, as contrary examples show (see Chapters 9 and 10). If inertia and conformism dominated, if clenched fists remained firmly ensconced in coat pockets, then individual people – citizens, consumers, media audience members – many of whom would have claimed to be sceptical of media output, bore a share of responsibility, as they did in 1914 and 1933.

Before his expulsion from the GDR (1976), the dissident songwriter, Wolf Biermann, addressed these words to passive fellow citizens there:

> So don't wait for better times now,
> Don't wait there, brave as you are
> Like the fool who, day by day
> Waits to cross at the river's edge
> For the waters to cease flowing,
> The waters that flow forever (Biermann 1973. Translation: JT).

They were equally relevant to those in the West.

Chapter 7

Acting as if ... Resistance to Dominant Discourses of Anti-Communism and Nuclear Escalation in the 1980s

We must commence to act as if a united, neutral and pacific Europe already exists. We must learn to be loyal, not to 'East' or 'West', but to each other, and we must disregard the prohibitions and limitations imposed by any national state (*Appeal for European Nuclear Disarmament* 1980).

The people of this country have been made dull and stupid by a diet of Official Information. But they are not all that stupid, and there is still a risk [...] that they might remember who they are, and become 'turbulent' before the war even got started (E.P. Thompson 1980).

The only way to contest the worst case is to envisage a better case, and then to summon up all our forces to work to bring that better case about (E.P. Thompson 1980).

Introduction

Edward Thompson, one of the major British twentieth century historians and a leading thinker-activist of the 1980s, is quoted here since these passages and those to be analysed below, dating from one of the most gloomy and crazy moments of the 'Cold War', restate basic premises concerning the power of public discourse on which this book rests, and echo key elements of the Krausian perspective on the mass media, with its apocalyptic tone. They also indicate the importance and effectiveness of rejecting the kind of over-theorised determinism which leads to paralysis and pessimism, and of becoming involved in acts of cultural resistance and liberation.

The shadows of the aggressively polarising discourses of the Reagan, Thatcher and Kohl governments with their omnipresent neo-liberalism and anti-communism, and the story of the culminating triumph of the West and humiliation of the East that they and theirs had so yearned and worked for, hang heavily over any view of the 1980s, seen through Western eyes. We should also remember, however, that the same decade was that of an extraordinary rise of counter-hegemonic expression, popular consciousness of global issues, and challenges to power elites and their dominant media of communication, coercion and control. These challenges include, among others, the peace movement, at its most spectacular in the West, and the citizens' movements for self-liberation against engrained authoritarianism, 'Cold War' dogmatism, and reactive armament in the East. It is discursive examples from these two areas that this and the following chapter address.

The cases so far highlighted in this narrative painted a dark-clouded picture of the effective, if not inevitable, mind control practised over twentieth century publics by power elites who determined its anti-human hegemonic discourses, with their grotesque distortions. It is now time to ask about the possibility, extent and nature of the role of counter-hegemonic discourses in processes of change – those which opposed the dominant, believed, self-nourishing stories which led to and sustained the unprecedented wars, atrocities, myths of nation, race and ideology, and the crazed logic of 'mutually assured destruction'.

The 1980s, with their climax in the momentous changes sparked off in 1989 which conjure up images of unprecedented mass civic action, provide potentially the most likely models of the successful dissemination of counter-hegemonic discourses at citizen level, leading to self-emancipation, an influential public sphere, and historic transformation. There are intimations here which merit careful attention. Synchronicity does not prove causality; alternative thinking, rhetoric and civic action may or may not have been significant linked contributory facets in a complex process, but if we ascribe real importance to *one* set of discourses – the hegemonic ones – as we do, then it is only consistent to examine the concrete effects on history of the *counter-hegemonic* ones. Likewise, if mainstream historians ascribe a key role to 'the people' in the revolutionary events in Eastern Europe in 1989 – as they do – then it is only consistent to include the role of articulate mass social movements in the West in any analysis of the transformations of that time.

Yet, looked at in terms of the 'final score', the peace movement of the 1980s could seem a poor example of significant opposition to hegemonic discourse. If the whistle blew to end the game of that decade at the end of 1989, then there was plenty of nuclear escalation and proliferation, and only small evidence of reduction of weapons of mass destruction to show. What is more, the US strangulation of the Soviet economy, and cultivation of frustration and dissatisfaction in the East by provoking its governments into diverting hugely disproportionate resources into military spending, could be said to have worked, as the Eastern Bloc and the Soviet Union started to disintegrate. Western hegemonic discourse, one could say, was as triumphant as it could possibly be, as it prevailed in the West, and gained largely uncritical acceptance in the East. At the end of the decade, the peace movement could hang up its boots and go home, exhausted and unfulfilled.

On the other hand, a deadly serious match had been played, a contest had taken place, and, of course, in history there is no final whistle (or none yet), although some asserted it. In other words, the triumphs of the elites of neo-liberalism over external and internal opposition, and of the powerful and resourceful nuclear imbeciles over the arguments of peace campaigners in the 1980s, were neither definitive, complete, nor inevitable. A challenge took place, the powerful had to expend continuous, costly and sometimes underhand energies against strong ideas and citizen pressure which threatened to undermine their schemes and investments. They were unmasked as fragile, nervous, paranoid, and occasionally rattled beneath their robust exterior. The 1990s showed that the US-led 1980s 'victory' was, in many respects, a pyrrhic one, and that the perspectives and achievements of the NATO powers' home-grown civic adversaries kept resurfacing in different guises, while they – particularly the US military, industrial, political and media elite – had to struggle increasingly to find military friends supine and co-operative enough, and military enemies credible and evil enough, to justify their naked strutting the world stage as number one superpower, generalissimo and global boss.

Any Peace Movement activists who had fallen asleep in 1985 and woken up in 2000 would have been astonished at how much of their agenda had been appropriated and progressed, and how much of the old mindset of their adversaries had collapsed or lost its focus. Of course, they would still have found their millennial counterparts vigorously engaged in 'hopeless' campaigns, and they would doubtless have noticed some veterans of the 1980s among them, still as passionate as before, and rightly so, for the Western power elites were still there, vast tragedies were still occurring, brewing and reproducing themselves. But at least, even if these power elites themselves falsely claimed all credit for the transformed geopolitical landscape, and even if they grossly mismanaged the subsequent opportunities in the 1990s, the 1980s global high wire act of superpower nuclear confrontation, and the gallows tension of imminent nuclear holocaust, formerly claimed as indispensable, had retreated somewhat, and those mad enough to be nostalgic about them had been sidelined.

The words and ideas of the 1980s peace movement may claim to be a seminal part of the mix of influences which brought this change about. It will always be difficult, maybe impossible, to quantify its role. The peace movement was part of what the Hungarian writer George Konrád called 'antipolitics' in that it did not seek formal political power; it was characterised by, as he put it: 'the emergence of forms that can be appealed to *against* political power; it is counter-power that cannot take power and does not wish to' (Konrád 1984:230-231). It acted to influence policy 'by changing [...] customary thinking patterns and tacit compacts, by bringing the pace-setters to think differently' (ibid.:224), and to upset a normality in which 'the politicians and their intellectual employees pollute the intellectual environment in the hope that the population whom they target through the media will be unable to think in any terms other than the ones they present' (ibid.:227). Such a movement has the power of the termite rather than that of the chainsaw; it fells trees, but even when the tree has fallen, the cause is not so easy to recognise or attribute if you do not know, or want to know, where to look.

Edward Thompson only ever saw himself as one among a broad group of alert and articulate thinkers, writers, academics, polemicists, journalists and activists who made peace and *détente* issues, combined with citizens' debate and international action, a key element of their lives in the 1980s. His reputation as a major historian and his incisive rhetoric on paper and on the platform did, however, lead to him being regarded in Britain and elsewhere as a focal figure within the initiatives for European nuclear disarmament and the various actions which went on under the heading of END (European Nuclear Disarmament). He is singled out at the beginning of this chapter for those reasons, and because he not only accorded in abstract a key role to counter-hegemonic discourse in processes of social, cultural and historical change, but he also intervened discursively and (anti)politically in a real and vital historical situation, contributing, and energising others to contribute to, and believe in, actual change, and to resist dominant media processes of passivication. The polemics, arguments and exhortations of his pamphlets, articles and books were thus not conceived as just verbal fireworks, full of ultimately impotent 'musts' and 'oughts', but as alternative discourse linked to generation of real pressure for actual change – not wishful sermons, but rigorously and passionately argued actions in themselves.

Here, analysis of short extracts from Thompson's essay *Protest and Survive* will illustrate this. Thereafter a broader look at 1980s peace movement publications and discourses moves the narrative from the individual to the collective level, and links the words of the campaign to its action, contrasting them with hegemonic discourses. Finally, a preliminary assessment will be made of the impact of this body of material on socio-cultural change.

Protest and Survive

Protest and Survive appeared in 1980. In terms of the British corner of the 'Cold War' nuclear stand-off, this was the moment at which the newly elected Thatcher government endorsed with conviction the deployment, and potential use by the US military, without British government permission, of new intermediate range US Cruise missiles at US bases on British soil (Greenham Common and Molesworth). On mainland Europe, decisions to station Cruise missiles in Italy, Belgium, the Netherlands and West Germany, and Pershing 2 missiles in West Germany – these latter capable of reaching Moscow within ten minutes of launch – added to inescapable perceptions, among sane and adequately informed citizens, of Europe in general and Britain in particular as the prime targets and nuclear battlefield in any nuclear war. There was a renewed high level of public consciousness of danger, and a spreading sense that the arrival of land-based Cruise and Pershing 2 missiles was a superfluous and demented escalation.

The majority of the mass media, in the very act of rehearsing the specious hegemonic arguments for even more 'deterrence' in the context of manifold 'mutually assured destruction', were at the same time having to provide information and details (albeit often distorted) which could only increase alarm and disbelief in any half-awake audience.

The revived Campaign for Nuclear Disarmament (CND) became the main focus for UK-centred argument and protest against these developments, with groups of activists forming all over the country, while the Labour Party opposition to Thatcher's Conservative government took up a position close to that of the peace movement, and helped, through its influence at parliamentary and local government level, to keep peace movement concerns high on the political and media agendas.

One of a range of such concerns was civil defence. If the risk of nuclear war was increasing, what arrangements, national, regional, local and domestic, were in place should it actually happen? What was the scenario that government envisaged?

Such questions led to the otherwise unscheduled Home Office pamphlet *Protect and Survive* being made available to the public in 1980, and consequently subjected to the widespread ridicule, persiflage and argued demolition that it deserved. Ridicule came, for example, in Raymond Briggs's comic book *When the Wind Blows* (1982), an antidote to *Tintin au Pays des Soviets* in the comic book Cold War. Argued demolition came in the form of E.P. Thompson's *Protest and Survive*. The government pamphlet *Protect and Survive* instructed the householder, in the event of a nuclear attack, to 'stay put' and prepare a fallout room and 'inner refuge' using doors, boxes, sandbags and heavy furniture, having stocked up with two weeks' supplies of food and water. It failed among other things to mention best estimates that the blast effect from a 'moderate' nuclear attack (200 megatons) would instantly cause 70 per cent of such shelters to collapse, either burying those inside or exposing them to fallout (Openshaw, S. et al 1983:221-224).

For Thompson, the very existence of such prepared official instructions, however crass, exposed the government's lack of faith in the West's policy of deterrence, of which it was such a passionate supporter; their publication to coincide with the decision to deploy Cruise missiles in Britain was an admission that such deployment *increased* the risk of attack, whereas in the theory of deterrence their presence should *reduce* the danger. The other idea that the Soviet leadership, on realising how well-prepared for attack the British population was, would be put off from making the attack in the first place – civil defence as a significant element of deterrence strategy – was some way short of the plausible.

As Thompson's title and approach indicated, it was not spurious and futile attempts at individual self-protection which were relevant to citizens, but cultural action against the whole fallacious discursive basis of the conflict. At the end of Briggs's *When the Wind Blows*, James Bloggs and his wife, conforming citizens, start *praying* incoherently as they lie dying in their makeshift shelter, constructed according to 'govern-mental' instructions; Thompson, in contrast, agreed with his Hungarian counterpart George Konrád, who wrote: 'Today, it is not enough to *pray* for peace; today one must *think* for peace – not piously, but radically' (Konrád 1984:223).

The following passages from *Protest and Survive* are central to Thompson's position:

> The deformation of culture commences within language itself. It makes possible a disjunction between the rationality and moral sensibility of individual men and women and the effective political and military process. A certain kind of 'realist', and 'technical' vocabulary effects a closure which seals out the imagination, and prevents the reason from following the most manifest sequence of cause and consequence. It habituates the mind to nuclear holocaust by reducing everything to a flat level of normality. By habituating us to certain expectations, it not only encourages resignation – it also beckons on the event.[...]

What threatens our interests [...] is seen as outside ourselves, as the Other. We can kill thousands because we have first learned to call them 'the enemy'. Wars commence in our culture first of all, and we kill each other in euphemisms and abstractions long before the first missiles have been launched. [...] We *think* others to death as we define them as the Other: the enemy: Asians: Marxists: non-people. The deformed human mind is the ultimate doomsday weapon – it is out of the human mind that the missiles and the neutron warheads come.

For this reason, it is necessary to enter a remonstrance against those who use this kind of language and adopt these mental postures. They are preparing our minds as launching platforms for exterminating thoughts.[...]

'Deterrence' is not a stationary state, it is a degenerative state. Deterrence has repressed the export of violence towards the opposing bloc, but in doing so the repressed power of the State has turned back upon its own author. The repressed violence has backed up, and has worked its way back into the economy, the polity, the ideology and the culture of the opposing powers. This is the deep structure of the Cold War.[...]

'Deterrence' has become normal, and minds have been habituated to the vocabulary of mutual extermination. And within this normality, hideous cultural abnormalities have been nurtured and are growing to full girth.[...]

What we cannot observe so well – for we ourselves are the object which must be observed – is the manner in which three decades of 'deterrence', of mutual fear, mystery, and state-endorsed stagnant hostility, have backed up into our culture and ideology. Imagination has been numbed, language and values have been fouled up by the postures and expectations of the 'deterrent' state. But this is a matter for a close and scrupulous inquiry.[...]

I am reluctant to accept that this determinism is absolute. But if my arguments are correct, then we cannot put off the matter any longer. We must now throw whatever resources still exist in human culture across the path of this degenerative logic. We must protest if we are to survive. Protest is the only realistic form of civil defence.

We must generate an alternative logic, an opposition at every level of society. This opposition must be international and it must win the support of multitudes. It must bring its influence to bear on the rulers of the world. It must act, in very different conditions, within each national state; and on occasion, it must directly confront its own national state apparatus (Thompson & Smith 1980:51-57).

These extracts demonstrate Thompson's clear progression from cultural-linguistic analysis and criticism, leading to a view of his contemporary culture as grotesquely distorted and dehumanising, to, first, a position of virtual pessimistic determinism, but then a rejection of this in favour of cultural action and mass mobilisation to influence and confront rulers in the interests of survival.

At the beginning of this progression, he discusses a process of effective passivication whereby the hegemonic hijacking of the way in which one is able to talk about a subject (the 'realistic' register which by definition denigrates all others as 'unrealistic', and the 'technical' register which can dismiss the 'non-technical' as incompetent) both reduces alternatives to silence, and cuts what then becomes the only 'acceptable' discourse off from the human response and the real life consequences. Once this alien discourse is imposed and routinised, it becomes possible to *speak* such words as 'nuclear holocaust' in terms of military strategy and megatonnage while excluding imagination of the suffering and annihilation which they entail. The more we make the possible use of nuclear weapons an assumed and natural part of our way of speaking of them, Thompson argues, the more we accept that they can and will be used, and the closer actual use comes. In addition, the more we demonise and dehumanise discursively 'enemy others', the more easily we can accept, even desire, their status as nuclear targets and their million-fold massacre. Echoing Kraus's First World War analysis with striking similitude, Thompson argues that the death of others in war occurs in our minds and in the death of our imaginations first, well before any shots are fired. The first and fundamental struggle is thus the discursive one against 'exterminating thoughts', and in particular against those who constantly and purposefully propagate and cultivate such thoughts.

Thompson's treatment of the word 'deterrence' is an example of how a stale, normalised word, which slipped so easily and frequently off the tongues of cold warriors, emptied of almost all of its real meaning and implications, and which was parroted in the mass media as a debate-clinching *solution* and guarantor of *security*, could be resurrected from its cliché status and unmasked for the real monstrous danger that it represented. By revealing it as a 'degenerative' rather than a 'stationary' state, he undermined the whole reassuring aura of it being something which maintained 'stability', 'balance', even 'peace' (all good and desirable things), and replaced this with associations of cancerous disease, of a situation getting progressively worse, and of inexorable decline towards death. More than this, he not only exposed deterrence as a *result* of deformed thought patterns, he perceived the physical act and result of constantly ratcheting up levels of potential mega-destruction as then reflecting back on culture and ideology, sealing minds into ever crazier concepts of 'normality'. A habitual 'stationary' definition of deterrence saw it as having the same 'stabilising' effect, and thus being equally peace preserving, at whatever level of destructive potential 'balance' was achieved. Thompson's 'degenerative' definition unfroze the imagination, revealing each successive escalatory step for what it was, another insane and perilous dance even closer to the edge of species extermination.

Thompson's appeal for protest seemed born of desperation, an instinctive belief against logic that survival and civilisation must be possible as long as there were people there prepared to struggle for it. Once that was accepted, focus was achieved, and mobilisation, action and the realisation through them of alternative logic, of envisaging a better case than the worst case could take place.

END Journal

He was by no means alone. Just as the umbrella organisation CND grew into a massive, inclusive UK-wide network of alternative information circulation, local campaigning and direct actions, and regular mass events, clogging London streets, Hyde Park and Trafalgar Square with hundreds of thousands of demonstrators, so END focused on activity at the European level, forging links through specialist lateral groups with both Western and Eastern peace groups and organisations, helping to arrange a decade of annual conventions in different European cities, and providing support and solidarity, again through its lateral groups, to those undergoing state harassment and intimidation for stepping beyond the much narrower limits of permitted alternative thinking and autonomous organisation in Eastern Europe. CND promoted its ideas nationally through the monthly magazine *Sanity*, supplemented at local level by a plethora of grassroots newsletters. END's mouthpiece was *END Journal*, again supplemented by smaller publications from its lateral groups, and complemented by international peace movement publications from a range of campaigning groups across Europe, including *ENDpapers*, published under the auspices of the Bertrand Russell Foundation.

A definitive history of the UK peace movement in the 1980s has yet to be written. Still less has a coherent account of international peace campaigns across Europe, in the USA and worldwide been produced. Suffice it to note here, to give an indication of the scale of the activity, that in the autumn of 1983, there were peace movement demonstrations in Austria, Belgium, Britain, Canada, Denmark, Finland, France, Ireland, Italy, Holland, Norway, Spain, Sweden, the USA and West Germany, amongst others, bringing over five million citizens onto the streets. At the London demonstration of 22 October, there were almost half a million people in the biggest demonstration since the suffragettes.

For the purposes of this narrative, only a tiny corner of this field, some texts from *END Journal*, will be examined to provide salient insight into influential alternative discourses, and to analyse rebuttals of powerful genealogies of untruth and insanity which would otherwise have traversed this section of the century uncontested. *END Journal* can neither be set up as representative of the mass movement, nor can the extracts to be used here be claimed as typical of the broad movement's ethos, but it did attract contributions from leading figures, thinker/activists of stature, and articulate specialists, finding its niche at the more intellectual end of the range, and promoting the international agenda of the movement. It can certainly be placed at the leading edge of peace movement journalism.

Thirty-seven issues of *END – Journal of European Nuclear Disarmament* appeared bi-monthly from END's cramped London office in the six and a half years between late 1982 and early summer 1989. Although entirely dependent on subscriptions, donations, and frequently in financial difficulty, it gained a high reputation for the quality of its contents. Its stated aims were to: provide the important facts about the arms race and the 'Cold War'; explore the debates and arguments for a nuclear-free Europe; and report on the activities and ideas of European peace and human rights groups and activists. These aims were largely reflected in the content throughout the journal's existence, although the emphasis shifted over the years. Earlier numbers were more involved with the anti-Cruise and Pershing 2 campaigns and thus more focused on specific work for weapons reductions and elimination, and then with SDI (the US government's Strategic Defence Initiative, popularly known as Star Wars). Later numbers concentrated on broader issues of East-West relations, *détente* from below, human rights in Eastern Europe, and reacting to the 'Gorbachev effect'. Throughout, however, there was a flow of detailed and first hand peace and disarmament information from all corners of Europe, East and West, including articles by contributors such as Olof Palme, the former Swedish Prime Minister, and Václav Havel, then playwright and dissident, later Czechoslovak and Czech President. Editor of the journal for most of its life was Mary Kaldor; selected extracts from her editorials, which formulate aims and record achievements, plus a small number of further key texts, chosen for their relevance to the themes of this book will be considered here.

The millions of peace movement demonstrators, activists and occasionally active supporters had a range of mindsets and motivations, but were united in their rejection of hegemonic discourses of 'defence', 'security', 'deterrence', and of the existence and deployment of nuclear weapons which, they were told via the mass media, were maintaining 'peace', and preventing attack by an aggressive, expansionist communist enemy. They were also united in their discovery of alternative discourses which they found more convincing than the ubiquitous media rhetoric of the powerful, and inspiring enough to induce them to take part in civic actions which they would normally not have undertaken. Although they were in almost all cases not numerous enough to elect governments which shared their perspectives, or to influence ruling parties towards adopting overtly alternative security policies, and one may thus argue that hegemonic discourses retained their hold on the majority, they were nevertheless manifestly a social force to be reckoned with. In several countries – including West Germany and the UK – the peace movement had its ideas adopted by main opposition political parties. Election results show that they *were* overall losers in terms of the ballot box in all the countries where it mattered most, but there are other criteria for judging success and failure in processes of social change, which amount to more than just consolation prizes or self-justificatory hindsight.

Not only mainstream, but also distinctly left-of-centre newstoriographies, as they blend into rapid-reaction histories, categorise the peace movement as a perhaps occasionally noisy, but ultimately fairly insignificant minority, whose discourses, although understandable, could be dismissed, and whose consequent actions could be ignored as significant factors in the flow of events. The *Guardian* journalist Martin Walker, in his book *The Cold War* (1994) portrayed the British peace movement as a 'loose and unstable coalition' which was 'never able to rally around a single cause they could agree to be for', and whose 'great weakness' was 'the range of its demands' (Walker 1994:263-4). Eric Hobsbawm, in his *Age of Extremes. The Short Twentieth Century 1914-1991* (1994) judged that: 'the movements for nuclear disarmament were not decisive [...]. At the end of the Cold War these movements left behind a memory of good causes and some curious peripheral relics' (Hobsbawm 1994:237-8). Timothy Garton Ash, in *In Europe's Name. Germany and the Divided Continent* (1993) gave the issue more space, posing, in his own way, pertinent questions:

> There are those who argue that it was Reagan's new-old policy of Cold War, re-armament and, yes, the Strategic Defence Initiative – 'star wars' – that compelled the decisive turn in Soviet foreign policy. And there are those who argue that, on the contrary, the true sources of 'new thinking' are to be found in Western détente policies, in impulses that came from the peace movement, and the parties gathered in the Socialist International. So was it SDI or SI? (Ash 1993:119)

Ash's answer is ambiguous:

> So far as Germany was concerned, Schmidt, Kohl and Genscher all stressed, in
> retrospective conversations with the author, the crucial part which they now believe their
> resolve to go ahead with the deployment of Pershing and Cruise missiles had played in
> compelling a revision of Soviet policy. Had anyone on the Soviet side endorsed this
> interpretation? Yes, said Chancellor Kohl, Gorbachev had. But had anyone on the Soviet
> side endorsed Willy Brandt's contrary interpretation? Yes, said ex-Chancellor Brandt,
> Gorbachev! (ibid:119).

If one turns to Gorbachev himself, the validity of the question, but the
ambiguity of the answer remain. In his 1999 book *On My Country and the World*,
the emphasis is on autobiography and the writer's personal role, but he does write,
in the course of a discussion of the end of the 'Cold War' and the development of a
new world order:

> Another sign of things to come may be seen in the enhanced role played in international
> relations by a new element in politics – major non-governmental organisations which in
> generalised form reflect the sentiments of world public opinion (Gorbachev 1999:213).

Here, he clearly recognises a role for social movements such as the peace
movement, and NGO-type initiatives which it created. He then makes the cryptic
statement: 'these new phenomena have a meagre influence in world affairs, but
even so they are quite important' (Gorbachev 1999:213). Even if we get no
indication of what 'meagre' or 'quite important' are in the mind of a world
statesman, and even if such a person who has been at the very top of the
hegemonic heap is more likely to stress and justify summit achievements than to
admit a significant role for positive impulses from 'below', we have here an
acknowledgement that it was not just Gorbachev and Reagan, holed up in
Reykjavik, who brought about 'a turning point in world history' (Gorbachev
1987:240).

It is not surprising that the peace movement's own documents and discourses,
represented here by *END Journal*, provide a fuller and at least sometimes more
positive assessment. Two facets of this will be interrogated here: first, the extent to
which specific campaigning aims were achieved and, where achieved, at least
partly attributable to peace movement activities; second, the extent to which peace
movement ideas and perspectives flowed into the discourse of, and were
appropriated by, policy and decision makers.

Fulfilment of Specific Campaigning Aims

This may initially appear simple to verify. Although a whole list of linked
campaigning issues (from militarisation of the North Atlantic to 'Star Wars') vied
for attention in the pages of *END Journal*, there were two, identified at the
beginning of the decade, which predominated: the issue of preventing the European
stationing of, then, when they arrived, getting rid of, the Cruise and Pershing 2
intermediate range missiles; and the issue of overcoming the 'Cold War' division

of Europe. At the beginning of the decade, both of these seemed like 'momentous challenges', as the Journal put it (END 1983/3:2), not to say virtually impossible dreams. But the movement seemed very determined, and to believe in its power to transform and have an impact at governmental level. 'The peace movement is here to stay. It is a new phenomenon in political life. It is truly international and truly local. The grass roots are speaking to each other', announced the editorial of Number 1, which went on to see in the movement's international appeal 'a rediscovery of individual responsibility, a shared sense of emancipation from the Cold War', taking up the Czechoslovak Charter 77 phrase, 'a renaissance of European citizenship'. The sense of empowerment is reinforced in the editorial of Number 3, which claims that 'the peace movements in Europe have clearly forced governments into a desperate flurry to re-assert their control over defence and armaments issues', and 'the resurgence in the West (and the emergence in the East) of non-aligned peace movements is disturbing and unfamiliar to the gentlemen in the Kremlin'. Within the context of such self-belief, the article goes on to define aims:

> Our project is a long-term project. But one with immediate, short and medium term aims. In the immediate term, there is the halting of the arms race. In the short term, its reversal. And in the medium term, the creation of a process of genuine, meaningful and lasting relaxation of tensions in Europe [...]. In the long term this is the only way forward for Europe and the world (END 1983/3:2).

The upbeat rhetoric and belief in the power of grassroots pressure continues in Number 4:

> The task of the peace movement is to liberate the 1980s, to avoid the trauma and menace of a new Cold War. We have to convince middle opinion that, whatever happens on June 9 [British general election. JT], whatever happens in Geneva [endless disarmament negotiations. JT], we shall continue, and indeed step up our opposition to the deployment of Euromissiles. There are tens of thousands prepared to go to prisons, there are millions more prepared to support them. We shall not be bought off by cosmetic agreements or sweet-talking politicians (END 1983/4:2).

There is a strong conviction here that the movement's alternative discourse, with its power to mobilise millions, could really force change in the strategic thinking of a superpower and its allies.

This, however, proved to be an illusion in the immediate term. 1982 saw the West German SPD, which, despite the opposition of its leader, Helmut Schmidt, was shifting towards peace movement positions, pushed out of government and replaced by a centre-right coalition led by Helmut Kohl. In Britain, Thatcher was triumphantly re-elected on the back of perceived Falklands glory. Over Western Europe, the Cruise and Pershing 2 missiles started to be deployed, and the following year, Reagan was elected for a second term in the USA. Elections in Italy and Canada confirmed the international predominance of the right. The defeat of the peace movement was clear, and its demise was confidently predicted. Hegemonic discourses accepting nuclear escalation and the renewed Cold War had certainly won a battle, and gained democratic credibility. The peace movement was depressed, but it did not collapse or lose belief in its cause; rather, it seemed ready to persist with its broader medium-term goals. Edward Thompson took stock with some sobriety in the *END Journal* editorial of Number 16-17, summer 1985:

> The appeal for European Nuclear Disarmament was launched in April 1980, and, after five years, it would be foolish to be optimistic.
>
> The challenge of NATO modernisation (Cruise and Pershing 2) first brought Western European movements together. In 1981, the West European protest had assumed epidemic proportions. By 1982, common understandings were developing with the powerful Freeze movement in the USA. It seemed that the pressure for disarmament must break through.
>
> Yet it did not […]. NATO's agenda was fulfilled. […]
>
> There are grounds enough for pessimism here. And yet it would be equally foolish to be too pessimistic.
>
> In its first stages, the new peace movement was in a mood of refusal, of nausea with nukes, and it did not achieve its immediate objectives. But it is now clear, to its opponents as well as to itself, that it has given rise to a movement of unexpected permanence which could lead on to enduring political transformations (END 1985/16-17:2).

It is an irony that, at the very moment when Gorbachev was coming to power in the Soviet Union, Western peace movement eyes were thus being directed to the middle distance, and minds to slower and less dramatic change. At the same time there was prolonged disbelief (and we can still only speculate on the deep cultural reasons why and how exactly the change came about) that within a short time of taking office in 1985, the new Soviet leader was declaring views and aims uncannily similar to those of the Western peace movement, and particularly END. Within four years, agreements had been signed leading to the first Cruise and Pershing 2 missiles as well as Soviet SS-20s, and others, being destroyed, and the 'Cold War' division of Europe was ending. In the final number of *END Journal*, which appeared a few months before the opening of the Berlin Wall, Mary Kaldor echoed, but transformed Edward Thompson's 1985 editorial, quoted above:

> When the END appeal was launched in April 1980, none of us imagined that, within a decade, our concrete demands – for the removal of Cruise, Pershing and SS-20 missiles – would be achieved, and our vision of ending the Cold War and of a nuclear free Europe a practical possibility.
>
> Yet it has happened. The disarmament talks underway could bring about big reductions in weapons; and the democratisation processes in the USSR and in Poland and Hungary suggest that the division of Europe might be overcome by the end of the century (END 1989/37:2).

Put in this way, the peace movement was victorious after all, but to what extent, if any, did it contribute to the victory? Kaldor was cautious, stating later in the same editorial: 'The role played by peace and human rights activists in the changes taking place in Europe is rarely acknowledged. Yet we expressed and contributed to a fundamental change in values and attitudes' (END 1989/37:2).

In the previous issue of the journal, she had been a little more explicit. She had been invited to witness, as part of a Western delegation, the destruction of the first Soviet missile to be destroyed under the terms of the INF [Intermediate Nuclear Forces] Treaty, which also ensured the destruction of the Cruise and Pershing 2 missiles in the West. Western hegemonic discourse, of course, wrote the peace movement out of any credit for this treaty. Reflecting the unequal newstoriographical contest of the moment, Kaldor commented:

> I am alternately bemused, depressed and awed by the ability of the establishment to rewrite the history of the INF treaty. It now seems widely accepted that it was NATO's determination to deploy Cruise and Pershing missiles in Western Europe that forced the USSR to accept the zero option (i.e. the dismantling of all medium range land-based nuclear missiles). It's as if the peace movement had never been; the millions on the streets in 1981 and 1983, the bitter debates, the peace camps – all seem to be forgotten (END 1988/36:18).

She clearly believed that the peace movement did play a significant role in making that treaty possible: 'what the movement did in the early 1980s was draw attention to the reality of nuclear weapons, raising public consciousness so that governments were forced to react' (END 1988/36:18). It is that unproven direct causal link between mass action and government action which is at the nub of this area of the unresolved debate on the power of counter-hegemonic discourse. At least the gallant Soviet commander of the base where the first missile was destroyed believed in it. When Kaldor congratulated him after the explosion, he replied: 'Congratulations to you too'.

Appropriation of Peace Movement Thinking by Decision Makers

The second area of debate concerns less direct and specific influences that peace movement ideas may have had insofar as they were taken over and appropriated by policy and decision makers. To what extent did governments actually, but more or less covertly, adapt or transform their perspectives in response to peace movement influences? To have this kind of influence was without doubt a peace movement aim. If it did not succeed (at least until Gorbachev) in having its outlook *openly* represented at decision-making level, then it could at least, over time, hope to have a persuasive impact on governments, whether through the force of its arguments, the pressure created by mass mobilisation, or through the desire of political parties to increase electoral appeal. Such discursive influence would have been subtle and unacknowledged, and possibly reluctantly taken on by elites, reformulated for their own purposes, while still leaving the peace movement idea as a salient factor.

It should be noted here in parenthesis that dirtier tricks such as deliberate attempts at distorting peace movement positions for counter propaganda and support for anti-peace movement discourses and actions, although they are interesting discursive phenomena, are not included in this debate. The peace movement could not be held responsible for malignant misuse of its discourses by those pursuing opposite goals – in either bloc. One example of this was the US zero-zero option on INF weapons in Europe in the early 1980s, which was put forward primarily as a propaganda ploy in such a form that the US government could present itself as the peace-loving superpower, in full knowledge that the then Soviet leadership could not accept it; another was Reagan's 'peace' rhetoric surrounding his 'star wars' initiative.

END Journal provides some evidence for the reality of indirect processes of influence. One of the peace movement's, and particularly END's links to the high levels of professional politics and decision making was Olaf Palme. The former Swedish Prime Minister was the central figure of the Independent Commission on Disarmament and Security, generally known as the Palme Commission. He was one of the first signatories of the END Appeal in 1980. Palme spoke to an END rally in September 1981, and some of his words then, which address the relationship between popular movements and politicians, are quoted in the *END Journal* editorial following his assassination on the streets of Stockholm in February 1986:

> Without the popular movement pressurising, hounding the politicians, you won't get anywhere. But without politicians wanting in the end to tackle the matter, and sit down with their adversaries and try to get the negotiating done, you won't get anywhere either. [...]
> I am speaking about the general issue of politics. Without accepting and respecting the dual role, the indispensable role of the clear-cut moral stand of the popular movement, and the necessity for people who do some of the practical work, without accepting that, you won't achieve anything in this world. I'm prepared to do this work and that's why we are sitting with the Russians and Americans and talking – trying to persuade them that this is nonsense. Some days, it's awfully tedious. I much prefer agitation. I love to be here, and I'd rather spend my whole life doing this. But you have to accept the different role between strong public opinion and the role of the practical politician. [...]
> I'd just like to say that I hope you will continue your fight for very clear moral principles, because sweet reason and human emotion is on our side. And if you don't do that, if you don't continue this fight day in and day out, this world might be very terrible soon. In the meantime, we will do our utmost in the world of harsh and dreary realities, to transmute as much as possible of those harsh principles into reality. You can never reach all the way, but you can get very far on the road (END 1986/21:2, 4).

Palme here ascribes a particular role to the peace movement as a provider of moral force and mass pressure which strengthens the hand of negotiators working for the same cause at the official political level. He sees this role as essential insofar as he is clear that it provides authority and credibility to sympathetic politicians who would be in a hopelessly weak position without it. This made sense within the structures of Western democratic politics. One only needs to imagine a movement of a strength, expertise and energy equivalent to the peace movement working *for* 'Cold War' hostilities and nuclear weapons escalation, and the strength which governments would have taken from that, to realise that Palme's argument carries weight. Given this, we may refer to Willy Brandt's 1989 volume of memoirs (Brandt 1989:354, 405), which claimed the influence of the Palme

Commission, and of his own Brandt Commission on Gorbachev's new thinking in foreign and security policy, and observe a chain of influence from the Western peace movement through to Gorbachev.

Further support for such an influence comes in an *END Journal* interview with Tair Tairov, a secretary of the World Peace Council (WPC) from 1980 to 1985, and thereafter an executive member of the Soviet Peace Committee (SPC). Although END had vexed and largely negative relations with these official Eastern Bloc peace organisations, especially in the pre-Gorbachev years, and although Tairov strikes an over-enthusiastic tone, giving what appears to be an inflated view of his and his organisation's significance, his assertions, made at the Lund END Convention of 1988, do contribute to an image of the time, and to the excitement, and sense of participation and rapprochement felt by committed peace campaigners of all kinds – including Soviet officials, to whom one could attribute all sorts of motivations – once the realisation that Gorbachev was really serious in his intentions started to sink in. They also come from someone on the inside of the new Soviet peace establishment, whose discourse was unlikely to contradict a Gorbachev approved perspective.

Asked whether he thought the ideas and proposals of the END movement had contributed to the development of new Soviet thinking, he replied:

Absolutely. If it wasn't for the peace movements in the West, there would not have been new thinking at all – they nourished the idea of nuclear weapons free zones, of a nuclear-free Europe, of a nuclear-free world. Without them, Gorbachev would never have proclaimed the idea of a non-violent, non-nuclear world – he knew that the soil was fertile. They created the historical arena in which he could go ahead.

From my position in the WPC I saw the new movements emerging, like CND, women for peace, the generals, the medical movement. Gorbachev has been watching this and thinking there is something developing in Europe which has never been seen before: you can't go on pretending that SS-20s are different from Cruise and Pershing 2. This is a direct consequence of the work of the peace movements.

I myself sent a cable to Moscow saying: 'Please, for God's sake make an oath not to test for half a year – it's a no lose game, we can't lose'. I was reprimanded by the SPC. They told me: 'It's none of your business, don't interfere, no, we will not stop unilaterally'. So I said: 'If you won't stop, at least don't test in August '85; every year, we test on Hiroshima and Nagasaki days'.

They said: 'Tair, forget the unilateral moratorium, but we promise we won't test at the beginning of August'. I sent another cable: 'Please, thousands of people from Australia to Canada are waiting, Bruce Kent, Daniel Elsberg, CND, SPAS [Swedish Peace and Arbitration Society. JT] are waiting – we have nothing to lose'. This was two weeks before the moratorium was declared, and I know it was read by all the top people, the Ministry of Defence, Gorbachev. When I read in the paper that Gorbachev had announced the moratorium, I really felt it was my lucky day. For me that was a positive lesson of Helsinki [Conference on Security and Co-operation in Europe, 1973-75, and the subsequent process of implementing its resolutions. JT]. My position there enabled me to try and convince the leadership.

I also worked out a No First Use proposal with Daniel Elsberg, and with Eva Nordland. I worked on the slogan: 'No to nukes in East and West'. The military in Moscow didn't like this slogan, but it opened the way for many people in Moscow to begin protesting against our own nuclear weapons. This is why I claim that the peace movement has contributed to new thinking (END 1988/36:21-22).

With these personal statements, which doubtless exaggerate his own role, Tairov nevertheless expresses the belief, confirming Palme and Brandt by a different route, that there was a key policy-influencing link between the discourses and actions of the Western peace movement, and the formulation and adoption of new thinking on nuclear disarmament and East-West relations in the Soviet Union.

This narrative has to leave that suggestion in suspension, pending further evidence. It may, however be of further significance that Gorbachev mentions Bertrand Russell and Albert Einstein among the key precursors of the new thinking. The roots of his vision may lie as much with the original and early seers of the insanity of nuclear weaponry as with their 1980s counterparts.

Even more unanswered questions lie with the figure of Ronald Reagan, who, following his ultra-hawkish image and actions of the early 1980s, and having established a position of US confidence and strength, suddenly, but temporarily, revealed himself as having all along wanted nothing more than to rid the world of nuclear weapons. He astonished all his closest aides at the Reykjavik summit, 'that bizarre weekend of bonding [...] which shocked US-Soviet negotiations into a whole new dimension' (Walker 1994:294). How, at this truly extraordinary and historic moment, perhaps a moment of truth within an age of untruth, which reportedly astonished Reagan's closest aides and caused his military and arms industrialists near apoplexy, did the manifestly cynical and empty presidential rhetoric of the early 1980s miraculously start to be taken literally and to convince its mouther-in-chief? There may be more clues towards an answer to this when the private correspondence between Gorbachev and Reagan is published in full.

Conclusion

This chapter cannot be conclusive and it has only looked into microscopic samples within a large subject, while posing big questions. It does, however hope to have contributed to showing that, within late twentieth century, Western mass communication structures with their powerful and pervasive processes for naturalising and propagating hegemonic discourses, which posed a threat to emancipatory public sphere debate and activity, alternative or subversive forms of democratic expression could not always be smothered, deflected, discredited, tamed or otherwise contained within the limited permissible bounds that power elites set for them. Stories of that period can be told in such a way as to suggest plausibly that dominant and refined anti-human orthodoxies such as those which pervaded the 'Cold War' could be effectively contested, even if to do so required close to superhuman energies, and the kind of constant vigilance, stamina and inventiveness that citizens' initiatives cannot generally maintain, and even if success was far from complete. In his 1983 pamphlet, *The Defence of Britain*, Edward Thompson wrote, in an optimistic portrayal of the British peace movement, of an 'alternative Britain, of citizens and not subjects which, in civilisation's eleventh hour, summoned up all the strengths of its long democratic past and cut through the world's nuclear weapons jungle' (Thompson 1983:34). In the same pamphlet, he wrote more darkly of the same peace movement:

> It was a necessary event. If after 38 years of gathering nuclear threat, and the insatiable and growing appetites of the nuclear armourers, some people had not stood up and started waving banners at each other across the globe, then one could properly have assumed that the human spirit had rolled over on its back and given up the ghost (Thompson 1983:3).

Cutting through the world's nuclear weapons jungle, or waving banners at each other? Or both – with the latter helping to provide the climate and impetus for politicians to embark on the former?

Chapter 8

A Collapse of Hegemonic Discourse. Resistance in Eastern Europe

An obvious sign that the times were ripe for change was the activity of dissidents. They were suppressed and expelled from the country, but their moral stand and their proposals for change (for example, the ideas of Andrei Sakharov) played a considerable role in creating the spiritual preconditions for perestroika. Of course, external factors were also important. Thus the Prague Spring of 1968 sowed the seeds of profound thought and reflection in our society (Mikhail Gorbachev 1999).

The East Germans [...] felt grateful to Gorbachev. But more important, they felt they had won this opening for themselves. For it was only the pressure of their massive, peaceful demonstrations that compelled the Party leadership to take this step [...]. And even the Party's Central Committee acknowledged at the beginning of its hastily drafted Action Programme that 'a revolutionary people's movement has set in motion a process of profound upheavals' (Timothy Garton Ash 1990, on the opening of the Berlin Wall).

Introduction

The collapse of a vast empire, and with it a social experiment, ideology, and way of life, is a rare thing to witness. The break up of the Soviet Union, and the bloc it controlled, although at one level not inevitable and the result of a series of specific actions, pressures and decisions in East and West which sabotaged the belated new thinking of Gorbachev and his supporters, can be seen, at another level, as the result of a massive, long term failure, and consequent popular rejection of a powerful hegemonic discourse. Despite ubiquitous and co-ordinated state-controlled networks for propagating the views of the ruling Communist Parties, the gap between what most people were experiencing in their lives and hearing through unofficial networks, and what they were being fed by their hegemonic, but unsubtle media and education systems, became so large and self-evident that confidence in the leadership and the ideology it was promoting had, for the majority, long since evaporated. It proved to be beyond restoration, even by the *glasnost* (openness) and *perestroika* (restructuring) promised by Gorbachev.

Even if, a few years on, millions living through the dire, often appalling consequences of the overthrow were wishing that they could turn the clock back, or a long way forward, they had, at the moments of decision, been utterly convinced that anything was better than what they had, and that getting rid of, rather than reforming their current system was a necessary first step towards something better.

The *fata morgana* of imminent arrival of idealised Western living conditions, and the extension of those much quoted 'blossoming landscapes' with which West German Chancellor Kohl seduced the East Germans, to the whole of the Eastern Bloc, provided the positive alternative discourse with which to replace the old.

What is of interest in the present context is the self-evident triumph of alternative over hegemonic discourses in the relatively closed context of the last years of the Eastern Bloc. This is a digression in the sense that the rest of this narrative has been concerned with the workings of hegemonic discourse in capitalist societies where media discourse has become a commodity, and has developed refined market-related techniques of selling and packaging its own untruths and distortions to become credible, desirable and attractive. It is included, however, to examine the circumstances in which an immensely powerful discursive hegemony was, following counter-hegemonic discursive mobilisation, rejected by the people it was designed to convince and control, leading to radical social change. Do these processes undermine quasi-determinist theories of media effects, and, by extension corresponding experience of tenacious and robust media power in Western societies? Could the apparent impregnability of media power prove in certain circumstances to be as illusory in the West as it turned out to be in the East?

We shall enter these issues by looking at the specific case of the development of counter-hegemonic discourses in the German Democratic Republic in the 1980s, and by carrying out some analysis on one alternative journal produced in East Berlin, *Grenzfall* (which means both 'borderline case' and 'the falling of frontiers') by the group *Initiative Frieden und Menschenrechte* (Peace and Human Rights Initiative).

The GDR was, a special case among a series of special cases in the collapse of the Eastern Bloc. Its use here, however, does in key ways also reflect events elsewhere, and does provide resonance and continuities with other sections of this book. It enjoyed the highest standard of living in the Eastern Bloc, but was also, geopolitically, its most precarious member, and the one most morally and existentially dependent on the Soviet Union. At the same time it had a common language, constant exposure to broadcast media from, and common historical and cultural links with, its Western neighbour, the Federal Republic of Germany, which was constitutionally committed to working for its demise. Its leadership was, for historical reasons, bound to be the Eastern Bloc's most loyal and committed member, seldom wavering from the Soviet line, least tolerant of internal non-conformists, and likely to be the most wary of Western influence. In this sense, it was as close to an ideal test case of the Soviet system as could be found. Having built the Berlin Wall, the most notorious symbol of the 'Cold War' East-West divide, its fate was bound to resonate well beyond its borders.

Since the failed strikes and uprising of June 1953, active opposition in the GDR had been for the most part muted and restricted to a small minority. Over the decades, and particularly since the building of the Berlin Wall in 1961, the great majority got on with life in political circumstances which were authoritarian, but material and social circumstances which, averaging out their high and low points, were experienced as tolerable and gradually improving. Frustrations were generally containable, or divertible into a broad subculture of private sphere activities. Once the Wall had been built, and the Berlin route to westward migration had been closed, persistent public critics had to choose between balancing on the knife-edge of reconciling self-restraint and subtle subversion on the one hand, or undergoing official harassment and, sometimes, expulsion to the West on the other. The widespread presence of the surveillance apparatus was routine, and had its coercive, but for most of the populace, undramatic effect in the inducement of conformity as well as the reduction of crime. I recall seeing a gang of East Berlin skinheads in the mid 1980s who were behaving quite aggressively and kicked over a rubbish container, spreading the content over the street. They started to move on, then looked around a little furtively and decided to go back, pick up the rubbish, and return it to its container. It was an isolated incident which remained in the memory for its subjective emblematic value.

In this context, a decision publicly *not* to conform, or to campaign for reforms outside recognised channels and limits, was difficult, and it is not surprising that only a relatively small number of people took this path. It needed strong convictions, independence of spirit, and a readiness to substitute a relatively comfortable, unremarked and uncontroversial existence for subjection to a range of threatening and disrupting treatments by the security police which could have wider repercussions on one's employment, family and circle of acquaintances.

Those who became involved in the numerous small autonomous groups campaigning for peace, nuclear disarmament, East-West *détente*, human rights, freedom of travel and expression, and environmental issues, in the 1980s, including the activists of the *Initiative Frieden und Menschenrechte*, joined the small minority who, over the years, took this risk. From 1986, well before there was any plausible prospect of revolutionary change, a number of unofficial journals, produced from these groups, started to appear. These were the home-grown discursive seedbed for the transforming events of autumn 1989, that 'brief flowering of civil courage, peaceful maturity and social self-organisation that was blighted [...] by the warm perfumed wind from the West' (Ash 1990:74) – the alluring propagation of Western hegemonic discourses.

Grenzfall

Grenzfall lays claim to being the GDR's first independent periodical, although many others followed it in the last three years before the opening of the Berlin Wall. These included *Nachtgebete* (Halle), *Aufrisse* (Berlin), *Arche Nova* (Berlin), *Briefe der FfF* [Women for Peace. JT] (Berlin), *Kontext* (Berlin), *Nachdruck* (Merseburg), *Die Mücke* (Leipzig), *Umweltblätter* (Berlin), *Ostkreuz* (Berlin), and *Artikel 27* (Berlin). *Grenzfall* and those involved in its production and distribution thus represent just one example of a much wider picture of reform and resistance activity throughout the GDR. The concentration here on this journal intends to represent the others, certainly not to devalue them.

Grenzfall appeared (almost) monthly from June 1986 until December 1987 (issues 1-15), then irregularly (issues 16 and 17) until May 1989. It had to be produced and distributed illicitly, and its publishers had only a typewriter, poor quality paper, and a hand-operated rotary copier, used on Protestant Church premises. Between 800 and 1000 copies of each issue were produced, distributed, and passed on from hand to hand. Regular publication ceased because on 28 January 1988, after a period in which the group's increasing public action was countered by intensified surveillance and harassment, five leading activists were arrested by the state security police, accused of treasonable activities, and of acting as enemy agents. Four of them were, as a compromise following solidarity activities from peace and human rights groups in the West, particularly members of END, and through the agency of the Protestant Church, pushed into temporary exile in West Germany and England as an alternative to long prison sentences. The fifth, forced into a similar dilemma, went into permanent exile in the Federal Republic. It was he, Ralf Hirsch, who, with Lev Kopelev, ensured an afterlife for *Grenzfall* by publishing privately a collected facsimile edition of issues 1-15 in 1989. Following these arrests and expulsions, only two further editions appeared; *Grenzfall*, but not the reform movement, had been effectively stifled.

This journal was a very small operation by Western norms, but it was highly significant in the GDR context, and the police reaction shows how seriously it was taken. Those in temporary exile – Bärbel Bohley, Vera Wollenberger and Werner Fischer – chose to swim against the tide and to return to the GDR when their exile time was up, arriving in time to play key roles, along with other members of the *Initiative*, in *Neues Forum*, and the mass GDR reform movement of autumn 1989. The activities of these groups, and the alternative discourses they produced, show that there was a social space in the GDR in which a significant will for reform of governance and structure of the system was expressed by those who had grown up and been socialised within it.

An indicative set of headings based on a scan for the most frequently appearing subjects reveals the following pre-occupations of *Grenzfall*:

1. Socialist democratisation and internal social change (equivalents of Gorbachev's *glasnost* and *perestroika*)
2. Environmental issues
3. Solidarity with opposition activity in neighbouring Eastern Bloc countries
4. Human and civil rights
5. Peace and disarmament
6. Freedom of expression and information

The theme which is conspicuous by its absence is that of German unification. The continuing existence of a radically reformed (but not Westernised) GDR is presupposed and unquestioned. The name which is far in front of all others in the number of positive references is that of Gorbachev, to the extent that there is some critical discussion in the pages of *Grenzfall* of the dangers of becoming over-reliant on him as *deus ex machina*. Four of the six key themes identified above will be looked at more closely here, and this will be followed by an analysis of the graphics used in *Grenzfall*.

First, socialist democratisation and internal social change, according to the Gorbachev model. *Grenzfall*'s use of Gorbachev's discourses of change and new thinking as a lever against the relatively rigid and reactionary, but threatened hegemonic discourses of the GDR leadership is central to its position, and exemplifies both its strength and weakness, as well as characterising its campaigning style. A key exemplary text comes in number 6, 1987, and takes the form of a 'Letter to Gorbachev'. It is a copy of a letter, signed by prominent members of the *Ininiative Frieden und Menschenrechte* – Gerd and Ulrike Poppe, Werner Fischer and Wolfgang Templin, as well as by Monika Haeger and Ibrahim Boehme (both later discredited on account of contacts with the security police), which was delivered by hand to the Soviet Embassy on 27 May 1987 on the occasion of Gorbachev's visit to East Berlin. In its commentary, *Grenzfall* uses the tactic of driving a wedge between the GDR government and its Soviet ally and model by emphasising that, in contrast to its subversive, even treasonable nature in the GDR, the letter was received in the Soviet Embassy in full consciousness of what was going on, and met with anything but cold rejection or consternation (Hirsch & Kopelev 1989:68).

In its content too, the letter emphasises a positive attitude to Gorbachev and his reforms as a means of undermining and isolating the GDR government in terms which it could not easily suppress without being seen to contradict the Soviet leader. Thus, the writers of the letter commit themselves to a socialist democratisation of the GDR, to internal political change coming from the grass roots, using quotations from Gorbachev to support this. Western-style socio-political reform is specifically rejected. The following extracts exemplify the style. Addressing Gorbachev, the letter says:

> The important changes in the Soviet Union are greeted by many people in the socialist countries with surprise, sympathy and hope [...]. Many of your proposals for transforming society in your country correspond to the demands of the independent peace movement and democratic opposition in the GDR.

Then:

> Our desire is certainly not to take over bourgeois structures on the Western model, rather to promote a social system which makes possible the unity of democracy and socialism.

And finally:

> Honoured Mikhail Sergeevich, your policy of restructuring finds such great resonance among our population because the problems you have identified are all too well known to us (Hirsch & Kopelev 1989:66-67. All *Grenzfall* translations: JT).

The letter is, on the one hand, a piece of autonomous direct action, but on the other, it is by its nature and motivation an appeal for action, reform and influence from above. It takes on Gorbachev's discourse uncritically, while spicing it with concepts borrowed from Western green and peace movements of the time. As such, it demonstrates elements of a bridge-building alternative East-West discourse. It should be underlined here that, while the *Initiative Frieden und Menschenrechte* welcomed Gorbachev's reforming rhetoric, and was able to exploit it for its own ends, it would have been opposed to any readiness by the Soviet leader to contemplate the demise of the GDR, and was fundamentally committed to indigenous reform from below.

The second key theme of *Grenzfall* to be considered here is that of the environment. Here too, the analysis will be restricted to a single representative article, this time from number 4 (1987). Typically for *Grenzfall*, this is again not just an article, but an action in the form of an appeal, an 'open letter to the governments of all countries' (Hirsch & Kopelev 1989:50). The readers should not only read, but also do something, in this case sign a petition to support a campaign for a referendum (as allowed under the GDR constitution) against the continued use and expansion of nuclear energy in the GDR. The instigators were Martin Böttger, Ralf Hirsch and Gerd Poppe. This was part of the worldwide reaction to the Chernobyl catastrophe, and the style reflects this; it resembles the campaign materials of any Western anti-nuclear movement and thus underlines the irrelevance of an 'iron curtain' in the nuclear age:

> Those who built nuclear power stations before Chernobyl, despite all the warnings, were irresponsible gamblers. Those who still support this technology after Chernobyl are dangerous terrorists and criminals [...]. BECAUSE WE NO LONGER WISH TO LOOK ON WHILE A HANDFUL OF POLITICIANS AND LOBBYISTS GAMBLE WITH OUR FUTURE AND THAT OF OUR CHILDREN, BECAUSE WE NO LONGER HAVE CONFIDENCE IN OUR POLITICIANS, BECAUSE WE BELIEVE THAT WHERE ALL ARE AFFECTED, ALL SHOULD DECIDE, WE DEMAND THAT THE PEOPLES OF EUROPE THEMSELVES SHOULD TAKE THIS DECISION (Hirsch & Kopelev 1989:50).

Here we see members of the GDR opposition, courageously in that authoritarian context, acting as E.P. Thompson had exhorted active citizens to in the Appeal for European Nuclear Disarmament, 'to be loyal, not to "East" or "West", but to each other', and to 'disregard the prohibitions and limitations imposed by any national state' (Thompson & Smith 1980:225). As with the letter to Gorbachev, we see the style of popular movement rhetoric rather than the phrases of politicians bearing the responsibilities of power – a mixture of utopianism and grassroots activism within the framework of a specific campaign – but they are a manifestation of a genuine moral and democratic impulse by people who stood to lose a lot by making public declarations of opposition to their government.

The third theme of *Grenzfall* to be examined is that of solidarity with dissident groups in neighbouring European states, including the Soviet Union. Every issue of *Grenzfall* included sections dealing with news of groups working in Poland, Czechoslovakia, the Soviet Union, and sometimes Romania, expressing support for them, especially in cases of harassment or persecution. As an example, a report in number 3 (1987) illustrates how Czechoslovak dissidents were, like those in the

GDR, faced with a government which wished to deny and refute the Gorbachev reforms. It expresses solidarity with VONS – the Czechoslovak committee for the defence of the politically persecuted – and its work related to the earlier arrests of Václav Havel, Jiri Dienstbier and Peter Uhl. *Grenzfall* states its view that 'it is through the mobilisation of national and international public opinion that the repressive practices of the government in its treatment of those who think differently can be resisted' (Hirsch & Kopelev 1989:43).

It is of interest here that in appealing to international – including Western – public opinion, the emphasis is on people's action against governments, not on diplomacy or government level action. *Grenzfall* also shows here that its prime identification is with the situation in Eastern Europe, and in reform movements in neighbouring Eastern countries. There is no sense of any ethnic or national identification with West Germany.

Expressions of solidarity with parallel groups elsewhere in Eastern Europe are frequently related to the fourth theme, that of campaigning for human and civil rights. *Grenzfall* (2:1987) contains a copy of a letter of solidarity sent by members of the *Initiative Frieden und Menschenrechte* and GDR unofficial peace activists to the Czechoslovak founders and promoters of Charta 77, on the occasion of its tenth anniversary. The letter is of interest on the one hand as a statement of solidarity, on the other as a declaration of autonomy and distinctiveness of the GDR activists.

An element of this distinctiveness was their desire to provoke debate with, and their constantly rejected hope to influence, party officialdom. This stubborn and much debated conviction that internal reform through dialogue was possible clearly made more sense to those involved in the GDR context than it did to their counterparts in neighbouring countries. It was a tough position to maintain, linked to their Gorbachev-inspired optimism, their roots in the Protestant Church, and their peace activism. A substantial part of *Grenzfall* 8 (1987) was devoted to the issue. Here, contributions from the Polish reformer Adam Michnik and peace activist Jan Litynski provide a considerably more sober and reticent view of Gorbachev. There were also dissident voices in the GDR which were considerably more sceptical.

Despite these latter, the predominantly less confrontational approach of the GDR activists, their continued critique of Western governments, and their refusal to support the possibility of German unification on Western terms, certainly did not enhance their public credibility once the headlong rush to unification had started. It was, however, consistent with their commitment to a radically reformed GDR, and their quite plausible expectation that, once the hardliners still clinging to power and determining hegemonic discourse were replaced, a younger, reforming generation, open to 'new thinking' and popular pressure, would come to prominence, and constructive dialogue, leading to real structural democratic change, would become possible.

The imagery of the cartoons and graphics appearing in *Grenzfall* provides visual representations of its critical perspective. Of particular interest for the group's self-definition, and for the kind of discursive challenge it was issuing to official rhetoric is the change of masthead after the initial issue. The first masthead portrayed literally the falling of a closed border, represented by a wall topped with barbed wire with, on the left, *Grenz-* (border) inscribed on it in upright letters, which then turned, on the right, into a pile of rubble, with *-fall* written on it in sloping, or falling letters.

The wall clearly referred to the Berlin Wall and the closed state boundary with the West. The graphic was thus implying the demolition of that boundary, and, by implication, the end of German division. This was abandoned in all other issues of *Grenzfall*, doubtless due to its susceptibility to misinterpretation of the agenda of the group producing the journal, which was certainly East-West *détente*, but equally certainly not German *unification*.

The new masthead for issue 2, which then remained, virtually unchanged, showed a low barrier consisting of a striped wooden pole stretched between two posts. It was not drawn as a barrier which could be raised, but was nevertheless one which was easily crossed. Moreover, the centre of the barrier was gnawed away and weakened, and twigs with leaves sprouted from that weakened central section. The ground beneath and beyond the barrier appeared to be riven with crevasses, and the barrier appeared to be there to prevent one from falling over the edge of a precipice. Thus, while the leaves sprouting from the dead wood appeared to show new life emerging from the weakening of old barriers, the message is ambivalent since the barrier was also seen to be there as benevolent protection against a dangerous, unstable landscape, encroaching from beyond. Eastern restrictions were subverted, while to the West was danger and potential disaster – literally beyond the pale.

Cartoons broke up the text of *Grenzfall* frequently in the first two issues, but were thereafter confined to one per issue on the front page. Thematically, they fell into five categories: indoctrination and censorship; successful subversion and opposition; cages and imprisonment; environmental pollution; and scepticism about reform from above. Here, examples are given of the first three of these.

The front page cartoon of *Grenzfall* 4 (1987) points to the provocative cat and mouse relationship between state authorities, and peace and human rights activists, and to the way in which *Grenzfall* taunted those who wished to silence or censor it. Although virtually powerless in terms of resources and equipment, it was, nevertheless, managing to distribute its message and defy official disapproval, demonstrating the power of the independent word in an authoritarian society. The rubric under the cartoon runs: 'Attention all police stations, I will now pass on the description of the weapon used in the crime: 35 cm by 30 cm, black with white keys, weight about 5 KG.' The drawing of a uniformed policeman speaking into a microphone while looking at a large picture of a typewriter pinned to the wall in front of him portrays the authorities mockingly as perceiving the humble typewriter – and by extension words – as a powerful weapon used to perpetrate criminal discursive activity, needing to be sought out, confiscated, and used in evidence. They are thus shown to be both paranoid, and wishing to suppress free expression and the means of producing alternative discourse, employing their whole network of control to locate the offending object. It is a direct portrayal of struggle between hegemonic and counter-hegemonic discourse.

Cartoons in two issues of *Grenzfall* (1987:10, 1987:11) which immediately preceded the arrests of key activists around the journal and the *Initiative Frieden und Menschenrechte* showed images of successful opposition to, or subversion of, state authority. The first showed a large figure holding a marionette, whose movements he would normally be controlling, in the process of falling over since the marionette has turned on the puppet master, entwined his legs in the strings, and is in the process of pulling them tight. This variant on the David and Goliath motif portrays the overthrow of authority through action on the part of the normally passive and controlled. It empowers the powerless as the oppressor is ensnared by the very means of control that he himself created.

The second showed a figure gleefully turning a hand-operated duplicating machine (a further reference to the group's primitive equipment) which is spewing out sheets of paper in the direction of a crowd of people consisting largely of truncheon and radio-telephone-wielding policemen and a machine-gun-toting soldier. The members of the crowd appear to be prevented from advancing as the sheets of paper from the duplicating machine fly towards them. One member of the crowd in civilian dress is making a thumbs-up sign and seems pleased, where all the others are frustrated at their inability to move in and prevent the dispersal of the papers.

Since the papers clearly represent *Grenzfall* in particular, and opposition discourse in general, this cartoon was an open provocation to the state authorities, presented as helpless and incapable of stopping its production. It may have been no coincidence that they moved in before another issue of *Grenzfall* could appear.

Three *Grenzfall* cartoons used the image of the birdcage. In the penultimate issue (1988:1-12), and the first to appear following the arrests of key figures around *Grenzfall* and the *Initiative Frieden und Menschenrechte*, the front page showed a sad-looking parrot in a cage with its plump, bespectacled owner, hand raised and finger pointing, standing close by, and saying: 'And now say after me: "I am free, I am happy".' The image is self-explanatory, but its unambiguous ironic portrayal of imprisonment, authoritarian structure, imposition of hegemonic discourse, and the requirement to mouth reality-denying mantras, portray the journal immediately as a still provocative place in which the opposite is happening, and as a defiant space where the will to resist such processes is alive. The editorial inside the front cover reads: '*Grenzfall* is dead – LONG LIVE *GRENZFALL*.' The message is that critical voices are not going to cave in when threatened by intimidating actions.

Grenzfall did, however, no longer appear after the spring of 1989, at just the moment when END Journal also ceased publication. Yet there was little time to lament the setbacks that these apparent failures represented. The rest of the year brought the processes of popular and largely peaceful liberation and falling of barriers across Eastern Europe that they had been campaigning for and to which they actively contributed. In the GDR, activists of the *Initiative Frieden und Menschenrechte* became key contributors to *Neues Forum*, which brought together people from a range of similar groups to organise and set the tone for the actions and demonstrations which pressurised the ruling party through the autumn. No longer backed by Soviet military force, and ultimately shrinking from violently suppressing its own people, the regime tried, too little and too late, to embrace reform, and was swept aside.

This would have been a suitable moment for the denouement of a stage drama. It turned out to be just a brief entr'acte, but had the curtain fallen at this point, the audience would have filed out satisfied that the hubris of the oppressors had been put down and that a new dawn was breaking. It is thus worth pausing to take stock. At this point – a moment of truth for those involved if ever there was one – a discursive and organisational power edifice had been demolished, its out-of-touch 'truth regime' exposed as the travesty it had largely become, and space had been created for a new grammar and lexis of social and political life to emerge. Reformers from inside the old ruling party sat around tables with members of autonomous reform groups; willing brains produced a fine new constitution for the GDR; the GDR media became excited and exciting – participators in rather than controllers of debate. One could in these moments of autumn 1989 make out an optimistic case which demonstrated that a seemingly captive public, despite the thrall of a robust and oppressive hierarchy of discursive control, *could* break out and defy hegemonic power. It is no wonder that there was a sense of euphoria – enlightenment in the sense of burdens being shed and shoulders being straightened, as well as the illumination of inner and outer spaces that had previously been obscured. These were brief moments of extraordinary and unique opportunity which deserve to be kept distinct from the interests and processes which *purposefully* rushed in to kidnap them. The adverb *inevitably* (see Chapter 9) rather than *purposefully* laid its claim to inclusion at this point, but that was neither the feel of the moment, nor is it the necessary judgement of analytical hindsight, which so likes to adjust itself in the light of subsequent events and new discursive hegemonies.

Conclusion

In the present context, the major questions that these moments pose are: Do they show us a set of circumstances in which hegemonic discourse and media power could be, and were, overthrown? Did the end of the twentieth century finally provide real evidence that controlling elites in their mass media disguises, albeit crude ones, *could* be unmasked, and their grip on public consciousness *rejected* through the spread of counter-hegemonic discourses and democratic collective action in a new embodiment of citizenship in the public sphere?

Simple answers would be satisfying, especially if they were positive. In fact they are threefold, intertwined, and give more intellectual temptations to pessimism than optimism.

First, the revolutionary events of 1989 took place in the specific context of the Eastern Bloc, where the power elites were monolithic and authoritarian, and the media part of them, unprovoked by market mentalities, had failed to realise sufficiently that seducing and entertaining the consumers is a far more effective means of controlling them, if that is what you wish to do, than boring and bludgeoning them. Print and broadcast journalists in the old Eastern Bloc did not gain credit by pleasing their publics, outdoing the competition, increasing sales or ratings, and *thus* satisfying their advertisers and employers; they did so by conforming to the requirements of the ruling party. This had the advantage to most readers and viewers that they were not seduced or lured into complicity with their mass media. They knew that they were getting a Party-controlled product. Most disliked the fact, and few were taken in by it. In these circumstances, no great insight or analytical acumen were required to be apparently media-wise; it was obvious that you searched between the lines or relied on alternative sources to get at 'real' information. In the GDR, most people watched West German television and found it more credible than their own country's product. If queues were to be found in East Berlin in the 1980s, they would, strange to Western eyes, often be found outside bookshops, when a limited edition of a new novel, play, or volume of poems by a critical writer had negotiated its way past the cultural minders onto the shelves.

One cannot transpose this set of circumstances into a Western, now globalised, context, where the immensely successful seduction and distraction of audiences within a competitive system in which the fittest survive, are, for most, naturalised phenomena, and where even the rump of public service broadcasting largely goes with the commercial flow. With a few occasional permitted exceptions, self-criticism by the mainstream media is cosmetic. Radical democratic critiques from the outside are ignored or brushed aside as paranoia or conspiracy theory, smeared as one or another kind of extremism, or 'counterbalanced' if a possible threat is perceived by tides of mainstream 'common sense'. As the previous chapter showed, even the more severe cases of hegemonic insanity can only be countered with immense effort and energy, and these struggles are unlikely to achieve easy or direct success.

Second, the revolutionary moments of 1989 were short-lived. Well-accustomed to smelling out the polluted waters of their own media practices, most East Europeans were far less prepared to resist the deceptive Eau de Cologne of Western media discourses, and initially far too enthusiastically allowed the civic space they had so well created for themselves to be opened up and impregnated by the other, apparently sweeter and more alluring hegemony on offer. As described in relation to the GDR in Chapter 9, a few weeks sufficed to turn the victory of a people who wanted to find their own way, and needed time to do so, into a precipitate victory for Western discourses. It was thus ultimately not the vulnerability of hegemonic mass media discourses in general which was confirmed in this period, but the superior effective power of media discourses corrupted and distorted by market forces and elite manipulation – the very thing that this narrative has observed throughout its course.

Third, despite all this, there may be found cause for encouragement and occasion for learning in the East European events of 1989. It may be remembered that even weeks before the dramatic events and the short timescale in which they took place, they seemed impossible. Apparently robust social systems, power structures and ideologies, we have observed, can – in this case in their entirety – submit to counter-hegemonic pressures for radical change in which popular action plays a significant role. If publics could, in huge numbers, see through relatively crude systems of hegemonic mass media control, they are doubtless, in the right combination of circumstances, and with requisite educational work over time, also able to get wise to cleverer and subtler systems. The lesson of the 1990s, however, is that counter-hegemonic discourses should not only develop radical critiques of manifestly inadequate and unjust structures and practices, but that they should also prepare inspiring and viable alternatives. That the evolution of such alternatives appears to preoccupy so few and meets with little resonance among the broad public would be cause for pessimism were it not for the example of those who have gone beyond it. As Alva Myrdal wrote: 'Pessimism is no good as a working hypothesis, except for historians who work after the fact. Those of us who live and want to work for the future must suppress those doubts that border on despair' (END 1986/21:22).

Chapter 9

Cold War Victory and
the Selling of German Unification

Except for the United States, no country close to Germany welcomed its unification. Had France, Britain and the Soviet Union been able to block or postpone unification, they certainly would have done so.

Americans hardly noticed at the time that among many Germans, too, enthusiasm for unity was very faint. The Social Democrats' chancellor candidate spent his 1990 election campaign warning (all too accurately as it turned out) about costs to come. The Greens of the time boasted that "everyone may be talking about Germany, but we talk about the weather". Writers and intellectuals in western as well as eastern Germany were apprehensive. Like Günter Grass and others [...] they were profoundly sceptical about unification from the start and opposed the shape of the unification process assumed after the spring of 1990 (Robert Gerald Livingston, Director of the American Institute for Contemporary German Studies 1993).

Introduction

What is remembered by most as the 'fall' of the Berlin Wall on 9 November 1989 is now habitually confused in popular memory with what is misleadingly known as German *re*-unification, and its images are simplistically retained in many minds as marking the moment when the 'Cold War' ended.

This was an event which was filmed and photographed as it happened. The blanket media coverage took place in full consciousness of the historic nature of the moment. Thousands witnessed it on the spot and millions across the world watched it on live television, awed by the symbolism of the occasion. Yet, despite the fact that the subject was seemingly covered from every angle, and that such a detailed record was gathered, and remains available to journalists, commentators, historians, and the public, an extraordinarily selective and distorted image was quickly constructed, and remains embedded in popular memory. A wide range of materials and accounts exists in archives and marginal publications, and, particularly in Germany, personal, family and local memories and experiences influence perceptions, but the predominant spin on these events – and the core of what most people say happened, if asked – was and remains an amalgam of resonant media images and hegemonic media discourse, a story moulded in the interests of the West German and US power elites.

In this version, the 'East German people' rose up against their dictatorial government, and stormed the Berlin Wall, attacking it with hammers and chisels until it was breached, and then poured through to 'freedom' in 'the West'. The long-separated 'German people' were re-united amid euphoria and popular celebration, following forty years of cruel division upheld by the morally and economically bankrupt Eastern communist regime. Thus the 'Cold War' came to an end in a spirit of universal rejoicing. Liberty had been brought to an oppressed people.

Whatever elements of caricature may be present in this portrayal, this *kind* of story, with its triumphalist subtext, glorifying the defeat of 'Communism' and offering conclusive proof of the moral superiority of 'the West' and its political and economic model, held sway in Western, thus dominant, post-'Cold War' collective consciousness in the 1990s. Publics – especially those personally affected – became aware of severe economic difficulties and major socio-political conflicts associated with 'transition' and 'adaptation' to 'Western structures' in the former East. These, however, could be portrayed – especially to those *not* personally affected – as 'teething problems'. They were blamed on vestiges of old 'Communist' mentality, on perceived historic eastern European and Russian anti-democratic predilections, or on 'new nationalisms'. Such catastrophes were seldom blamed on the ruthless way in which Western elites pressed home their victory, or on their unscrupulous exploitation of the new power relations for profit and advantage. In the West, the nefarious individual and collective consequences of Westernisation for millions of men, women and children in the former Eastern Bloc were usually downplayed or ignored. Yet for millions in these regions, the 1990s brought insecurity, economic hardship, in many cases real poverty with social, health and education services in free fall, and even, as in Chechnya, war of unrestrained barbarity.

For most East Germans, virtual annexation by West Germany initially seemed a price worth paying for a measure of protection from the turbulence reserved for their former Eastern Bloc neighbours and partners. But although the Western hegemonic story of their good fortune told them they should be satisfied, reality, for most of them, told them that they were not. The majority of them voted in 1990 for Western solutions in the Western-style elections which they had so wanted, but it emerges, when one looks more precisely at the circumstances, and at the manipulation that characterised their choice, that they were misled and deceived. There were moments of genuine popular euphoria surrounding the demise of the old regime in the GDR, but the subsequent collapse into the seemingly friendly arms of the West was rapidly revealed as a delusion, which had seduced them into abandonment of all control over their destiny, and speedily turned them into an economically and socially retarded and colonised region, dependent on grudging, if substantial handouts from the taxes of their wealthy Western cousins, to whom they were expected to be cravenly grateful.

The word 'inevitable' was often used in the 'word politics' of this context. It set the seal on what had happened, assuring us, and them, that it could not possibly have taken place in any other way, and that it was now too late to change course. At the same time, it snuffed out alternative discourses which might have led to questioning of the *status quo* and possible policy changes. The well-placed insertion of 'inevitable' is an invaluable and ubiquitous tool of passivication.

Thus, what could have been moments of truth and self-emancipation for the peoples of the former Eastern Bloc in general, and for the GDR in particular, were unceremoniously transformed into moments of imposition of a *different* hegemonic discourse which rapidly showed itself to be, in its own way, as untrue to the hopes and aspirations of the majority as had been the previous one. Western elites, instead of encouraging the development of autonomous structures and solutions appropriate to their regional contexts, for the most part marched in with victors' discourses, victors' justice, and victors' rights of exploitation of whatever spoils were to be had. The trope of anti-communism, cause of so much twentieth century misery, instead of being decently buried alongside the old Soviet system, danced on its grave, rubbed salt into the wounds of its survivors (if that metaphor is now again permissible, see Chapter 4), and used the occasion to trumpet brazenly the undisputed newspeak of its now 'proven' superiority. This, even as it happened, could be recognised as a mistake of incalculable dimensions. While alternative courses offered no instant panacea, and would doubtless have encountered complexities of their own, the deliberate treading of pathways which led to easily foreseeable humiliations and crises in the former Eastern Bloc, and contemptuously overran all alternatives, could not be condoned or defended. The course of falsehood was set early on, with the most decisive, pivotal moments in the contest for discursive hegemony occurring between November 1989 and March 1990. Germany, particularly Berlin with its Wall, the most powerful and photogenic symbol of 'Cold War' insanity, and its wealth of stories of divided families and daring escapes or escape attempts, was the place on which world media interest, and debate (such as it was) was most firmly focused.

The Imagery of German Unification

Analysis of salient media texts, drawn from the mass of revealing 'ephemera' that appeared, demonstrates the managed take-over by US/West German discourse at the expense of all others.

Filmed and still pictures of the Berlin Wall, particularly shots showing the Brandenburg Gate, with celebrating crowds of people by, on, and climbing onto it, flashed around the world on the 9-11 November 1989, burning indelible images into millions of memories. These were shortly followed by pictures of people taking pick-axes, hammers and battering rams to the graffiti-covered concrete. Variations on these images were shown again and again in subsequent television reportage, documentaries, weekly and periodical journals, and on the covers of instant books, rushed out to construct and profit from the occasion.

In the mid to late 1990s, I showed such images to several groups of students, and then to a number of well educated, but non-specialist adults. In virtually every case, I received answers indicating that these pictures showed 'the East Germans' storming and knocking down the Berlin Wall on that evening when it 'fell', and Germany was 're-united'. It was a straw poll of no significance beyond itself, except that it confirmed the self-evident: that a useful myth had been successfully created which, although untrue in every detail, had gained currency through the presentational work of the mass media.

'The East Germans' did not, of course, storm the Wall. A poorly phrased press announcement emanating from a just completed meeting of a rattled, but reforming, GDR *Politbüro* revealed, among other things, the imminent end of travel restrictions. (It should be remembered that travel restrictions for GDR citizens had already been somewhat relaxed such that many tens of thousands of GDR citizens had already visited the West in the first nine months of 1989. Visa-free travel for Austrians and Hungarians visiting each other's country had also been in operation for several years.)

Once this press announcement was broadcast, several thousand of the over one million East Berliners went to the standard crossing places, and, amid mounting excitement, requested the border guards, who knew nothing of the announcement, to open the barriers and let them through. There was clearly much official confusion as to the detail of the announcement, particularly as regards the timing of its implementation. What was happening had evidently not been intended to proceed in this way, but eventually the guards raised the barriers, and the euphoric crowd swept through, symbolically asserting the right to travel to the West. The vast majority of them returned home after a few hours of celebration, drinking, socialising and window-shopping, and many of them apparently managed to get to work the next morning.

Meanwhile, news of the announcement was broadcast on the Western media, and this brought several thousand of West Berlin's two million inhabitants onto the streets, while, as in the East, most stayed at home, and watched the 'history' happening on their doorsteps on TV, or missed it altogether. A good proportion of those who did go out gathered at the Brandenburg Gate; a few of those had had the presence of mind to bring household hammers and chisels, and started to chip away symbolically at the western side of the fortification – approximately three metres high and equally thick at that spot – while others clambered up onto it. Of course, the Berlin Wall did not physically fall that evening. Those who brought pick-axes made great subjects for photographers, film crews and mass media editors. They had a great impact on global media consumers, but very little on the actual concrete. Along with everyone else, the leading West German weekly *Der Spiegel* carried such pictures, confirming in its text that the crowds on the Wall were *West* Berliners (*Der Spiegel* 46/1989. 18-20 and cover picture). The Wall in front of the Brandenburg Gate was, prosaically enough, not actually demolished until the following spring. On that day, heavy East German industrial plant drilled and tore at it for almost three hours before a significant opening was made. On the Western side, about two hundred tourists and Berliners had gradually gathered. As the breach was slowly enlarged, an advertising banner was revealed with the slogan used at the time by a leading US cigarette manufacturer: 'Test the West'. Although originally coined to associate the cigarette with the wide open spaces and pioneering spirit of the North American far west, the slogan had fortuitously gained local significance in the Berlin 1989-90 context. Here, it unmasked the underlying meaning of the end of the East-West divide, the opening up of Eastern markets, with US multinationals rolling their wagons into the Wild East. This was an unintentional moment of truth as history merged indistinguishably with marketing. But even then, it contained a lie, for, to make any sense, the banner would have had to be facing eastwards. But what did that matter? It was ideally placed for the cameras.

The euphoria captured by the world's media on 9-10 November 1989 had at the time nothing to do with German unification in the minds of the participants. Only later were events concertinaed, with stories constructed in such a way as to create a seamless narrative of inevitability in which unification and the 'fall of the Wall' became so closely linked as to be virtually synonymous, with popular anti-communist revolutionary action rather than US-dominated global geopolitics presented as its chief cause. Far be it from *this* text to underplay the extraordinary courage, determination, importance and sacrifice of those in the GDR who had lately united as *Neues Forum* (see previous chapter). It was they who had on the previous Saturday, 4 November, been behind the organisation of the huge demonstration on East Berlin streets which, along with other GDR events, especially in Leipzig, had convinced the *Politbüro* of the need for radical change if the government was to survive. But these were not the opportunists of unification, nor the bit-players and spear-carriers of its blockbuster production. The 4 November demonstration, the largest East Berlin had ever seen, had been a massive call for *GDR reform*. None of its speeches, and none of its banners called for German unification. It was simply not on the agenda. Five days later, when the detested travel restrictions were removed, few, if any East Germans would have stated that their innermost desire was the precipitate take-over and annexation of their state and society by West Germany. As confirmed by Livingston's statement at the top of this chapter, such an outcome was far from a general wish, let alone a foregone conclusion, except perhaps in the schemes of the US and West German governments, their business backers, media colleagues and political acolytes, that is, those most capable of bringing it about. Most East and West Germans, as well as concerned neighbours, were at best dismissive or sceptical.

We are thus faced with a situation in which, within eleven months, events were so skilfully directed, reacted to and seized upon as to transform what initially seemed to most to be an advisedly slow, long-term, and delicate process towards, perhaps, a loose German confederation taking into account both external worries and internal sensibilities, into an unstoppable triumphant stampede towards the goal of unification on Western terms, sealed on 18 March 1990 at the GDR elections, and signed on the following 3 October .

As the more rough-hewn newstoriography of Western takeover of the GDR and the Eastern Bloc as a whole was discursively fashioned and filtered into the dominant historiography of Western solidarity and righteousness, so, within the same process, untruths, inaccuracies and distortions were integrated into the structure of popular memories – despite the good and accurate work of some historians, writers and analysts. Likewise, much that could expose the manipulative process was not commented on, and plenty that did not conform to the orthodoxy fell by the wayside.

The recalling of a few pieces of this historical jetsam may serve as a small antidote to those unquestioned authoritative narratives which present the whole process as if a natural phenomenon – 'the people' – took over control and grasped 'freedom'. The fact that in this scenario 'the people' delivered just those outcomes that the US neo-liberal power elites and their dependents, notably in West Germany, most desired, that is, a shattered empire, and the chance to reconstruct and exploit it ruthlessly along lines that would multiply their own power and wealth, was a remarkable 'coincidence'.

The alternative to the disingenuous hegemonic 'people power' narrative is one which sees some degree of public manipulation – largely via the media – playing a role in the eventual rush to unification, and in its international acceptance.

After all, between November 1989 and March 1990, a radical *volte face* in East German public opinion took place. The at first dominant *Neues Forum* approach promoting major internal political reform within a continuing GDR was replaced by a decisive majority in favour of adopting the *Deutschmark* and proceeding to rapid unification on totally Western terms. On the international front, by October 1990, initial opposition to the US/West German governments' pro-unification position in the top echelons of power in Italy (Andreotti), France (Mitterrand), Britain (Thatcher) and the Soviet Union (Gorbachev) had been twisted into acceptance. One does not need a conspiracy theory to find it unlikely that all of these underwent autonomous and unrelated Damascene conversions, replacing their prejudices or thoughtful independent judgements with positions which happened to comply with those of superpower hegemonic discourse.

Michael Hofmann demonstrates cogently in his essay 'The Unity Train' (Nowell-Smith & Wollen 1991) the way in which the mainstream German media interacted intimately with the Kohl government in the creation of an unstoppable pro-unification bandwagon within Germany. He points to several ways in which media interventions crucially influenced events and public opinion while shoring up Chancellor Kohl's then precarious political position in West Germany. He shows in particular how critical public debate was suppressed and reduced to the voices of a few individuals (for example Günter Grass) as the whole spectrum of media opinion from right to centre-left swung behind the Kohl line on unification. In place of real debate, he argues, it was the resonant media metaphor of the unstoppable train to unity, along with the constant televising of scenes of rejoicing crowds, often the result rather than the cause of the presence of TV cameras, that created the emotional momentum behind Kohl's coercive and duplicitous promotion of rapid unification on Western terms. Television, according to Hofmann, also increased pressure for unification by focusing on, and thus encouraging, the mass migration of East German citizens to the West, and by constantly plugging the need for the GDR to adopt the *Deutschmark*. Furthermore, in the four-week pre-election period in late February and early March 1990, Hofmann sees mass media persuasion as crucial. At this moment, the conservative Alliance, supported by Kohl, surged dramatically upwards to overtake the Social Democrats, by convincing the GDR voters that it was worth tumbling without further reflection into the arms of the West in order to be showered with the promised benefits of the Western currency, West German living standards and lifestyle within the shortest of periods. Hofmann concludes that the political symbolism of the unification train, a constant media motif with its strong connotation of 'inevitability', became 'the self-fulfilling prophecy of the year' (Nowell-Smith & Wollen 1991:68).

On the international scene, a parallel process of narrowing an initially wider spectrum of media and public debate on unification, including some strong opposition, took place as non-conforming views were progressively marginalized.

A brief look at French reporting in November 1989 exemplifies this, and demonstrates also how national media first built up distinctive perspectives, then bowed to hegemonic pressure. The immediate aim of much of the French *classe politique* was to influence public attitudes towards a negative view of possible German unification. This reflected historic fears, the European self-image, and the rhetorical, if not actual, independence from trans-Atlantic foreign policy of the French establishment. Thus, for example, in the conservative *Le Figaro* (11.11.89:1. All translations: JT.), J. Rovan, a strange bedfellow for the GDR reformers, stated: 'Today, reunification is not on the agenda'. The left of centre *Libération* also wished to influence its readers towards negative attitudes. Ambivalent towards the president and the Socialist Party, it cast doubt on the words of Mitterrand and Jacques Delors, who both, despite misgivings but seeing the way things were going, cautiously accepted, *in the long run*, the *principle* of unification. It dubbed their weasel words: 'A flood of reassuring statements serving above all to calm the worries of their authors' (*Libération* 13.11.89:13). *Le Monde*, however, acquiesced in the Mitterrand position.

Writ large in the right of centre French press campaign was the potent concept of the Fourth – sometimes referred to as the Fifth – Reich, a comparison bound to evoke images of defeat, occupation and German domination of Europe. Thus, in *Le Figaro*, we could read, even before the opening of the Berlin Wall, under the alarmist headline 'Towards the Fifth Reich':

> The shock wave of Gorbachev's revolution is hitting the other half of Germany. In the Federal Republic, all they are talking about is reunification [...]. The hypothesis of the birth of a Fifth Reich, which frightened Mauriac so much, will not go away (*Le Figaro* 8.11.89:13).

Similarly, the centre-right weekly *Le Point* ran the headline: 'Towards an Economic Fourth Reich', and, evoking the idea of German revenge for 1945, described 'a reunified economy of 78 million producers and consumers, [...] sitting up there at the top table with the United States, Japan and the USSR' (*Le Point* 20.11.89:72ff). Another article in the same issue of *Le Point* saw the European centre of gravity slipping eastward, away from France: 'from Paris to Berlin, from the Rhine to Prussia' (ibid:59).

Such attempts to whip up historic fear at the prospect of German unification were balanced elsewhere in the press landscape. For example, ex-Foreign Minister, Jean-François Poncet wrote in the conservative weekly *L'Express*: 'In this basically happy situation – the end of the Cold War to the West's advantage – we should not resurrect old phobias about Germany' (*L'Express* 17.11.89:65). Similarly, in the left wing weekly *Le Nouvel Observateur*, J. Juillard's article was almost lyrical in its desire to calm fears. Under the headline 'Europe is a love story', he wrote: 'Since it became our ally, partner and friend, Germany can no longer inspire disquiet in us [...]. The only feeling that [its success] should arouse is not jealousy or unease, but the desire to emulate' (*Le Nouvel Observateur* 16.11.89:78).

In looking at these extracts, the important thing in the present context is not so much to measure their individual qualities and limitations, but to note how, at this moment, there was still open debate. Certainly, important areas of that debate were *not* touched on in these particular reactions, some aspects of which were specific to France, but the sense is still that commentators were expressing their real weighty concerns, and that final decisions had yet to be made. International comparisons show that France, in this respect, was no exception. But just as the East Germans were speedily bundled onto the unification train, so international leaders and agenda-setting media, whatever their initial misgivings, soon found themselves under pressure to concur with the US government's push for 'Cold War' victory, and support for the ambitions of Kohl and the economic elites he represented. Neither Thatcher with her atavistic nightmares, nor Gorbachev with his geopolitical dreams could sustain credible resistance. The hegemonic discourse of the most powerful narrowed the debate to a single option, smothering the rest, and, paying only token attention to diplomatic niceties, forced it through to fulfilment.

Thus, by summer 1990, 'victor's discourse' had become 'the truth' and the signing of the Four Plus Two Agreement on 12 September 1990, the necessary international prerequisite of German unification, ultimately came to seem like a formality. A flood of warm, sentimental feeling surrounding the unifying of a people who had been divided was evoked for public consumption, forming, for those moments, the perfect cover for the expansionist ambitions of Western power and neo-liberal capital.

The highly manipulated and stage-managed nature of the stampede towards unification, with its sustained exploitation of the feelings of joy and spontaneity which characterised the initial moments of liberation, stifled detailed and realistic public debate about the future, and concealed the motivations of the powerful. This is well illustrated by the *Spiegel TV* video documentaries, *Protokoll einer Deutschen Revolution* (Protocol of a German Revolution). While these three 90-minute tapes purport to serve the documentary function of providing an accessible, more detailed account of the dramatic events of the period than other parts of the media, they are, in fact, primarily propaganda, deeply soaked in pro-unification newstoriography, symbolism of German nationalism, and the discourse of inevitability, even destiny. Here, we shall look more closely at sections of Part 3: *Die Letzten Tage bis zur Einheit* ('The Last Days up to Unity') (1990), covering the period immediately preceding 3 October 1990. It is a hurriedly compiled and extremely tendentious example, in terms of structure, content and text, of the transformation of biased news and reportage material into a distorted history, and can only be seen as an exercise in selective memory making, wearing a thin disguise of objectivity.

The opening sequences could be a piece of ironic self-persiflage if they were not, all too evidently, intended to be taken seriously. To a background of Wagnerian music, the first image is of flag-waving crowds in front of the

Reichstag at the unification ceremony. The crowd pictures signify massive public support, the music evokes ancient national myth and tradition, while the flag-waving portrays popular national enthusiasm. The latter is reinforced as the picture cuts to a close-up of a screen-filling Federal German flag unfurling against the night sky in a gentle swelling breeze: a nation is re-born. The music continues as the title appears, linking these opening scenes to a soft focus aerial panning shot of the Brandenburg Gate. As the camera circles around the sunlit monument, we make out people walking freely backwards and forwards across this area which was previously closed off by the Wall. The people have long shadows, and the whole atmosphere of the scene evokes a new dawn, although, given the direction of the shadows, for *this* new dawn, the sun is rising in the west. Crowds, flags, shadows, aerial shots, Wagnerian music – the reminders of the famed opening sequence of Leni Riefenstahl's documentary of the 1934 Nuremberg Rally, *Triumph of the Will*, while obviously unintended, are nevertheless manifold and manifest. They are later reinforced in a scene in which Kohl, filmed in close up, and from below, accepts the adulation of crowds, who are shown straining to touch him, shake his hands, and congratulate him. The film even shows them laying their hands lovingly on his car as it moves away, in an expression of devotion.

Archive film of Berlin falling into Soviet hands in 1945 is now edited in, with the subsequent 45 years of Soviet dominance of East Berlin treated as a continuation of the war. Then comes the comment, against another shot of the German flag flying on the new united German Reichstag: 'Now, in autumn 1990, 45 years on, the Second World War is ending for a second time. Those who were then losers have after all become victors'. Even in context, this is a startling statement. Clearly the reference to 'losers' is not to the Nazis, whom one tends to think of as the losers of the war. Given the nationalist glow of the opening of the film, the reference may be to the German people, now 'victors', because united and once again able to assert national identity. Or, given the tone of the rest of the film, the reference may be to East Germans, now finally delivered from the 45-year punishment of continued totalitarian rule into the joys of Western freedom, democracy and prosperity. Whichever was intended, the statement is loaded with dubious ideology, scarcely appropriate to the documentary genre.

Following the opening sequences, the structure of what is to come becomes clear. There is a section on each day of the final week of the GDR, leading up to 3 October 1990. The sections are each divided into three parts, the first showing archive film of selected extracts of the GDR news exactly one year before in 1989, the second showing specially filmed reportage of the winding up of different aspects of the GDR, along with reactions to it, the third showing preparations at the Reichstag for the unification ceremonies, and then the events themselves. The sections are linked by short comments and clichés which reinforce the ideological message for the audience, voiced over the ironic background of the GDR anthem, and further aerial shots of Berlin, tracing the course of where the Wall had stood. The archive extracts from the GDR news programme *Aktuelle Kamera* of September-October 1989 are the pretext to show scenes where the old GDR leadership could be gloated over. The static and repetitive style of the programme reinforces perceptions of relative dullness and backwardness compared to the

Federal Republic, while the shots of Honecker, Krenz and the rest of the leadership, still in power, celebrating and congratulating themselves on the solid achievements of 40 years of GDR socialism, unaware of what is about to befall them, are nothing but an exposure of these already humiliated figures to further condescending ridicule and over-egged victors' discourse. Similarly, the scenes of the GDR packing up and discarding the old, receiving and taking on the new, with expressionless faces acting out old routines for the last time, changing uniforms, re-spraying police cars, clearing out offices, all emphasise the worthlessness of the old and the superiority of the new. The climax of this repeated structural contrasting of 'bad old' and 'good new' is a scene in a Dresden (GDR) restaurant around midnight on the night of 3 October, the official moment of unification. As midnight approaches, the GDR national anthem plays, and the guests carry on eating, drinking, smoking and chatting. Midnight sounds, and the anthem is abruptly stopped in mid phrase. As the clock finishes striking, the Federal German anthem begins, and immediately all stop what they are doing, stand up and sing, or listen respectfully. The audience is left in no doubt by the film's artificial presentation as to where its real loyalties should lie, and which is the *real* national anthem.

Showing the preparation of the Reichstag for the unification ceremony and for its future use as united Germany's parliament, as well as the ceremonies themselves, also provides a framework for emphasising Western domination. The new leaders are contrasted with the old (not present, but mocked in the archive footage). An East Berlin flag factory is shown making up West/United German flags, and the commentator cannot resist the remark that although they have unlimited stocks of material for the *red* stripe, they are not sure whether they will be able to find enough for the black and gold. From an East Berliner, it would have been a nicely satirical piece of ironic self-deprecation; from the Western commentator it is a sarcastic dismissal of yesterday's Eastern identity.

The content of the film shows consistent choices to dwell on the most negative aspects of the GDR, and to show contempt for anyone expressing that it might have had its more positive aspects. For example, one passage dwells on the case of a young woman, arrested in September 1989 for putting up home-made anti-government posters; extracts of her trial are shown, and her account of her arrest and cross-examination provides a pretext for a lengthy diversion into how the GDR security police kept samples of individuals' body odour for future identification by sniffer dogs. Not exactly a savoury aspect of GDR society, but also not necessarily one which an observer wishing to provide a fair valedictory picture would automatically focus on with such evident relish, and at the expense of other material.

At various points in the film, those described as suffering from GDR nostalgia are shown and dismissed – the butts of incredulous mockery or arrogant cliché. Thus, when women's groups from East and West combined to organise a demonstration which would publicise an alternative view of unification, a short extract is shown, foregrounding the unconventional dress of the participants and their less than friendly attitude to the media. The whole event is summed up in a tone of bored superiority: 'In East Berlin's "Lustgarten" some people wanted to meet up in order to demonstrate *against* all forms of hostility to foreign women, sexism, racism, nationalism, militarism, and *for* a few other kinds of "-isms".' Another East Berlin demonstration receives the comment:

> A funeral procession. They're singing the anthem of the *American* civil rights movement, 'We shall overcome'. The supporters of the old system are appropriating symbols of freedom in order to demonstrate against the tearing down of the Wall and the *Stasi*-state.

They are included in the film in order to be mocked, not to provide a credible counter-balance to the bias of the rest of the film.

The text and imagery of the film are replete with victor's discourse. Shortly after showing images from the moment of currency union, where joyful East Germans burn old GDR banknotes for the cameras, and grasp eagerly at their treasured new Deutschmarks, the audience is helped to its conclusion, as the GDR national anthem plays, by the comment, referring back to its words:

> It was supposed to rise out of the ruins of the world war, the GDR, its face turned towards the future. But somehow it didn't do anything right, or even left. At best it turned into a dreary mixture of Kindergarten and Gestapo [...]. Socialism with a Prussian face, and a large portion of self-deception.

A little later, more archive pictures of the leadership during the fortieth anniversary celebrations of GDR achievements are followed up by remarks in which the commentator crows with ponderous irony: 'Within a year of this, what they *did* achieve was that which counts as the highest possible achievement of socialism – the withering away of the state, only not exactly in the way that the Marxist classics envisaged it'. Such are the half-educated comments of predators, toying with their dying prey without fear of further resistance.

Finally comes the remark which sums up the whole point of the film. It denies the whole manipulative process that took place between the opening of the Berlin Wall and the formal event of unification, and claims the whole thing to be a foregone conclusion, fulfilling what has by now come to be seen as the will of mass popular revolutionary action to destroy a tyrant state. As the actual moment of legal unification passes in relatively low-key fashion, the commentator explains why: 'Everyone is there waiting for something which actually already happened a long time ago. The 9 November 1989 was the real day of unification.'

Conclusion

The makers of this film, along with producers of voluminous other comparable materials and perpetrators of media processes criticised in this chapter would doubtless claim that they just filmed and edited together what was there, and produced an accurate record of what was going on. But then, we recall, that was exactly what Leni Riefenstahl said of 'Triumph of the Will'. Although *her* film was better crafted, and her *cause* more malign, her spirit and manipulative techniques live on in future generations of media hacks. Whether audiences (not just German ones) have got much better at seeing through them is questionable.

Chapter 10

The Longevity of Wartime Discourses and Identities.
The Case of Britain and Europe

Just because we're always making jokes about how dangerous Germany is doesn't mean to say that it isn't (*Evening Standard* 1.10.1992).

In the anti-Europe campaign Kraut bashing performs a particularly important function. Cheap anti-German propaganda is ideally suited to instill the European debate in Britain with the desired negative spin. The calculation is simple: the greater the fear of the Germans, the stronger the aversion of the British against involvement in the European project (Jürgen Krönig, London correspondent of *Die Zeit*, in Tenberg 1999).

Eurosceptics perceive Germany [...] as the chief threat in a European hegemony. They see it as controlling the currency they have sworn to shun forever. Worse, Germans are perfectly comfortable with the F-word, federalism. [...] Diplomats with experience of both countries believe that the British prejudice is worse than 30 years ago. Paradoxically, the more the Second World War retreats into the past the more its legacy seems to poison modern attitudes (*The Observer* 26.3.2000).

Introduction

A truism about propaganda, in the current usage of the word, is that it is generally created and succumbed to by someone else, normally foreign, and/or of a different ideological colour, for example, 'the Germans' in the Nazi period, 'communists' in the 'Cold War' period. We perceive *ourselves* as independent-minded enough to see through it. It could not work *here*.

Yet the definition of 'here' is, ironically, itself a product of what might be called propagandistic identity creation. To pick out just one example, it seems to be common among some self-consciously or stridently 'British' people to pride themselves, along with their 'island heritage', on a self-image of stubborn individualism and resistance to anything to do with mass action or mass persuasion. Bolstered by a selective national(ist) historiography which places them on a superior level of righteousness and glory *vis-à-vis* all European neighbours, let alone the rest of the world, this minority, which seems easily pumped into a majority in times of national crisis when otherwise slumbering instincts are awakened by massive media campaigns, feels itself to be in possession of a profound truth, and believes it has incontrovertible evidence to prove it. For its adherents, this set of beliefs has nothing to do with propaganda, mass communication, manipulation or persuasion. It is truth, transcending all that and in no need of such props.

While the once sturdy myths of national superiority in, for example, France, Italy, and especially Germany, have within living memory been severely battered by events, and largely discredited in mainstream politics and media as the dangerous fantasies that they are (to be partly replaced by the weaker, supranational 'European' identification), the British superiority myth, supported by selective and aesthetically adjusted accounts of wartime heroics, was constantly upheld, and has proved slow and reluctant to question itself. Through the 1990s, when many realities contradicted them, such pretences could still be brazenly promoted in the British media, to the bemusement of mainland European counterparts, and come across as more real and desirable to many in Britain than the more egalitarian, but less virile and apparently more superficial, alternative of greater integration into the European Union, and a broader framework of international law and convention. Public and media debate took place largely on these terms, and distracted from discussion of substantive issues.

Into this brew must be added the potent associations of the word 'appeasement'. It invariably takes British minds back to one moment in 1938, and in particular to one media image, that of Prime Minister Neville Chamberlain descending from an aeroplane on his return from Munich, waving the piece of paper – the compromise over Czechoslovakia – signed by Hitler and himself, which, he proclaimed, would guarantee 'peace in our time'.

This media image reverberated through the rest of the century in the minds of the public and decision makers. While, as one of the first TV 'on the spot' reports, it is part of media history, and was in itself a historic occasion, its visual recording of that moment for mass consumption, its endless repetition and re-insertion into the narratives of key subsequent historic moments, have brought it an iconic status, and a life and influence of its own within British historiography (feeding into newstoriography) and popular memory. In most minds, it is the only thing for which the unfortunate Neville Chamberlain is remembered – the fatally naïve and timid act of believing that the dictator could be appeased, when a firm, decisive stand against his expansionism would have kept him in check. This act, encapsulated in the TV images, is taken as a warning never to appease dictators for fear of the opprobrium of history. Conversely, it is taken as a pretext and justification by all subsequent leaders who, for whatever reasons, feel the need to go to war.

These media images of Chamberlain haunted Thatcher, Major and Blair as, in turn, Galtieri, Saddam Hussein, Milosevic and Saddam Hussein again, were all conflated into 'Hitlers'. As soon as the Hitler comparisons were made, and the Chamberlain images had been recalled (and re-run on television), military action became instantly justified and inevitable. For British leaders, even pale comparisons with the iconic and untouchable Churchill, himself the subject of a catalogue of endlessly repeated heroic imagery, were clearly to be preferred.

There is thus a degree (unquantifiable though it may be) to which those early TV images of appeasement and war justification have contributed to future judgements and public attitudes. However one judges the Falklands, Gulf (x 2), and Kosovo killings, that piece of newsreel may be seen to have precipitated the action and stiffened public support for it. Here, a historic media report loops round, helps by specious association to create new historic events several decades on, contributes to future public acceptance of violence, and strengthens the national will for it.

A late indicative example of Britain's engrained and opportunistically sustained propaganda myth – for, whatever it seems to its believers, and despite countless real acts of ultimate bravery and sacrifice it has inspired in the past, its constant appropriation in the present can be analysed as no more than that – appeared in the London *Daily Mail* of 11 October 2000 in the form of an essay by Paul Johnson entitled: 'In Praise of Being British.' This may serve as an entry point for tracing motivations for revival of the myth and the form of its particular manifestation in 1990s and turn of the century Britain – the subject of this chapter.

The Best of British

Those induced to rely on feelings of British superiority as a significant component of their sense of collective identity felt under threat from at least three directions in the 1990s: the rise of regional consciousness and moves towards regional political devolution, especially in Scotland and Wales; the increasingly multi-cultural nature of British society; and the moves towards greater integration into a strengthening European Union. Any of these three could be perceived as weakening, even destroying, certain ideas of essential British identity. Together, they could be woven into a substantial threat. Popular conservative newspapers such as the *Daily Mail*, which sold mainly to broad 'middle-of-the-road' (see Chapter 6), 'middle brow' audiences and supported the interests of the europhobic establishment Right, did not hesitate both to inflate and exploit this perceived threat by exciting embattled, xenophobic and anti-European feelings, and to present glorified myths of British superiority.

There was a long series of pretexts for such fulminations both before and during the 1990s, and the new millennium brought no sudden enlightenment. The autumn of 2000 alone, overshadowed by an imminent UK general election in which the EU, the euro and asylum seekers were likely to be big issues, saw British nationalist media polemics sparked off by the Danish 'No' in its referendum on introduction of the euro, the UK contribution to the proposed EU rapid reaction force, and the run-up to the European Council meeting in Nice which promised pivotal debates on further EU integration. But in the midst of this came the publication of the government-commissioned Runnymede Trust Report: *The Future of Multi-ethnic Britain* (October 2000). Paul Johnson's essay was part of the *Daily Mail*'s reaction to this, and a resonant example of positions taken up by the heavily dominant right of centre press.

On and around 11 October 2000, the *Daily Mail* picked up on the publication of the report. It was a closely-worded 400-page document, prepared over three years by a commission of experts addressing current and future issues of concern in Britain's multi-ethnic society. The predominant media reaction, the *Daily Mail* included, was to take about four phrases from the 400 pages, and instrumentalise them for hysterical chauvinistic polemic. In particular, the report's alleged characterisation of Britain as a 'community of communities' rather than as a 'nation', and its alleged assertion that 'to be British is racist' (*Daily Mail* 11.10.2000:1) – both so distorted as to be seriously misleading – were extracted from context and reported as its main conclusions. These then got turned into an assault on the report's authors (ibid:6), and its Labour Party sponsors, accused of being anti-British (ibid:7), and uncaring about British history and traditions (ibid:12).

Paul Johnson's essay was the culmination of the coverage on that day (ibid:12-13), setting itself up as a right-thinking, patriotic counterblast to a traitorous report and government which could think of nothing better to do than undermine and ultimately destroy British identity by re-writing 'our' glorious history in a negative light, and selling 'our' birthright of freedom and independence. The editorial alongside Johnson's essay somehow associated the Runnymede Report with what it saw as the government's 'pathetic eagerness to abolish the pound – and Britain's national sovereignty' (ibid:12). A closer look at Johnson's essay reveals more precisely the message that the *Daily Mail* was sending out to its readers. Its layout on the two-page spread adjacent to the editorial is already indicative. Beneath the large headline, literally a 'banner' headline in that the word 'British' in 'In Praise of being British' is overprinted with the pattern of the national flag, is a collage of eight historical portraits, there to represent the 'Best of British'. The thinking behind the choice is not entirely clear, as the group includes both Charles I and Oliver Cromwell, who were on opposite sides in a bloody civil war in the 17th century, with the latter ultimately having the former beheaded. However, the inclusion of the multi-wived anti-Papist Henry VIII, Elizabeth I, whose navy defeated the Spanish Armada, the Duke of Wellington, whose army defeated Napoleon, and Queen Victoria, who presided over the heyday of British imperialism, leaves a strong message that defence of one's own territory, coupled with rampantly overrunning other peoples', is what defines the 'Best of British'.

The essay itself can be analysed under three headings: promotion of the British nation and tradition as superior to all others, and rejection of any alternative evidence; one-eyed celebration of Britain's historical openness and generosity in its integration of persecuted foreigners into its pluralist tradition and tolerant value system; pride in Britain's gift of its language and culture to the rest of the world.

Promotion of the British Nation and Tradition as Superior

From the start, the essay positions itself as the defender of the rightness of 'our history' against those who would re-write it, and of our 'sense of nationhood' against those who would 'destroy' it.

The attack on those who would dare to re-write British history by taking a critical stance towards aspects of it is vicious. The Runnymede Report is branded 'a brutal exercise in Labour racial theology' which is not only 'anti-democratic', but also has 'a distinct smack of totalitarianism about it'. Anyone who produces a version of the national history which questions 'our history' is likened to a rogue's gallery of foreign *bêtes noires* – Lenin, Hitler, Mao Tse Tung, Saddam Hussein, Gadaffi and Milosevic, lumped together by the writer as totalitarian re-writers of history.

Following this insulting attack on the Runnymede Commission, of which the chair and several members were from British ethnic minorities, Johnson asserts the superiority of 'our' British history writing over the way in which 'European nations' do it. He writes: 'By contrast, Britain, unlike many European nations, has a long tradition of unbiased, objective and truthful historical writing, avoiding propaganda and hagiography' (ibid), then: 'Britain was the first truly free country in world history, and because our history has always been free, we can trust it' (ibid).

For Johnson, 'our' history, which we can trust, demonstrates Britain to be the centre and originator of world civilisation. For example, he tells us: 'The first parliaments were an English institution. We have since exported them all over the world, and in many countries they have taken root' (ibid:13), then:

> We were the first country to establish the universal rule of law [...], in due course, the rule of law became the essential element in the United States constitution, and in the British Commonwealth, which encompassed a quarter of the globe's surface (ibid).

Our history, we hear, springs from the British qualities of 'a strong sense of justice, fair-mindedness, tolerance, a global outlook and national feelings of responsibility towards the poor, the unfortunate and the oppressed', and not only that, 'we have established an unrivalled record for advancing human knowledge and the frontiers of civilisation' (ibid). Finally, readers are assured:

> British history is the story of freedom and respect for the law, and Britain's relationship with the world beyond our shores is the story of benefaction, not exploitation, of justice, not oppression, and of the desire to enlighten, to improve, to teach and to help (ibid).

It was disappointing that Johnson omitted from his list those other stereotypical British qualities of humility, modesty and understatement, but one does not want to be churlish. The important message here to the British public, and anyone else who might be reading, is that as long as no one questions undoubted British moral, cultural and historical superiority in every respect, and as long as everyone else shows suitable deference and gratitude, we will all get on just fine.

Celebration of Britain's Openness and Generosity

Johnson denies that Britain has ever been racist or xenophobic, citing as proof the facts that the slave trade was illegalised in Britain in 1807, and that the British population has always been 'a mixture of cultures and nationalities'. Be that as it may, he does not hesitate to compare the British record favourably with that of others. Apart from the Danes, he states, (the Danes were, of course, in favour because they had just voted 'no' in their 'euro' referendum), the British were the first to outlaw the slave trade, and went on to enforce the law on the high seas, teaching a firm lesson in humanity to the French, Spanish, Portuguese and Americans: 'It took us 70 years to stamp it out at sea', he says, 'but we did it at last' (ibid). He omits to mention that Britain had been among the worst offenders.

Again, we cannot possibly be racist or xenophobic since free Britain has for centuries been a haven for refugees from oppressive regimes abroad. In fact, in Johnson's view, huge numbers of foreigners have cause to be grateful to us and have shown that gratitude by integrating into and reinforcing our tradition of freedom; he provides us with an impressive list:

> Being the first free country, we have taken in refugees from all over: French Huguenots, Dutch Calvinists, German Lutherans, Portuguese Jews, Italian Democrats, survivors of the Russian pogroms, Poles fleeing from communist tyranny [...] – we have been taking in outcasts and helping the helpless for half a millennium (ibid).

The extraordinary and totally false image here is of centuries of European oppressed immediately thinking of, and flocking to, welcoming Britain, and nowhere else, as their only refuge, and of no one ever leaving Britain or British territories because they felt persecuted. It is also doubtless pure coincidence that Johnson manages to cast in a negative light relative to Britain the historical traditions of all the major EU members who were currently pushing for closer integration, thus encouraging his readers to view them as undesirable and untrustworthy.

Finally, it is of interest that he does *not* include *current* asylum seekers on his list of welcome immigrants. The key point for his readers is, however, that *good* foreigners are those who are grateful to us, look up to us, accept 'our' history and tradition, and learn quickly to do things in *our* superior way.

Pride in Britain's Gift of its Language and Culture to the Rest of the World

To cap his argument, Johnson implies that the English language is a unique vehicle of truth and civilisation. In his discourse, it is foreigners – fascists and communists (and of course their Labour Party admirers) – who re-write history, twisting *the truth* to their own perverted ends. The language in which 'our' history is written is, it seems, somewhat like that of the Bible, divinely revealed truth which therefore cannot be re-written, or, as he puts it: 'it can be re-written only by inserting bias and dogma, propaganda and downright lies' (ibid). English, one infers, has the quasi-mystical destiny of becoming a world language. Gathered in over the centuries from all corners of the globe, it is now bestowing itself back, a gift of true culture to the waiting multitudes. 'The English language itself, with words from scores of different languages,' writes Johnson, 'is our title deed to multiculturalism. One reason it is now establishing itself as a world language is that virtually the entire world has gone into its making' (ibid).

In other words, since English is fashioned from many other languages, and has absorbed so many influences, true multi-culturalism consists of everyone else speaking English and recognising the superiority of the British way. In Johnson's world, all problems of intercultural communication can thus be solved in an instant as long as two simple principles are observed:

1. Everyone should speak English.
2. Everyone should gratefully adopt the British way of doing things.

The serious point to be made here is that, although Johnson wrote this article in a strident and caricatured style for a popular newspaper, all too easy for the relatively sophisticated to ridicule and demolish among themselves, he also knew himself to be addressing a huge readership which, by and large, agreed with him, and whose view of the world he was hereby reinforcing. Critical minds may react with incredulity, but he was, in the year 2000, making a sufficiently coherent and informed case, seemingly grounded in historical evidence, to communicate to millions of *Daily Mail* readers, fed for years on this kind of discourse, that he had found the right words to express what they really felt.

Germanophobia and Europhobia

There had been substantial buttressing of this kind of perspective in 'post-Cold War' Britain, through the 1990s. This period was characterised by the synchronicity of the impact of united Germany, easily the EU's largest national population and market, on the European balance of commercial and political power, with energetic moves to promote EU convergence and enlargement, to the east. It did not take much paranoia – and there was no shortage of that – to put these two developments together and envisage a new, German-dominated EU with its political centre of gravity shifted eastwards to Berlin, and its economic centre of gravity, a *Deutschmark* disguised as the euro. In such a scenario, Britain could easily slip back into its historic role of embattled island nation, with its sterling national characteristics, fending off the continent, and reprising its determining twentieth century role of saving the world from the Germans.

That the dominant British media should have made efforts to revive and magnify a wave of anti-German feeling through the 1990s as a useful component of campaigns to separate the UK from deeper EU integration thus comes as no great surprise. It fitted unproblematically with the nonsensical, but widely unquestioned media-promoted view of Europe as a set of juxtaposed rival national boxes, each with separate essential, unchanging and conflicting identities which stretch back into the unfathomable mists of time, and will stretch on, as if genetically determined, through countless generations to come.

Such a view emphasises the small percentage of culturally determined perceptual pluralities, behavioural differences, and cultivated exclusive identities between European regions, frequently as manifest intraculturally as interculturally, at the expense of the high percentage of commonality, harmonious intermingling and cross-cultural fertilisation which describes more accurately what is actually happening.

Adoption of the former perspective in the British context leads directly to *a priori* germano- and europhobic mindsets, and emphasis on divergence, suspicion and retreat into splendid isolation. Adherence to the latter implies, on the European level, a sympathetic approach to convergence, at least in the social, cultural, environmental and ideological fields, but also, with due attention to structural and pragmatic considerations, the political, economic, diplomatic and legal ones.

These were the battle lines in the British debate over 'Europe' in the 1990s. The dominant Murdoch empire, comprising *The Times*, *The Sunday Times*, *The Sun* and the *News of the World*, followed by Conrad Black's *Telegraph* group, and the *Mail* group, led the anti-Europe press pack, with only the relatively small *Guardian* group being committed 'pro-Europeans'. In broadcasting, the still dominant terrestrial channels were dragged by the parameters set for the debate into seeking 'balance' between strident europhobia and conditional support for slow development towards a circumscribed, toughly negotiated, inevitable-rather-than-desirable co-operation.

A basic success of the anti-Europe camp was its achieving of routine and unquestioning acceptance of the discursive separation of 'Britain' and 'Europe' in the formulations of most of the media, politicians, experts and the population. Virtually everywhere, the naturalised shorthand, which opposed 'Britain' and 'Europe' as two discrete entities, prevailed. Although geographically, historically and culturally part of Europe, and a full member of the European Union, Britain, in its everyday language, reinforced by constant media usage, insisted that it was separate. The significant niceties of speaking of 'Britain and *the rest of* Europe', 'Britain and *mainland* Europe' or 'Britain and its *partners in the European Union*' were largely eschewed. Parallel to this in the broadcast media, particularly television, the 1990s provided virtually constant identification of Germany and Germans with Nazism and Nazis; despite the great interest and importance of developments in newly unified Germany, the number of films and documentaries covering the Nazi period vastly outnumbered those analysing contemporary Germany. Emblematic of this was the fact that, in the week before the 1998 Federal German elections, particularly significant because of the likely change of ruling party, ending the Kohl era, and possible first time integration of the Greens into the governing coalition, British television devoted no special programme to the event. Instead, it decided to start a re-run of the BBC series, *The Nazis. A Warning from History*, whose main selling point was that it showed to a greater extent than previous accounts the involvement of 'ordinary Germans' in Nazism and its atrocities. In comparable vein, on the Monday before the election, Murdoch's top-selling *The Sun* newspaper made front-page reference to the 'jackboots' of the EU marching across Europe in its presentation of the vacuous controversy about whether the Queen's head should appear on euro notes. Such decisions, and such output, were typical of 1990s British media bias; a reflection of it could be heard from English football fans in the 1998 World Cup in France, who taunted their French counterparts with chants of: 'If it wasn't for the English you'd be Krauts', a boorish statement which, if reflected on, succinctly reveals significant assumptions in terms of historiography and identity politics.

In this context, combining the two elements of anti-European and anti-German rhetoric – instrumentalising the latter in the cause of the former – was only a small step. Old, tested, and still active viruses of British germanophobia were transposed in the mass media to reinforce the related xenophobic disease of europhobia. The 'logic' being put across was as simple as it was mendacious. The old germanophobia told us that 'the Germans' were 'expansionist', 'anti-democratic', and 'authoritarian', and a threat to British power and autonomy. The newer europhobia perceived the European Union likewise as 'expansionist', 'anti-democratic', 'authoritarian', and a threat to British power and autonomy. Therefore (media consumers were to conclude) Europe *was* Germany. Germany was already secretly dominating Europe and had obtained by peaceful means what it had failed to gain in two world wars. The European threat was the German threat. In this perspective, the European Union was unmasked as Germany in disguise, gaining thereby a sinister and fearful history, and a tangible stereotypical Germanic identity of a kind which has been deeply embedded in British consciousness over at least five generations.

Germanophobia in the British mass media, we should remember, can be traced back to their early days as the mass circulation commercial press around the turn of the twentieth century. The most popular British newspaper of the time, Lord Northcliffe's *Daily Mail*, held its readers enthralled, six years before the outbreak of the First World War, with a serialised story of a German invasion of Britain. In this narrative, the German army took a bizarre ziz-zag course across Britain as each episode described the effects of the invasion in towns where Northcliffe wanted to increase the *Daily Mail*'s market penetration. The theme of German occupation of Britain was taken up again in Saki's popular novel *When William Came* (1914). Thus, even before the First World War, the image of the militarist, expansionist, threatening German was established in the popular mind, as German economic strength threatened the British position as leading European power. The two world wars then spawned many variations on, and intensifications of, these themes, exploiting the new technological means of radio and film to the full. After 1945, the rapid West German rise to become Europe's most successful economy in the 1950s and 1960s, overtaking the far less dynamic British performance, was again the pretext for media provocation of germanophobic emotions. Countless films, comics, press articles, cartoons and broadcasts evoked the war and established the poisonous image of the German as Nazi, or Nazi in disguise.

The 1990s saw a chronic rash of newspaper scare stories, editorialising and cartoons inflating the perceived German threat. An editorial from the conservative *Daily Telegraph* of 30 April 1996 reflected the tone as well as any. Occasioned by a visit from Chancellor Kohl to Prime Minister Major, its title 'Britain vs Germany' needs no more exposition than its text, of which the following is an extract:

When the German Chancellor calls on the British Prime Minister these days, one senses at once who is in charge. Dr Kohl's dominance derives partly from his long experience, his prestige as the creator of a united Germany, and from the weakness of Mr Major's domestic political position [...]. But these impressions of German superiority, which are not at all pleasant to a British mind, could not be sustained if they did not reflect reality. Why is Germany 'top nation' in Europe, and what should be done about it?

Germany deserves, and has now received, the political benefit of her post-war economic success [...], with their country's reunification, the Germans now compose Europe's largest nation, and one whose boundaries, for the most part, are no longer defined by defeat. For a country which within living memory behaved more disgustingly than any other in history, this is an amazing achievement. And because Germany did behave in this way, her post-war leaders have until now been clear that their country's road to political recovery lies through the European Community. Dr Kohl has devoted his career to the idea of a united Germany in a united Europe. Its consummation will come, he believes, with Economic and Monetary Union: the sacrifice of the untrammelled power of the Bundesbank will be worth making because it will forge a federal Europe which Germany controls (*Daily Telegraph* 30.4.1996).

The *Daily Telegraph* reinforced its message with a cartoon showing an enormous and somewhat wild-eyed Kohl squeezing the breath out of a limp, diminutive and helpless Major in a huge bear hug, as British and German flags fly in the background. The caption reads: 'At the heart of Europe'.

The discursive merging of 'Germany', 'Europe' and 'threat' is self-evident. Highly tendentious material such as this contributed to the anti-EU climate in 1990s Britain, and to sustained campaigns in the second half of the decade which helped keep public opinion firmly against joining the European single currency, whatever the rational arguments for or against it. The discourse here is not at the level of informed debate, even if it pretends to be. Rather, between every line, it seeks cynically to appeal to threatening memories and historic fears, falsely equating them with a very different present momentum and motivation.

The propaganda effort of James Goldsmith's Referendum Party in the 1997 British general election based itself on similar techniques. Never intended to be a serious political player in terms of votes (it actually polled between 8 and 9 thousand), it nevertheless succeeded in a number of ways in becoming a significant discursive influence on the British scene:

1. It heightened the profile of the discourse of radical opposition to the EU in the electoral campaign.
2. It forced the split Conservative Party to intensify and sharpen its anti-EU stance.
3. Its promoters and backers were people of influence, members of the economic elite whose influence extended far into the corridors of established power in terms of both politics and the media. Its leader, multi-millionaire entrepreneur James Goldsmith, was a man of enough wealth and sufficient friends in high places to ensure himself high profile media coverage.
4. Its real aim and achievement was not to gain itself parliamentary seats, although it claimed to have lost the Conservatives up to 40 seats, but to drag the whole public European debate, especially in the media, in a europhobic direction, which it

did successfully, gaining, or at least helping to gain, promises of a referendum on the single currency from both Conservative and Labour parties, and demonstrably influencing media discourse.

The campaign video, distributed free to thousands of households, showed clearly how its originators associated the EU with 'threat', and with 'Germany'. Writing in the campaign newspaper, *News from the Referendum Party* (April 1997:1), the leading industrialist and establishment figure Alastair McAlpine (who was to become the new leader following Goldsmith's death), wrote when referring to EU publicity of a 'propaganda effort to match the best of the Third Reich', blatantly tarring the EU with the Nazi brush.

For the purposes of this brief analysis, five points can be made about the content of the video. First, this is an overtly anti-EU and europhobic diatribe, but we only see one national flag in it, the German one, while Germany is referred to as 'Europe's dominant nation'. Second, in the text, only one other European country apart from Britain is named, and referred to repeatedly – Germany. Third, the creation of a European super-state is presented as a German plan, and when a map of Europe is shown, initially each country is shown in a different colour, then blue monochrome spreads over the continent from a point in south-west Germany. Fourth, the only other political leaders seen, apart from British ones (it is a British election), are Kohl (twice), Kinkel and Waigel, ministers in the German government. Fifth, a combination of 'suspense' music, commentary reinforced by a large lettered screen print-out of the quote from Kohl: 'Within two years we will make the process of integration irreversible', accompanied by visuals of the bulky figure of Kohl advancing menacingly on the retreating camera, flanked by a couple of sinister heavies in dark glasses, is clearly designed to evoke the association of an aggressive, threatening Germany, forcing integration and uniformity on the rest of Europe in the name of the EU.

Further observation reveals that in several sections of the video, the existence of a hidden, threatening German agenda is shown to be lurking beneath an apparently anodyne European project. The video sets itself up to tell us the 'hidden truth' of a Germanic super-state spreading its uniformity across Europe. It can be noted that in Kohl's first appearance, he is presented centre screen and full frontal, while Major is in a subordinate position to one side of the frame, and in profile. As this image is shown, the words 'cunning', 'deceiving' and 'empty promises' form part of the text, and are therefore deliberately associated with Kohl, inviting comparisons with Hitler's meeting with Chamberlain in 1938.

It seems that people with views similar to those expressed in this overtly propagandistic video gained a disproportionate influence on British media output in the 1990s, for there were many other manifestations of this kind of distorted story in media content and discourse, barely hidden in, for example, popular entertainment and documentaries. The two following cases out of many possible examples illustrate this.

The first was a sketch on one of the shows of the TV-hypnotist Paul McKenna, broadcast in his 1997 series. This was a prime time ITV show in which Paul McKenna apparently hypnotised members of the public, and then had them play out bizarre roles or situations to the amusement of the audience. In every case, the hypnotised people lost habitual inhibitions and failed to observe social taboos or usual behaviour patterns, and this was the source of amusement.

One needs to think through the political mindset and motivation of those who set up this particular sketch, which staged a spoof Eurovision Song Contest (the annual 'so bad it's good' musak-fest which, better than any spoof, invariably seeks and finds the lowest common denominator of European popular music-making in the name of intercultural collaboration). The three hypnotised volunteers had been told they were representing France, Italy and Germany respectively, and had all been asked to sing the Cliff Richard song 'Congratulations', but in the style of the country concerned. Thus, the context of a caricatured 'Europe' was constructed, in which stereotypical characteristics were part of everyone's assumed common knowledge, and what the British audience, with its own desired sense of superiority, and its own media-derived normality, really felt these 'others' to be like, was released and mutually reinforced under the supposed hypnosis.

There was no surprise that the 'French' contestant was petite and sexy, the 'Italian' one was dark-haired, swarthy and operatic, and that, of course, the 'German' one was blond, blue eyed, and a Nazi. They were clearly selected by the programme makers to correspond to, and strengthen, distorted stereotypes of national, even racial (in the Nazi sense), difference. It does not require subtle analytical skills to see that the 'German' constructed in this scene is designed to engrain further all the traditional germanophobic prejudices evoked by the anti-EU propagandists.

It is to be noted from the whole sketch that while the caricatures of the 'French' and 'Italian' contestants were merely silly and superficial, the lampooning of the 'German' character was highly political and offensive. To portray present-day Germans as goose-stepping Nazis, and arrogant, humourless, domineering little Hitlers, clearly considering themselves to belong to the master race, is, after all to implicate them in some of the century's most barbaric excesses. When the most affectionate thing the 'German' on the show could think of to say (or rather shout) was: 'You are all going to die', the audience howled with laughter at what was a hackneyed and quite chilling reference to the sadistic killer Nazi of a hundred war films and a thousand comics. It evokes associations between 'Germans', death camps, and wartime atrocities. Yet this was a portrayal of a young German, born about 30 years after the end of the war, who was thus 'unmasked' as no more than a Nazi in modern clothing. This was reinforced by the Nazi-saluting, goose-stepping performance of the song, and the 'German' character's assumption that in this competition between European countries, it was 'of course' the German who was superior and the natural winner.

To the uninvolved observer, the sketch was a demonstration both of the success of long-term attempts at implanting stereotypes, and of a further media penetration by the europhobic lobby, which aimed to strengthen these stereotypes and prejudices, and reinforce a quasi-racist nationalism, concealing their intent in light entertainment and harmless fun. One might have thought that this grotesque 'Eurovision' sketch would, once broadcast, have been forgotten in embarrassment.

Not so; it was selected for repetition in the compilation programme of highlights *The Best of Paul McKenna* in July 1997.

For the second indicative case, we move to BBC2, and a supposedly serious-minded historical documentary about Nazi architecture entitled *Jerry Building*, broadcast in prime time (twice) in 1995. The theme was legitimate and interesting, and would most appropriately have been presented by a reputable historian of the period. Instead, the BBC decided to turn to the then culinary correspondent of Rupert Murdoch's *The Times*, to front a programme which was no more than a thinly disguised germanophobic polemic, peddling again the pernicious view that there was an unchanging, specifically German identity that characterised both Nazi Germans and present-day Germans. The political context of the programme was, again, the post-Maastricht, post-German unification European convergence debate, and within this, the programme makers were seeking to arouse fears in the British public of renewed German expansion across Europe through its domination of the EU, in the full knowledge that already implanted stereotypes made this a cheap and effective way to nurture europhobia. One recalls that in the 1997 British general election, the narrator's employer (*The Times*) told its readers to vote for anti-EU candidates, whatever their party.

The opening section of the programme set the tone for the whole. The initial shot of a slab of concrete with the words 'Jerry Building' inscribed on it, dropping down from above was an intertextual reference to the contemporary *Volkswagen* advertisement which featured a car dropping down from above. Thus an immediate visual association indicating continuity between the Third Reich – the ostensible subject of the programme – and a typical emblem of modern, prosperous industrial Germany (with, however, its origins in Nazi Germany) was invited. The title, with its use of Gothic script, and the word 'Jerry', harked back to the hostile stereotyping of the Germans in the propaganda of two world wars, while the concrete was reminiscent of military defences, bunkers and architectural brutalism.

The first words of the programme ensured that the audience did not miss the message: 'Nazism did not die in the ruins of Berlin in 1945, nor on the gallows at Nuremberg in 1946. It merely buried its uniform, slipped into mufti, and sauntered into the post-war world.' Here too, the audience was presented with the quasi-racist view that 'the Germans' were unchanged and unchangeable, still Nazis underneath the surface, and out to dominate Europe.

The next images were of the 1930s holiday complex, constructed during the Nazi period at the German seaside resort of Prora. The camera work made it look like a prison, with shots of an interminably long corridor and the narrator walking along it slamming doors as he went. The image creates an audio-visual association between Germanness and clichés of authoritarianism and mass conformism. A few seconds later, this was reinforced by archive film images from the fascist period of young girls engaged in mass gymnastics to the accompaniment of military music. The point was then further laboured by the narrator's comment that: 'There are no private individuals any more.' Again, the Nazi past and contemporary Germans were merged in the text as the audience was told of 'the tragically obedient German people, with their taste for all that is compulsory and all that is communal'. Within all this, the not overly athletic culinary correspondent was intentionally made to stand out as the antithesis of all that – the individualist, non-conformist, humorous, and above all free Englishman, visually contrasted with muscular, obedient Germans, and quite unable by nature to fit in with mass gymnastics, or anything communal. His text, when talking of Robert Ley, the Hitler Youth leader, ran: 'His big maxim was, "there are no private individuals any more [...]". Ley's notion of leisure was compulsory communal games, compulsory communal walks [...], compulsory communal gymnastics.' The repeated alliterative juxtaposition of 'compulsory' and 'communal', and their association with 'German' was presented as quintessentially un-British, and resonated closely with contemporary europhobic discourse, and the nightmare of a future 'compulsory communal' Europe that it painted. The subsequent image of the narrator throwing away his beach ball in disgust purveyed the unsubtle message to the viewers that they too should not play ball with such ideas.

Conclusion

This chapter has used the example of Britain in the 1990s to argue that national identities – one's own and one's view of others – can be exposed as constructed and manipulative tissues of distortions and selective historical references, woven – largely via the media – into collective consciousness. It also contends that decisions dependent on majority public acceptance of these distortions can and do lead to, or sanction, precipitate or ill-conceived actions by power elites, including warlike ones, which determine subsequent events and patterns of existence, including life and death, at the same time as distracting from proper analysis and debate, and a better quality of decision making.

Chapter 11

The Balkans Revisited

All participants lie in war. It is natural. Some often, some all the time. UN spokesmen, Croats, Serbs, Muslims, the lot. Truth is a weapon more than a casualty. Used to persuade people of one thing or another, it becomes propaganda. The more authoritative a figure, the bigger the lies; the more credible his position, the better the lies. Why waste time listening to an officer in a headquarters crank out the party line when you could see the reality of a situation for yourself in the dirty bunkers up the way? That others chose not to go to the scene of the fighting was understandable. It was dangerous and frightening. On one level there was no match between death and 600 words on page 14. […]. Sometimes it seemed the more I wrote, the more distanced I became from the war, packaging it out to faceless men in a London office like the middleman in a business deal, handling the goods without consuming (Anthony Loyd 2000, on his work as a war reporter in Bosnia in 1993).

Introduction

One of the final major news events of the twentieth century was the Kosovo bombardment, a further twist of the 1990s tragedy of former Yugoslavia which provided a gruesome symmetry to the century whose early years had been so traumatically overshadowed by crisis in the Balkans. For this narrative, renewed concentration on this area provides an opportunity to compare the modes of public deception then (see Chapter 3), with the end of the century, following the exponential development of the mass media, the media industries and media technology, and equally decades of opportunity for mass media practice, analysis, criticism and regulation, and generations of opportunity for the development of a critically and ethically conscious public sphere in the media age.

The skeletal finger of pessimism beckons as it is parallels and continuities which become increasingly apparent, rather than contrasts and progress. 'Serbien muss sterbien' ('Serbia must die') was a brutally chilling slogan in the Viennese press, combining a memorable, punning 'rhyme' (the German for 'to die' is *sterben*, not *sterbien*) and crude wit with jingoism and a light-hearted incitement to inhumanity. In all these attributes, and in its intended effect, it seems to be taking a leaf out of Rupert Murdoch's British tabloid, *The Sun*, in its incitement of NATO to military action over Kosovo in the summer of 1999, with its headline 'Klobba Slobba' – except that it dates from the outbreak of the First World War. Eighty-five years separated the headlines. Nothing separated their intention, or their techniques.

We may remind ourselves that Kraus fulminated against the enormity of rosaries being made out of shrapnel and shells being made out of church bells. From Bosnia in 1993, Anthony Loyd wrote:

> Television sets were eviscerated then packed with explosives and nails, the resulting 'TV bombs' laid at the flanks of positions and wired; coke cans were converted to hand grenades with such frequency that the UN made it conditional for their troops to crush them after drinking as their rubbish tips were being raided to supply the HVO [Bosnian Croat army]: recycled consumerism flicking back on destroy (Loyd 2000:167-68).

The TV bomb was perhaps the most powerful metaphor for late twentieth century war – the technological means of mind control became the mechanical means of destruction and death – a reprise of Kraus's 'Tinte, Technik, Tod' ('Media, Machine, Massacre').

Kraus's insights stemmed from his experience of the media's role in the 1912 Balkan Wars and the First World War. One could legitimately wonder what the media-saturated world of the 1990s had to add. Was the difference merely of *volume*, not of principle? Was it the case that, although the 'cancerous loquacity' had become globalised, spreading to sicken most of the body of humanity, the disease itself still bore the same name?

More evidence will be provided here to suggest that, while the technology had changed and spread out of all recognition, the manipulation of discourse, the hypocrisies, delusions and corruption of language and image, as well as the role of journalism and the media, remained broadly constant in their processes and effectiveness throughout the twentieth century. If this can be shown, the vital focus for research and analysis – the point where it has the capacity to impact on cultural change – shifts. Rather than concentrating on the power of dazzling innovations in media technology itself, it focuses on the way in which glittering new technology has been continually and effectively subjugated to the power of the corrupted word and image within hegemonic struggles to maximise control of minds, consumer thought patterns and routines.

Kosovo - How the Truth became 'the Truth'

A critical analysis of the BBC TV programme: *Kosovo: How the War was Spun*, broadcast on BBC2, 16 October 1999, forms the basis of the argument.

By October 1999, the summer's bombing adventure in Kosovo seemed, in the fading memory of most media consumers in Britain and elsewhere, to be no more than a distant, but justified conflict which *we* won with almost no losses; but the BBC offered its public – or that minority of it which found such fare preferable to Saturday evening quiz shows – a three-part retrospective. The first of these, entitled *How the War was Spun*, looked at the media handling of the war.

The overt assumption behind the programme was that the audience was already 'on message' and willing to sympathise with NATO, and the BBC in particular, and to understand their genuine difficulties in getting the real, honest truth about what was happening over to the public.

Viewers were, it seems, presupposed to have empathised with NATO spokesman Jamie Shea's initial well-meant, but under-resourced struggles to provide them with a convincing and coherent version of NATO propaganda (also known as 'the truth', since it contradicted Serbian 'lies'). They were expected to accept that the massive bolstering of the propaganda effort with the arrival of Blair's spin supremo Alistair Campbell and his international team after the Serb 'propaganda coup' following the NATO bombing of a Kosovan refugee convoy, was ultimately a positive development, serving the greater good, even if it did practise some minor distortion of the news in the process. This had been NATO's first war, the viewers were supposed to understand, and, despite its military prowess, it had, in its straightforward honesty, unlike the devious Serb leader, Milosevic, seriously underestimated the importance of the media war, and had had to act energetically to remedy this. In this programme, consumers were thus given a selective peep behind the scenes of *how* the war was spun, but were not invited to ask *why* the war was spun, or whether it should have been.

Despite this 'overall' message of the programme, corresponding to establishment requirements, it also put over a secondary, more sceptical subtext. It was, after all, made by involved journalists who preferred to profile themselves as fearless investigators rather than lickspittle stooges of NATO spin doctors. A 'free' society has, after all, to portray its journalists as free agents. Thus, some significant tension was shown between the NATO 'information givers' and the journalists, and on-the-spot dilemmas faced by journalists were portrayed. Different participants in the (dis)information chain were, in the very act of justifying or making excuses for *themselves*, blaming or passing the buck on to *others*.

Finally, the programme chose to show us the perspectives of the military, and the retrospective view of its representatives of what they knew, and how they perceived, and wished to manage, the information-flow emanating from their actions. Here, they constructed themselves as straightforward men of action, doing the job they had to do to the best of their ability, but only reluctantly involved in the, for them, alien world of the media. One honest-to-goodness NATO general named Leaf, the commander of the Aviano air base in Italy, epitomised the programme's appeal to audience sympathies with this stereotypical and disingenuous self-characterisation of the honest soldier:

> I grew up in a very small town in Wisconsin, never expected to be on worldwide TV, and I stood up on the podium and asked myself: 'Who's watching?' And the answer was: 'Everyone'. Then I was taken aback. There really was no spin-doctoring, believe it or not' (BBC2 1999).

A more critical approach to the programme's discourses shows us, however, chains of examples of Kraus's 'death of the imagination', and the separation of 'word' from 'world'. These same examples are capable, unless viewers made the necessary conscious critical effort, of reassuring them of the goodwill of all concerned, even if there had inevitably been mistakes and tensions in the confusion of fast-moving events. But a second look at the text uncovers in microcosm the deeper, media and language-linked cultural flaws which span the century.

Four short extracts from the programme, moving up the 'information' chain, will suffice here to illustrate the point.

At the beginning of the 'information' chain (in the absence of a ground war) was the pilot. Even if he was 15,000 feet up, he was the nearest anyone in NATO got to the war. He and his crew dropped bombs. The process is documented by their cockpit videotape. The programme's narrator, the BBC correspondent Edward Stourton, told us: 'The pilots played a role in the information war from the start. With Kosovo closed off, their debriefings provided one of the few sources of information about what was happening' (ibid). Even First World War reporters got closer to the action than this.

So who *were* the primary sources of information, the first filters through which 'the truth' passed on its way to the public? The programme brought us, courtesy of NATO, Captain John Meitner, a veteran of numerous NATO bombing missions over Kosovo and Serbia, reminiscing about his war. Representing 'the pilots', he said: 'It's a lot of fun. I mean, I love my job. I would never consider doing anything else. It's ... er... it's kinda like ... er... playing a video game and riding a rollercoaster at the same time [laughs]' (ibid). Viewers did not know how much death, mutilation, agony and destruction Captain John Meitner was instrumental in causing. Nor did he. As he presented himself, his way of remembering, his discourse and choice of metaphor were totally divorced from reality. He saw his killing of other human beings as a cross and a cloud of smoke on a video game simulation, his piloting of a lethal machine carrying high explosives which he dropped on populated towns, chemical plants or oil refineries, causing death, mutilation, and family tragedy to civilians, and short or long-term environmental damage, as a particularly exciting fairground ride. His imagination had seemingly been surgically removed, turning him into a happy, enthusiastic, well adjusted, likeable, regular guy, and killing machine. For this reason he, as presented on the programme, betrayed no consciousness of moral responsibility for what he had done. Yet his primary accounts formed the basis of the Western consumers' most credible source of 'truth' about NATO's conduct of the war.

To put this in perspective, we may refer to personal accounts of what *was* happening on the ground. Such accounts existed, but were, of course, not published or broadcast during the war. A series of e-mails, sent from Pancevo, 17 kilometres from Belgrade, between 24 March and 10 June 1999, the duration of the bombing, by the cartoonist Aleksandar Zograf, gave a picture of what life, and death, were like for those beneath the flight paths of the Captain Meitners on their happy-zapping fairground rides, which, although filled with its own subjectivities, showed up the sanitised and cliché-ridden pilots' reports, which supplied NATO and the Western media with their 'truth', for the deceptions that they were. These extracts set the tone and speak for themselves:

> 23 April 1999: At 2.06 am, we were sitting in our room, talking. Then we heard the awful sounds of a plane. It was so loud that we all hid under the bed, thinking that it would hit our building and kill us all.

Then we heard strong detonations. Our windows started rattling. The lights went out. We heard several more explosions [...].

We saw smoke, fire, then we reached the building. Firemen, police, civil defence people were all already there trying to help the survivors.

We saw a woman shouting from the ruins: 'Please, I am here, help me!!' some men tried to get her out. She was walking around like a lunatic, shouting: 'Where is Jelena? Jelena, she is still in the building!!'

Then we saw someone falling from the second floor. We saw a man who was hanging upside down from the first, or second floor, I dunno. His head was all covered in blood. His legs were literally crushed by a concrete block. Everybody tried to help him. He is (or was) around 20-25 years old.

People were running around dripping with blood. Fire and smoke all over the place. Blood could be seen everywhere. A real massacre.

Then a friend of mine shouted: 'This man is dead!!' I didn't turn my head to see him because I thought I was about to faint. My friends went a bit further, and saw a corpse lying without a head. We also saw a pair of (women's) legs lying crushed under another concrete block. I think that she was already dead, even though people tried to pull her out.

It was terrible. I don't know if I described it well enough. I am still shaking and I'm unable to think. People were lying wounded all over the place. I can still smell the mixture of blood and smoke. (Zograf 1999:51-53) [...]

31 May 1999: Yesterday morning, we heard a strong detonation. It seemed that the whole apartment building was shaking, and everybody guessed that it was a projectile that had fallen in the Pancevo area. The area which was rocketed was in fact some 20-30 kilometres away, which means that very powerful projectiles were used. I can only imagine what it felt like in the targeted area. There were countless NATO attacks during the night and day yesterday, but the most awful, most frightening one was in a quiet little town of Varvarin, where the small bridge in the centre was bombed while civilian traffic was flowing across it. It was market day, and an orthodox Christian holiday, and the town was full of people who came from the surrounding area. The strike was renewed just a few minutes later, while passers-by were coming to the rescue of the people who were injured by the first strike! (I guess that the pilot must have seen that the bridge was crowded with civilians and vehicles?) Eleven people were found dead, and 40 injured, but as the traffic was very busy, and many vehicles fell in the river, the real number of victims of this glorious action is yet to be defined. As we learned from the similar cases when the bridges were bombed by NATO in this war; some of the bodies were found floating in the river several weeks after the bombing. And still, NATO officials have already confirmed that the bridge was a 'legitimate military target'. OK, OK, just do your job, guys, we still believe that it is a humanitarian mission you're on (ibid.:81-82).

In NATO-speak, such events, unseen by their perpetrators, emerged as ever from the linguistic mincers as 'collateral damage', or, if some descriptive detail slipped through the net, as 'Serb propaganda'. Neither Zograf nor Meitner, nor the world's media consumers were aware at the time of the ten tons of depleted uranium dropped on Serbia/Kosovo during this campaign, likely in the longer term to cause the death of in the region of 10,000 people; but then that was a mere trifle compared with the estimated 3,000 tons dropped on Afghanistan three years later.

The debriefing of Captain Meitner and his fellow 'top guns', unable to see or conceive of what they were doing, was, however, only the first link in the 'information' chain. Their perverse version of events passed through many processes before reaching our screens. We may recall, after all, that when the Aviano air base did ultimately provide a cockpit tape of the infamous bombing of the refugee convoy, it turned out that they supplied the wrong one. Whether this was a mistake, or an attempt at deliberate disinformation, was never clarified.

Let us then turn to the top of the military hierarchy, the Supreme Allied Commander, General Wesley Clark, for his considered view of how what he called 'the truth, the whole truth, and nothing but the truth' of the war reached the public. In the confusion of his formulation, careful listeners could discern the very process of the separation of 'word' from 'world' taking place, the process which ensured that all they, as citizens of societies calling themselves 'democratic', had ever heard from NATO had been precisely *not* what the disingenuous General Clark claimed they had been getting. Rather, it had been, as is constantly forgotten, no different from every hot and cold war of the century, whether in 'authoritarian' or 'free' societies, a version of events wilfully manipulated with a range of techniques to render the war desirable and acceptable, and the deeds of the side being supported credible and justified, while blackening those of the other side.

In other words, however advanced the technology, however ceaseless the media coverage relative to earlier wars, the discourse and imagery had only a distant relationship with reality. These were the Supreme Allied Commander's words. With one breath, he said: 'We discovered early in this campaign, in fact we knew inherently, that the right way to fight a propaganda offensive is not with more propaganda, it's not with a lie. It's to tell the truth, the whole truth, and nothing but the truth. And this as rapidly as possible' (BBC2 1999). Here, one may note in passing that, before correcting himself, he almost stated that the rightness of telling the truth was a NATO discovery dating only from early in the Kosovo war. Then, in the next breath, he said: 'but you need some smart people who can tell you what piece of truth you're looking for [...] and who can package it and know how to distribute it in such a way that it answers the requirement' (ibid). And of these 'smart people', he said: 'I don't call them spin-doctors. They were people who understood which pieces of information were important to provide the truth to the public' (ibid). It was doubtless logical that, once you had 'smart' bombs, you needed 'smart' people to construct 'the truth' about them for the public, which was clearly not 'smart' enough to be allowed to do it on its own.

Although the Supreme Allied Commander would doubtless not have claimed to possess expertise on the relationship between language, truth and reality, he would probably have had to admit on reflection that what he was describing here with such an air of sincerity was not *giving* the truth, the whole truth and nothing but the truth to citizens, but wilfully *depriving* them of it. In so doing, he was preventing them from reconstructing in their minds a full and accurate picture of what was actually happening, in order to make a properly informed judgement about its acceptability.

The General thus abdicated the responsibility, or passed the buck, for packaging the 'information' provided by the military to the 'smart people'. Initially these were 'Doctor' Jamie Shea, and subsequently, Shea's much-enlarged team, the NATO MOC (Media Operations Centre), with British Prime Minister Blair's principal spin-doctor, Alistair Campbell, as its guiding genius. It should be remembered that, following NATO's confused and obviously dissimulating response to its bombing of the refugee convoy, Blair and Clinton, perceiving this as a major propaganda coup for Milosevic, had decided that 'a better job needed to be done', and that, in the words of Pentagon spokesman, Ken Brown, 'Shea needed help' (ibid). Thus, Alistair Campbell had been drafted in, and had set up an international team of 25 high-powered PR people – the MOC – which quickly took hold of ensuring that there were, in the interesting words of Joe Lockhart, White House press spokesman, 'no more information mis-steps' (ibid). This piece of jargon, which could be interpreted as 'no more letting inconvenient pieces of the whole truth through to the consumers', signalled a near total control and co-ordination of the news agenda by those who were interested not in public information, but in using any means, including factual distortions and deliberately misleading statements, to justify and bolster the NATO position.

Looking back on it, Shea did not even pretend that he was there to convey accurate information or the reality of the war; rather, he said somewhat plaintively: 'I try to be a good NATO spokesman. I try, I try to present our case. I try to defend it' (ibid). Within the NATO Media Operations Centre, there was one member of the team occupied full-time with 'making up good lines'. A US-American member of the team, National Security Council spokesman Colonel P.J. Crowley, said: 'You also have to provide at the end of the day that sound-bite that will make sure that you're part of the 10 o'clock news in London or the 6-30 news in Washington' (ibid). Democratic citizens might have asked, had they known at the time, how all this fitted in with General Clark's statement that NATO provided 'the truth, the whole truth and nothing but the truth' to the public.

The whole process of NATO information filtering and distortion, from the imagination-free Captain Meitner flying over Serbia, to 'smart' Dr Shea at his news conferences, took place up to this point certainly with the media in mind, but without their intervention. The final stage between the reality of the war and the public reception of it involved its transfer to our screens, radios and newspapers via journalists and editors.

In twentieth century wars, in 'democratic' societies as elsewhere, the mainstream media, it must be clear by now, seldom dissented from, and generally actively supported, their own side. A pretence of, or even a belief in, journalistic independence may have been maintained, but it was rare for oppositional positions to be accorded more than token space or credibility. This was as true of the 1914 war as it was of the Kosovo war. Kraus's magazine, *Die Fackel*, appeared with pages blanked out by the censors; his main work on the war could only appear after it was over. The main newspapers peddled, embroidered on, and were the principal distributors of state propaganda. In Kosovo, although overt official censorship of the media had been substantially replaced by filtering and blocking information before it reached the media, and by systematic anti-Serb propaganda, the overwhelming majority of the British mass media – honourable exceptions being John Pilger and Robert Fisk – played an actively supportive, or at best supine role with regard to the NATO version of events. The NATO version was given, on the whole, *a priori* credibility, while virtually every report out of Serbia came with a health warning and a proviso that it had been passed by the Serb censors, and was thus discredited. Stories of Serb atrocities were instantly believed. Stories of atrocities by NATO were treated as Serb propaganda.

In *How the War was Spun*, four months after the events, the chief BBC correspondent at NATO during the bombardment, Mark Laity, admitted this unashamedly, positioning himself, with hindsight – disingenuously, given that he was an experienced reporter of previous wars – as having been naïve and gullible in the face of NATO lies. *De facto*, he was thus, as the voice of the BBC, the unquestioning purveyor to the British people of NATO, and thus British and US government propaganda – a highly manipulated version of events which, as we have seen, bore little relation to the reality of the war. Laity's retrospective statements here threw light on the penultimate twist before the story reached its public. He described how he saw 'the enemy', with perceptive, 'no one can fool me' insights into their devious propaganda methods:

> I took from very early on that there was a propaganda war here, and my judgement was that the Serbs were capable of deliberately misleading. We knew, and subsequent events proved ... er ... beyond doubt ... that the Serbs were killing a lot of Albanians, deliberately, and so, if they killed Albanians deliberately, and could blame it on NATO as well [smiling] it's a kind of double whammy (ibid).

To take just one analytical point from this statement, the repetition of the adverb 'deliberately' exposes his bias. When the enemy killed, committed atrocities, or deceived in war, it did it on purpose. When our side did it, it was an unfortunate error, or side effect, in the honest pursuance of a good cause. Thus Laity said of Jamie Shea:

> I did not feel that Jamie lied to me at all. But I clearly wasn't getting the right story. And it seemed to me that, whether he was being deliberate or not, and I don't think he was, he, as representative of the NATO machine, was falling down on the job (ibid).

So Jamie was OK because he was not misleading deliberately. He was just the victim of impersonal forces and circumstances. Telling a false story was not lying when it was the NATO spokesman who did it.

It sounded like an opportunity for an intrepid BBC investigative reporter, suspicions aroused, to step in and really get to the heart of the matter, pose those penetrating questions, and not give up until he had found out what was really going on. Mark Laity thus recalls:

> When they [NATO] first started ramping up the results, I was quite sceptical. I started phoning people up, and said: 'This is looking pretty good, suddenly. Why are you, you know, suddenly getting such good results from *your* point of view? And can we believe them?' and they said: 'It's different to previous wars, you know. We've got videos; we're doing much careful examination.' And these were *good* people I was talking to,

not PRs. And so, in the end, I made the judgement that battle damage assessment was more accurate this time. [laughs] I was wrong, I mean, I just got it wrong [smiles] (ibid).

And because the intrepid Mr Laity 'got it wrong' – that is, chose to swallow the NATO story from beginning to end because someone 'good' on the end of a phone told him that, for the first time in the history of mass media war reporting, one of the participants was providing reliable and accurate damage assessment because it 'had the video', taken at 15,000 feet while flying at several hundred miles an hour, the British TV news consumers were fed lies as if they were truth. Four months after the event, the smiling Mr Laity was, despite this confession of what looks like gross professional incompetence, still the BBC's defence correspondent, although subsequently he was to move on – to work for NATO.

From this evidence, we can trace a process from Captain Meitner's videos to our TV screens, and see demonstrated that 'the world' (the reality of war), became progressively further separated from 'the word' (the discourse of the reporting). Only a small proportion of the public appeared to realise that this was happening, let alone worth protesting about, although it was a clear denial of the democracy and freedom of information in whose name the war was ostensibly being fought in the first place.

It is not surprising that the BBC, the makers of *How the War was Spun*, tactfully missed out its own final editorial role in the presentation of the war to the British public. It gave us, in this programme, no interviews with news editors, nor did it show us footage that it edited out of the news at the time. It apparently did not even think to examine, let alone question, its own role.

Subsequently, some criticism of the BBC was expressed. *The Guardian* (5.10.99:5) quoted Steve Hewlett, Director of Programmes at the rival Carlton TV, and former BBC employee, as saying of the BBC coverage of the Kosovo war (in comparison with the French coverage which he had seen) that: 'It was so sanitised that it made me question whether the event had happened at all in the way I had previously seen.' In the same *Guardian* report, Martin Bell, BBC Defence Correspondent during the Bosnian war, went further, unconsciously echoing Karl Kraus in 1914, when he stated that broadcasters make war more acceptable as a means of resolving conflicts in a way that might *not* be the case if more graphic images were shown. Of his own experience in the Bosnian war, he stated: 'We were not allowed to show anything of substance at all', and concludes: 'It has a political effect' (ibid).

Anthony Loyd confirms the censorship in his account of the Tuzla bloodbath in the spring of 1995 in Bosnia:

The shell fired by a Serb gun to the west of Tuzla came in low [...]. As the sun dipped below the horizon it landed in the old town's main square, thick with youth.
The explosion sent shrapnel scouring through the crowd and picked up the square's cobblestones in a cyclone of secondary death [...]. They [the camera crew] got out of the vehicle in the darkness and pushed their way into the chaos of the square. In the narrow walled confines they were confronted with a scene such as few see in any war; the ground was slippery with blood and flesh, strewn with limbs and pulped bodies that still smouldered with the blast. Seventy-one were dead, nearly three times as many

injured. The oldest of the dead was thirty-six years old, the youngest four [...]. Only when the last bodies were recovered did the pair send their footage from the TV station and return to the hotel. They washed the blood and human tissue from their boots in the shower and sat together in shocked silence in their room.

I found them like that the next morning [...]. On the tape, I saw most of what they had seen, the frightful mutilation and chaos, heard the pleading of the dying and the cries of the bereaved, only without the aggro of being punched and spat at.

We all wondered if it had been worth it the next day. Their footage was deemed unacceptable to be seen in Britain. They had been unable to edit out enough of the horror, unable to film a single body that was not too mutilated to be watched in a British home after dinner (Loyd 2000:279-281).

There were both economic and political reasons for this sanitisation. In economic terms, news, as has been shown often enough in this narrative, was and is a commodity, its form and content determined by its commercial value. In terms of TV news, this means ratings; commercial pressures mean that ratings are more important than truth. Steve Hewlett again, with his insider's view, was quoted as believing that fear of a backlash from squeamish viewers – that is, people switching off if some reality of war is shown – led to the broadcasting of a distorted version of the realities of the Kosovo war. In political terms, showing any real war would quickly turn the public against it and every war. Robert Fisk, who reported on Kosovo for *The Independent*, again echoing Kraus in 1914, expressed the view subsequently (BBC Radio 4 2000) that if media audiences were to be shown the reality of war, instead of a sanitised, distorted version of it, then they would be so shocked that they would never support another war again, a development which governments – especially those of leading arms manufacturing and exporting countries like the USA and Britain – would not wish to encourage. As things are, of course, real war is not shown on the media, and majority publics accept, some even enthuse about, wars, when hegemonic discourses promote and require them. There were no mass anti-war demonstrations on the streets of London or Washington during the Kosovo war. Nor, of course, were there in Belgrade, where similar – but cruder and thus less convincing – mechanisms were at work, but where fear was also a greater factor. The words of Aleksandar Zograf, surviving Captain Meitner's bombs on the ground in what remained of Serbia, provide a salient insight: 'I should say again and again, that we are living in a savage world, hiding behind the happy face of mass communication' (Zograf 1999:62).

Since then, the Kosovo campaign has been regularly held up in the mainstream media as a success, and this claim, having seemingly gained majority public acceptance or acquiescence, has been repeatedly used by political leaders and their acolytes as a justification for subsequent military actions.

Conclusion

This may be a bleak, desperate vision of a global Potemkin village at the end of the twentieth century; it is, however, sustained both by much of what has emerged in the preceding chapters, as well as many of the analytical positions described in Chapter 2. But it is not an invitation to curl up (a)pathetically in front of the television to enjoy the Glorious Sunset of Civilisation Show – sanitised, of course, in between the sport, game shows, 'reality TV' and advertisements. It would not have been worth writing a book to conclude with that. The following chapter and the conclusion set out to examine the situation at the beginning of the twenty-first century, to envisage alternatives, and to draw lessons from the experience of dynamic discursive forces for counter-hegemonic, socio-cultural change.

Chapter 12

Twin Towers of Babel. 'War on Terrorism' and 'Anticipatory Pre-emption'

I truly only manage to observe public affairs indirectly because unfortunately so much journalistic rubbish lies in the way; sweeping it away is a laborious, but necessary task (Karl Kraus 1899).

Had the great broadcasting institutions and newspapers on both sides of the Atlantic not merely channelled and echoed the agendas and lies of government, but instead exposed and challenged them, the Bush/Blair attack on Iraq would have been made untenable (John Pilger 2003 *The Independent on Sunday* 6.4.03).

Introduction

The early twenty-first century event that dominated the 'mediatised' world and the subsequent media landscape was that known simply by its date '9-11' or '11 September', a journalistic naming which came to signify the baptism of fire of the new millennium, giving meaning to the new era far more potently than artificial January 1 fireworks.

That moment in 2001 is deeply engrained in media consumers' minds as the image of the airliner disappearing in slow motion into the second of the New York World Trade Centre towers, edited into pictures of the collapse of the towers. Further indelible images of tiny figures jumping to their death from the upper floors remind of the human desperation of those moments and of the almost three thousand who lost their lives.

The shock and aftershocks of this event were sufficient to justify its pre-eminence in the news and world political agenda. However, its location and capture on live TV, coupled with its symbolic value and political appropriation by the US government for its long-term internal and global ends, meant that media coverage was magnified far beyond appropriate proportions at the expense of other tragic and barbaric situations of yet greater dimensions.

Instead of provoking Western media consumers to thoughtful investigation of why it happened, and alerting them to burning issues of global inequalities, injustices and exploitation, the coverage flooded their minds with an elite-promoted global scenario of conflict between good and evil. The image of the omnipresent, threatening enemy, justifying all sorts of discursive, economic and military excesses, but missing since the demise of the Soviet Union and the communist threat, was now re-discovered in a new guise. It was named, in a phrase invented by US presidential spin-doctors for journalists to etch onto public consciousness, the *'axis of evil'*. Likewise, a *'war on terrorism'* was declared, which, we were told, was likely to last longer than the 'Cold War', and had to be waged against a stateless and omnipresent oriental opponent, hidden in our midst and plotting to destroy us. Parallels with old anti-Semitic mythology, as also appropriated by the Nazis, are both inevitable and unmentionable.

Against such an enemy, previous laws, conventions of war, modes of diplomacy and democratic practices were no longer applicable. The task for the 'civilised world' (the USA and its acolytes) could no longer be expressed in reactive words such as 'self-defence' or 'deterrence'. The new, more aggressive stance was legitimised by the concept of *'anticipatory pre-emption'*. This meant that one had to act to prevent a threat before that threat even became apparent. It provided the pretext for the establishment of military control over, or 'bringing order to' strategically and economically valuable parts of the world, once they had been branded as 'terrorist' or 'evil'. Playing on an over-excited, media-induced paranoia, this opened the door to publicly approved imperialist expansion, with its accompanying trail of mass death and destruction, in the name of world peace, stability and liberation.

These three resonant clichés, 'axis of evil', 'war on terrorism' and 'anticipatory pre-emption' are simple, media-friendly slogans, each hiding a world of deceit in their claim to be based on values of freedom and democracy while mobilising support for actions which deny these values. They are constantly written into the 'victor's' sanitised newstoriographies and self-righteous historiographies.

We may note that the word 'axis' recalls the 'axis powers' of the 1930s and 1940s, Hitler's Germany and Mussolini's Italy. This sets up misleading (and often used) associations between Saddam Hussein and Adolf Hitler, and hence potent warnings against 'appeasement'. Likewise, the word 'evil' reminds of Ronald Reagan's 1980s description of the Soviet Union as an 'evil empire'. The whole phrase thus evokes and combines the twentieth century's twin defeated monsters, fascism and Soviet communism, and mendaciously lays their shadow over the newly created monsters of the twenty-first, preparing the way for justification of all-out war against them.

The new equivalent evil '-ism' against which the fight must be carried forward is expressed in the resonant, but empty, phrase 'war on terrorism'. 'Terrorism', a method to achieve an end, clearly cannot be compared with 'fascism' or 'communism' which designate ideologies and political systems (themselves mutually incompatible). It is thus a self-evident nonsense, a piece of linguistic trickery, to set up a historical continuity between US wars, fought first against one, then against the other, and now against the third, as if each successively justified the next.

'Global imposition of ideology through military expansion', and 'appropriation of economic assets of oppressed peoples', were characteristics of 'the enemy' in the discourses of the great twentieth century wars against fascism and communism. The discursive task of apologists of US foreign policy during the G.W. Bush presidency, particularly the influential coterie advocating the Project for the New American Century, was, however, to transform such heinous ambitions into selfless, emancipatory acts of US munificence and humanity in the face of shady, alien threats of primitive barbarism. 11 September 2001 delivered them the perfect scenario, and the iconic, dark-robed, bearded figure of Osama bin Laden provided them with the ideal embodiment of evil to justify their 'liberating' mission and the necessity of 'anticipatory pre-emption'. He became the pretext for the bombardment of Afghanistan and the installation of a US-compliant government in Kabul. The next target was Iraq, with its already demonised leader, Saddam Hussein. He was accordingly inflated into a major threat to world security on the basis of improbable links with Osama bin Laden and unlikely possession of ready-to-use weapons of mass destruction, and thus transformed into a pretext for invasion. When a power elite can advocate and have its forces carry out a 'pre-emptive' invasion for the 'liberation' of a people, in the full knowledge that it is killing uncounted thousands of innocents on the basis of an unproven threat, and when it can simultaneously persuade the majority of its citizens via the mass media that it is doing the right thing, then insanity and cultural bankruptcy rule, and the door to atrocity is wide open.

While the overall European reaction to these developments was mixed, with strong oppositional positions developing, particularly among French and German political, economic and media elites and broader publics, that of the Blair government in the UK was that it *'stood shoulder to shoulder'* with the US government. Cartoonists mocked the misleading image, with its deluded implication of equivalence, but the phrase still passed into uncritical mainstream usage. Those with longer memories recalled that it was listed among what Eric Blair (George Orwell) described in his 1946 essay 'Politics and the English Language' as 'a huge dump of worn-out metaphors which have lost all evocative power and are merely used because they save people the trouble of inventing phrases for themselves' (Jackall 1995:426). This fawning loyalty to US elites at the centre of UK political power was manifest both in its unwavering acceptance of the discourse, and in its proactive determination to join military action against the newly defined enemy. In his enthusiastic stance, the Prime Minister himself wished to be seen as leading from the front, thus appearing less to be acting as President Bush's 'poodle', as the momentarily re-radicalised *Daily Mirror* put it. However, as the government's figurehead, he still faced the task of ensuring that he took a majority of parliament and the country with him. In the pre-invasion months, the superficially unanswerable establishment line was to indicate that it was democratically encouraging public information and debate so that the public could make up its own mind over time. What it did not say was that it sought to control the framing and discourse of the information and the terms of the debate. Foremost in this process was the BBC, still frequently seen worldwide as a trusted source of unbiased information.

This chapter will thus first look at two BBC programmes which were symptomatic of its pharisaical posture. Following this, examples will be given of the more overt discursive hypocrisy of the great majority of the UK press as it cheered and misled the country along the runway to war. Finally, examples of the unprecedented volume of counter-hegemonic materials originating in the UK will be assessed.

At the centre of the BBC's current affairs analysis is television's time-honoured weekly show *Panorama* which aims to stand out from the rest of reporting by the objectivity and *gravitas* of its approach. Two editions of this programme, one from autumn 2001, in the immediate aftermath of 11 September, the second from autumn 2002, as the world was being prepared for a US-led attack on Iraq, will be analysed here. They have been picked out from other programmes on the same themes since they each seek authority and democratic legitimacy by incorporating public participation and thus an aura of genuine dialogue and interaction with the public. Both reveal how what initially seem to be programmes structured with impeccable balance and plurality are in fact disguised acts of persuasion for the standpoint of the UK government, designed to contribute to the luring of sceptical viewers into support for, or acquiescence in, the US/UK government position.

Operation Veritas: How the Truth was Brought from New York to Islamabad

The grotesquely named 'Operation Veritas' was, in the words of the UK Ministry of Defence, the UK's contribution to the US-led Operation Enduring Freedom which began on 7 October 2001, the military operation against Osama bin Laden's Al Qaida terrorist organisation and against the Taliban regime harbouring them in Afghanistan. Here we apply the name, just as grotesquely, to an example of the UK government/media propaganda effort to reconcile the British people to that brutal bombardment of the world's poorest country by the richest, abetted by UK forces.

At first glance, it was a textbook case of the BBC's balanced approach to a subject. Observing, in the wake of 11 September, the confrontation between the Western and Moslem worlds, and wishing to promote contact and *rapprochement* between them, BBC1's *Panorama* decided to set up a live debate between ordinary citizens in New York and Islamabad, ostensibly to investigate the 'clash of cultures', and to serve as mediator in a process of furthering mutual understanding at 'people to people' level with our Pakistani allies. The programme was broadcast on 24 October 2001, as cluster bombs, bunker-busters, daisy-cutters and an estimated 3000 tonnes of depleted uranium were being dumped on Afghani citizens, polluting their land and water supplies.

In setting up the programme, the producers evidently paid great attention to demonstrating a scrupulous observance of balance.

A group of US citizens sat in New York, their contributions managed by a white British presenter, Nicky Campbell. A group of Pakistanis sat in Islamabad with Indian-born British presenter, Nisha Pillai, in charge of that side of the discussion. The New York group could be seen as a carefully chosen cross-section, containing not only representatives of the white mainstream, but also both genders, US Moslems, people of colour, people from the peace movement, and workers engaged in clearing-up operations in the ruins of the Twin Towers. The Islamabad group also set up its own kind of balance, with half of the group having been involved in direct action and recent street demonstrations, and half classified as moderates. Among the women, one chose to appear veiled. There was a manifest desire shown in the selection of both groups to represent a broad range of opinion.

As well as the discussion groups, the programme provided a balance of experts, one from the USA, one from Pakistan. In the studio, underlining the BBC/UK self-positioning as intermediary, was ex-Foreign Secretary, Robin Cook. Anchorman was the doyen of BBC presenters, David Dimbleby.

As the programme developed, the debate was switched back and forth between New York and Islamabad, the experts had a couple of slots to make their comments, and Robin Cook was likewise brought in for the British government standpoint.

This had to be the BBC at its much vaunted fairest and best, doing what it was renowned and praised for throughout the world, and showing the positive democratic value of globalised mass communication technology by promoting live citizen participation and dialogue across continents. Yet a closer look at the programme unmasks a quite different agenda. What will emerge is that the programme actually functioned as a disguised Anglo-US government propaganda exercise, and a forceful assertion of US hegemony masquerading as fair debate. It did this by branding Pakistani Moslems as brainwashed dupes, while pushing the Bush government's 'for us or for terrorism' stance. Furthermore, far from promoting dialogue and understanding, it deliberately set up a 'clash of civilisations' confrontation, and made sure that the West/US won it by allowing a verbal carpet-bombing of Pakistani-Moslem standpoints, and a rubbishing of their positions while permitting some response, but not an adequate one.

The underlying imbalance of the programme is revealed by a closer look at the detail of its structure, and at the discourse it employed. Five observations exemplify the deceptiveness of the supposedly fair structure:

1. The opening sequence sets up polarised oppositions leading to false images and identifications. The series of images shows us, on the one side, Bush and the New York discussion group of 'typical Americans', and, on the other side, Osama bin Laden and the Islamabad group of 'typical Pakistanis/Moslems'. Demon figure bin Laden is thus from the outset falsely associated with Islam in general, and the Moslem interlocutors in particular – a mendacious representation which is hardly an invitation to conciliatory dialogue.

2. The choice of experts and discussion hosts betrays both desire for confrontation and use of hierarchical gender categorisations. The chosen US expert is the male, hard-line, neo-conservative hawk from the Bush administration, Richard Perle; the chosen Pakistani expert is the non-polemic female diplomat Abida Hussein. We have here the predictably uneven pairing of a bullying propagandist with someone who had come onto the programme to discuss the issues rather than shoot sound-bites. Equally, the New York host is male and somewhat bullish, whereas the Islamabad host is female and constantly forced into defensive postures. These choices by the programme makers underline the 'dominant, authoritative West' versus 'subordinate, less credible East' assumptions of the programme.

3. The series of contributions from the groups in New York and Islamabad both begin and end in New York. The New Yorkers are thus crucially permitted both to

set the initial tone, and to have the last word. Despite the range of US citizens represented, we note that the aggressively anti-Islamic mainstream whites, those least likely to want to listen to and understand the views expressed in Islamabad, are physically placed more visibly than the others in relation to the main camera position, and are repeatedly drawn into the talk by the host, consequently dominating it. For example, of the 16 minutes 45 seconds of the programme allocated to the New York group (already about a minute more than the time permitted to the Islamabad group), only 1 minute 25 seconds is allowed to the token peace movement representatives.

4. Similarly, the experts' interventions are dominated by the Western side. Perle and Cook, with their different perspectives, are allocated both the first and the last words, with their combined comments lasting for 10 minutes (Perle with a dominant 6 minutes 15 seconds in four interventions, Cook with 3 minutes 45 seconds in two interventions), while Hussein gets only 4 minutes 20 seconds and three interventions. Moreover, in the first two of her three interventions, Hussein is crudely cut off in mid-sentence by Dimbleby, whereas Perle and Cook are treated with greater deference and are not interrupted.

5. If the total time allocations across the 50 minute programme are added up (discussion groups and experts together), the totals come to 20 minutes and 10 seconds, about 40 per cent of the programme, allocated to the East, and 26 minutes 50 seconds, 53 per cent of the programme, allocated to the West, with three minutes taken up by the introduction, links and conclusion. That 6 minutes 30 seconds difference, about one eighth of the programme's time, is a quantitative measure of the BBC's 'balance' on this occasion.

A combination of editorial decisions made prior to the live transmission, and choices made during it, thus subtly undermined the Pakistani side and put the US side in the driving seat even before the participants opened their mouths.

Examples of the language used in the programme set the domination of the East by the West in even starker profile. From the start, the 'clash of cultures' rather than any attempt at understanding and real dialogue is emphasised. US/Western rectitude is set against presumed Islamic/Eastern violence, envy, rage, self-delusion, coupled with accusations of sympathies with the supposed mastermind of the 11 September atrocities. In the opening sequence, Dimbleby praises Bush as: '*Sticking* to the *bold* war aims he *set out* from the *start*', indicating Bush qualities of determination, courage, decisive action and consistency. Then we are shown Bush himself saying: 'this conflict is a fight to save the civilised world and values common to the West, *(pause)* to Asia and to Islam.' One might detect a positive gesture here, but on the final word 'Islam', and as if to undermine immediately any hope of dialogue, the programme editor changes the image from Bush's talking head to crowds of Islamic/Asiatic children burning an effigy of Bush. The powerful images deny the conciliatory afterthought in Bush's words, as the thinly disguised discourse of 'clash' that pervades the programme takes over.

The first visit to New York confirms this. Nicky Campbell, the discussion leader, has already lined up those with the most strident pro-US government ideas to kick off the 'debate', Nicki Hayden and Lisa Ponte. He turns to them first, addressing them by name, and returns to them several times in the course of the programme. They oblige with highly inflammatory 'us and them' generalisations. Asked to explain Islamic 'rage against America', their responses are replete with confrontational clichés:

> *Hayden:* [...] It is *our freedoms* that *we* enjoy *here*, *our many choices*, and a *misconception* on the *other side*.
> *Ponte:* [egged on by the presenter] ...*they* think *our* women are *too liberated*, *our* press is *too free*, *our* free market is not a system *they* ascribe to, so *absolutely, they have it in for the American way of life*.

By the time the discussion switches to Islamabad for the first time, the bludgeoning anti-Islamic tone has thus been set, and the Pakistani group is forced into reactive debate to deal with the falsehoods and defend themselves against stereotypes. Seeking common ground or putting across a reasoned argument has already become difficult. Yet they for the most part avoid counter-attacks, and make points about not being anti-American, just opposed to current US government policy in Afghanistan. At this time, no conclusive evidence against Osama bin Laden had been made public, and US military action was killing thousands, and terrorising an innocent neighbouring population. Throughout the programme, they try to bring the debate back from confrontation and into genuine dialogue, but are not listened to by those in New York.

Back in New York, Lisa Ponte and Nicki Hayden are again immediately brought in by the host:

> *Campbell: Lisa*, let me bring you in *first*. You may well not have got the right guy if they're right in Islamabad.

The questioner again picks on a 'clash' issue, and we can note easily in the replies the markers of total certainty, belief in superior morality and intelligence, possession of truth and reality, and corresponding denigration of the Islamic others:

> *Ponte: Oh give me a break*, Nicky. The evidence is *beyond reasonable doubt*...
> *Hayden: We* have a *free* press *here in the US*, unlike *their* country; *we* have it from all sides, the left, the right, the middle. *They* only hear it from Al Jazeera and the *Arab* [sic] sanctioned newspapers.

Then Ed Koch, ex-mayor of New York intervenes:

> *Koch:* I think that what *they're* saying is so *silly*, it *boggles the mind*...

Other, less aggressive New York interventions are for the most part smothered by this kind of onslaught, and ultimately drowned out by the US government expert, Richard Perle, who makes his contempt for Islam, and the Islamabad participants crudely clear. Asked by Dimbleby if the US can win the war on terrorism without the support of Moslems, he replies:

Perle: Of course we can. We're going to defend ourselves against these sorts of attacks whether we have the support of the Moslem world or not. We are not going to fail to defend ourselves because someone in Islamabad is unconvinced [...]. If [bin Laden] has declared war on the West, then it really doesn't matter at the end of the day if the people of Pakistan agree with that or not.

He thus expresses nothing but disdain for those whom the programme is ostensibly bringing into contact with him for dialogue. The US is the top world power and will impose its will. Those who are not with the US government are for bin Laden. The threatening tone is not even disguised.

Perle's bullying words, which leave even Robin Cook embarrassed, capture the dominant insulting tone of the US side of this supposedly balanced and constructive debate:

Perle: I have sat and listened now to nearly 40 minutes of rubbish, much of it from Islamabad. Unbelievably ill-informed people, perhaps because they don't have a free and vigorous and open press, and access to information [...]. So I am really tired of hearing the ramblings out of Islamabad. If that's the thinking in Pakistan, so be it. No rational argument. And certainly no change in American policy is going to convince people who think that the earth is flat.

What happened here? Was a well-intentioned live BBC programme hijacked and sabotaged so that it turned into the opposite of what had been hoped for? It certainly left the two sides further apart than when they started, contrary to the stated aims.

This could not have been the case. Both the framing of the programme, the order of appearance, the time allocations, the behaviour of the presenter in New York, and the very fact that Richard Perle, with his well known views, was permitted to appear, show that the BBC was complicit in the direction that this ultimately biased and unfair programme took, and that its ostensible neutrality was merely a disguise for functioning primarily as a mouthpiece for US propaganda.

In the eyes of critical observers, the BBC may have long lost its credibility as a bastion of balance and fairness, but it still manages to maintain a good measure of public and international trust in its integrity. This programme was an example of its duplicity in the covert pursuit of power-elite agendas. Despite claims to the contrary, it is likely on this occasion to have contributed more to war than to peace.

It is of interest that on 3 March 2003, during the lead-in to the invasion of Iraq, *Panorama* repeated this format with a similar link-up between Amman and New York. This was a notably better programme which appeared to have taken note of published criticism of the previous one, but it was nonetheless no more than a tiny oasis in the desert sandstorm of the BBC's coverage in these pre-invasion months. The Corporation's overall agenda was clearly to tame a highly sceptical public into accepting that military action was inevitable and justified, to stifle the opposition and discredit the counter-arguments. BBC coverage of anti-war demonstrations was the smallest in Europe and even smaller than the negligible coverage of some major US TV news channels such as NBC.

Panorama Interactive: the BBC's Hall of Mirrors

The second programme to be looked at was billed as *Panorama Interactive* and broadcast on 29 September 2002, following a *Panorama Special* on Saddam Hussein the previous week. This was at a moment of intense media preoccupation with Iraq and its leader, manifested in a powerful campaign to alert consumers to threats posed to the world by the Iraqi regime. It was, we were told, in possession of, and ready and able to use, weapons of mass destruction; it had links with the Al Qaida terrorist network. The recent and distant crimes of Saddam Hussein and his henchmen, particularly their use of chemical weapons against Kurds and Iranians in the 1980s war with Iran, were ceaselessly repeated. This diabolical package was co-ordinated with US government declarations of intent, backed by the UK government, to engage in war on Iraq to bring about 'regime change'. The coming attack on Iraq was presented as part of the continuing 'war on terrorism', with that country being placed at the heart of the 'axis of evil', and thus becoming the prime target for 'anticipatory pre-emption'.

Despite significant anti-war opposition, G.W. Bush, with his coterie of advisors and mainstream media friends, could already be encouraged by his high personal poll ratings, and confident that a combination of middle-American support and widespread indifference and ignorance would allow them to claim public approval and guarantee that they could act with impunity. Surveys showed that well over a third of US citizens had been persuaded that Saddam Hussein was involved in the 11 September attacks, despite the lack of any evidence to support this.

In the UK, however, the task of successfully presenting a demonising newstoriography around Saddam Hussein and swinging consumer opinion around to acquiescence in the notion of joining a preventive US-led invasion was not so straightforward, requiring the deployment of a less strident approach and the figleaf of UN approval (UN resolution 1441 was imminent). Opinion surveys showed strong opposition to war, especially without UN backing. The governments and publics of the most influential European neighbours, Germany and France, were clearly reticent about support, let alone participation. Given the backing of the Conservative Party, there was a large parliamentary majority for UK government support of the US government line, but the weight of recalcitrant public opposition evidently needed addressing, as a blatantly under-reported anti-war demonstration by about 400,000 protestors in London on 28 September, the day before the *Panorama Interactive* programme, showed.

The BBC's contribution to the 'information' campaign and the 'debate' was substantial. In that week, there were not only the two *Panorama* programmes, and heavy coverage in the regular news slots, there was also a *Newsnight Special* (BBC2) on 24 September, and a *Question Time* (BBC1) on 26 September, both exclusively devoted to the subject. *Panorama Interactive* was also immediately followed by an *Iraq Debate* on the commercial station, Channel 4. The machinery of information and debate was clearly in overdrive, and rightly so in a democracy at a moment when key decisions about attacking and inflicting death and destruction on another sovereign country which posed no proven direct or imminent threat, had not yet passed into action.

It was of crucial importance in this situation that particularly the BBC, but also other broadcasters, should be, and be seen to be, neutral, fair and non-coercive. Not only did democratic practice and the BBC's reputation as an independent organisation depend on it, but also a sceptical public would not be taken in by what it could easily recognise as a biased approach.

The conceivers and designers of *Panorama Interactive*, presented as 'the first of its kind' thus went to elaborate lengths (just as they had done a year before with the New York-Islamabad link-up) to demonstrate overtly their even-handedness. One can imagine the programme makers compiling a tick-list of all the democratic credentials such a programme could muster, in combination with a maximum of technological wizardry, then mixing the whole into the most impressive and convincing demonstration of BBC twenty-first century democratic public service broadcasting ever.

The studio design reflected visually the programme's overt interactive intent. The centrepiece was a semicircle of four people, backs to the camera, in shirtsleeves and wearing headphones, seated at computers, evidently busily receiving thousands of electronic messages from 'us', the public – a prime visual focus on interactivity. At the top of the screen was to be seen a line of spotlights, their beams probing out into the ether like searchlights, and simultaneously channelling in that vital commodity, public opinion. Central to the backdrop was a large red screen, with 'Panorama Interactive' emblazoned on it in bold letters. This was flanked by six yellow windows, three on each side, soon to be filled by the talking heads of six BBC correspondents, beamed in from across the world. The long-running *Panorama* had for many years been marketed as the British viewing public's 'window on the world'; here was the literal visual representation of this. Seated beyond the shirtsleeved message receivers, and facing the camera, were two more BBC journalists, Jane Corbyn and John Simpson, also busying themselves with laptops. Pacing dynamically around the studio, addressing the various contributors, were the two presenters, Nisha Pillai and Gavin Esler.

The whole programme was live and studio-based, apart from the inclusion of brief extracts from recent Bush and Blair statements, and the occasional interspersion of a series of pre-recorded questions from the public, gathered by BBC journalists on the streets of a representative range of British cities, including Birmingham, Bristol, Cardiff and Glasgow.

The aim was already clear. It was to get questions on the Iraq crisis, direct from the public, in real time, addressed by expert, on-the-spot commentators who were best placed to give authoritative answers. Channels of live communication were to be opened up between the viewers and those best placed to inform them. In addition, we were soon told, and shown, views and comments from the public would be rolled instantaneously across the bottom of the screen as the programme proceeded, and the public would be invited, in the course of the programme, to vote on what was seen as the key question of the day: 'Is war inevitable?'

The democratic nature and cutting edge technological credentials of the programme were emphasised with its opening words: 'Welcome to this *very first Panorama Interactive*, a special edition *driven by you, the viewers.*' The BBC was evidently here pushing at the frontiers of democratic broadcasting. It was trumpeted that here, it was the *public* which was in control of the programme, *not* the BBC: 'We've been receiving *your* e-mails, *your* text messages and *your* phone calls with *your* questions, and *your* concerns.'

Referring to the assembled commentators, Nisha Pillai underlined the programme's role as servant to the active public: 'The reason we've gathered them all together is to put *your* burning questions on Iran (sic) directly to them.' Then Gavin Esler continues: '*You* can continue to give us *your* questions and *your* comments throughout the programme.' The computer people in shirtsleeves and the presenters were there, it was implied, as neutral conduits between public and trusted experts. Who knows, the feel was, what unpredictable direction this programme might take? For this was spontaneous public sphere interactivity, facilitated by a non-interventionist programme concept, crowned by a democratic viewers' vote, with the result announced at the end: 'And as *you* watch this programme, we'll be asking *you* to vote whether *you* think war is inevitable.'

Correspondingly, there were, throughout the programme, references to e-mail questions from named viewers, and updates on how many thousands of communications from the public had been pouring in.

As with the first *Panorama* programme, one has to ask oneself what greater effort the BBC could have made. Does it not have here a robust case for asserting its free and pluralistic socio-cultural role? Does this not compare favourably with best mass media practice anywhere in the world?

In response to these questions, several more arise. Was the much vaunted viewer power real or illusory? Was the range of questions and answers properly representative of the full range of serious debate on the subject? Did the programme show a process of free unruly public debate, or was it an exercise in trying to tame it? Was this a genuine innovation in broadcasting democracy, or just a piece of covert government/media persuasion masquerading as a public consultation?

It is clear from what can easily be deduced from the broadcast evidence that the assertion of viewer control was false. The only element of the programme of which the BBC was not firmly in control was the result of the vote at the end.

The framing, format and visual presentation were decided by the broadcaster. The programme proceeded according to a set of pre-arranged themes, known to the presenters, the computer operators and, at least in outline, to the experts. The questions which were addressed, and the way they were posed, could have been predicted by anyone with a knowledge of mainstream media priorities. BBC reporters had been out and about on the streets of British cities before the programme and had gathered questions from the public. It is not surprising that many media consumers' questions fitted the preferred themes of the programme, and could thus be picked out and screened to give the impression that it was the public which was determining its direction; but if the programme was genuinely proceeding according to live messages received while it was on air, how was it that these pre-prepared clips could be inserted so neatly as each new theme was introduced? Towards the end of the programme, Gavin Esler announced that about 6,500 contacts from the public had been received during the programme. Was the pre-planned order of events and priority given to particular issues changed in response to instant analysis of these contacts as they came in? It is unlikely. In the same breath, Esler stated that one in four of e-mails received had pointed out the hypocrisy of the US and the UK insisting on Iraqi compliance with UN resolutions, but not Israeli compliance. Yet this major, but 'off-message', issue was evidently *not* on the pre-ordained list, and was not discussed further. Had the programme been doing what it claimed, debate of these contributions by the public would have been given prominence.

The BBC also controlled the responses to its chosen questions by the simple device of using only its own employees to answer them. In the six windows sat six pairs of safe BBC hands; Jane Corbyn and John Simpson in the studio, with their long BBC careers, could be relied on to remain within the spectrum of opinion acceptable to the Corporation. No figure opposing US/UK policy was to be seen or heard anywhere on the programme despite the fact that all indicators of public opinion were showing majorities in opposition to war. This *Panorama* was no 'window on the world', rather a hall of mirrors, with experts reacting to the expected with the predictable in the interests of the power elite.

Let us take the issue of Iraq's weapons of mass destruction as an example. Of all controversial issues in the Iraq debate, this was the central one on which the justification for military action hinged. The BBC was as aware as anyone of this. Its senior managers and news and current affairs staff, its programme planners, producers and editors all knew that the existence of weapons of mass destruction in Iraq in 2002-3 was hotly disputed in claim and counter-claim, and that there was no solid evidence of their presence in the Iraqi armoury, or of the regime's ability or intention to use them even if it had them. They knew that UN weapons inspectors believed that 90-95 per cent of such weapons and capabilities had been removed or destroyed by the time the inspectors were withdrawn in 1998, that the Iraqi nuclear weapons programme had been eliminated, and that any residues of chemical and biological weapons, dating from the 1980s, would be degraded and useless. This was merely a matter of reading up easily available public information.

Yet the US and UK governments were asserting the opposite, without offering proof, as a pretext for war. While much of the public questioned these assertions, and any programme claiming to be driven by the public should have automatically raised doubts about them, *this* programme did not. In response to an e-mail message from 'Neil in Manchester', quoted by Gavin Esler, John Simpson said: 'It always seems to me that the real problem behind all this is that if you stir up Saddam Hussein, you ... he'll *use* the weapons that he *undoubtedly has*, secretly, and that he's been developing, *without any question at all.*' Simpson was then backed up by fellow BBC journalist David Shukman: 'Imagine British forces gathering in Kuwait or Saudi Arabia before an attack on Iraq, and Saddam Hussein feels his back is against the wall, he may well *use* the chemical and biological weapons that we *know* he has, as John was saying.' Several other statements in the programme were predicated on the assumption that the Iraqi military possessed and would use these weapons. Nowhere in the programme were these assumptions, which parroted the UK/US government position, in any way questioned. The central issue was raised, but the answers closed it down; it was not debated, the public was told to believe.

It was only when it was too late for the uncounted thousands of Iraqis who were slaughtered during the invasion and for the many further thousands of injured and bereaved, that is, only after the acclaimed 'liberation' of Iraq, that admissions started to be made in the mainstream media which undermined the previously unassailable hegemonic story, and pointed to the deception of the public by its leaders. Thus, in *The Guardian* of 31 May 2003, we could read:

> Lieutenant General James Conway, the Commander of the 1ˢᵗ Marine Expeditionary Force said that he had been convinced before and during the war, shells with chemical warheads had been distributed to Republican Guard units around Baghdad. 'It was a surprise to me then – it remains a surprise to me now – that we have not uncovered weapons, as you say, in some of the forward dispersal sites', he told reporters in a video conference at the Pentagon yesterday. 'Believe me, it's not for lack of trying', he added, 'We've been to virtually every supply point between the Kuwaiti border and Baghdad, but they're simply not there.' 'We were simply wrong', he added (*The Guardian* 31.5.03:21).

Neither the BBC, nor the other parts of the mainstream media which had been asserting the opposite, issued any statement that they had been 'simply wrong'. Still less did they confess to misleading the public by purveying a grossly distorted version of the state of knowledge about Iraqi weapons of mass destruction, and to making an active contribution to the process which led to invasion, carnage and huge long-term damage.

Likewise, the widespread belief that a key underlying motive for the threatened war was the US government's desire to gain control over Iraqi oil resources was brought up, only to be ridiculed as Iraqi propaganda and a far-fetched 'conspiracy theory'. The US/UK government line was mouthed with blithe certainty while alternatives were not afforded any credibility.

Thus Nisha Pillai introduced the 'oil' section of the programme as follows, distancing the BBC from the whole idea of bringing it up at all: 'Some of our viewers are pretty sceptical too about why the USA is gunning for Iraq. Wendy from Bath is pretty typical here. She says: "This war has nothing to do with 9-11 or any threat to the West, it's all about oil, oil, oil." Then, turning to the Baghdad window/mirror, she sneered: 'That must play down pretty well in Baghdad, ay Caroline?'

In this way, arguments about the significance of oil among the motivations for invasion were instantly devalued through association with the official Iraqi position and the insinuation that anyone taking the issue seriously had been naïvely taken in by Iraqi propaganda. It is indicative here that *Panorama*'s six window/mirrors were filled with five experienced male correspondents and one inexperienced female correspondent, and that she, the least authoritative figure, was the one who happened to have been charged with representing the Iraqi standpoint in Baghdad. It will also be noted that when President Bush, who flaunts an 'action man' image, refers to Iraq with a pronoun, he uses 'she'. There is a long discursive history of rapacious colonisers feminising the colonised – a pattern to which the BBC was here witlessly conforming. In her reply, Caroline Hawley played the role flawlessly, reporting her Iraqi contacts as asking helplessly: 'What have we done now? What have we done over the last decade?' – the reaction of victims of abuse faced by a violator who will not take 'no', or even 'yes' for an answer, but will carry out his assault anyway.

It would not, however, have been credible just to dismiss the oil issue as enemy propaganda, so the presenter turned to the more seasoned male expert, Evan Davis for hard economic analysis. He, with voluble plausibility, half admitted that oil was a factor, only to deny immediately any direct link with the current crisis and resort to the last put-down of any journalist who has run out of serious argument – that of 'conspiracy theory'. Here was neither 'conspiracy' nor 'theory', rather a body of credible evidence and argument, but branding them repeatedly with these words effectively forestalled analysis. Having planted this cliché, however, he quickly moved on to another, that of the Iraqi threat to the superpower. Reinforcing the incestuous 'hall of mirrors' ambience, he said: 'As Matt Frei said earlier, I don't think you need a conspiracy theory to explain American motives here. We know that the Americans are very security conscious, and that's what changed in the last year, rather than a Western desire to get its hands [...] on oil.' With this, the item 'oil' had been dealt with. There had been no serious analysis of the case, just a message to the public that oil was, at most, a marginal issue and not to be taken seriously as a motivation for war.

The end of the programme provided a moment of comic discomfiture as the BBC emperor's brand new interactive clothes were revealed as illusory by its viewers. The entire show had been framed around the question 'Is war inevitable?' This was a carefully chosen power elite formulation, deliberately designed not to elicit votes based on the ethics or desirability of the looming war with Iraq, which the programme makers knew they would 'lose'. Instead, it wished to extract from the viewers a lowest common denominator of resignation that no more could now be done to halt an unstoppable momentum to war; and it hoped with the whole programme, and a culminating 'yes' to its question, to reinforce the mainstream pro-war newstoriography and to consolidate the process of public passivication. The desired viewer reaction was thus one of acceptance, and a feeling that any further opposition was pointless. In the course of the programme, consumers had been told what to think on key issues and reassured that war would not lead to tax rises. They were to see it as a regional conflict that was unlikely to impact on their lives in the UK, especially if Saddam Hussein was removed quickly. Finally, they had been presented with a war scenario suggesting small US/UK troop involvement and rapid victory: 'I'm *sure* they don't want to put conventional troops in any great numbers on the ground, tanks or anything like that', said John Simpson.

To make things absolutely clear, a final round of the experts was undertaken, asking them for their answer to the question: 'Is war inevitable?' Seven of the nine trusted authorities replied: 'Yes'; one replied: 'Probably'; the last replied 'No, but only in the sense that nothing is inevitable'. The message of the programme was unequivocal.

Then came the result of the viewers' poll. 19,000 had voted. Gavin Esler let slip that it was: 'Quite a surprise', that is, not the result that the BBC, in its hall of mirrors had been confidently assuming. 35 per cent had voted 'yes', and 65 per cent had voted 'no'. The presenter was unprepared for this: 'We didn't ask if this was *desirable*', he stumbled, implying that the viewers had answered the *wrong* question, the one the BBC had not dared to ask. Then he mumbled: 'This is not a scientific poll', suggesting that the result was not a proper reflection of opinion. Finally, he came out with the incredulous deduction: 'Two thirds completely disagreeing with *all* our experts here'. What impudence! How dare they?

This was a moment when the extent to which the BBC was out of touch with its viewing public was exposed. Caught up in its self-referential, conformist bubble, it had badly misjudged, and underestimated, the politically articulate consumers in the *Panorama* niche market. As the coming months were to show, levels of public resistance to this war, despite relentless, but not unanimous mass media propaganda, remained resolutely higher than the experience of previous pre-war campaigns would have led elite circles to expect. This culminated in around two million people demonstrating on the streets of London and Glasgow on 15 February 2003, joining the largest global demonstration of the media age.

In response to this commentary, an apologist for the BBC might argue that this was indeed a case of democracy at work, and proof positive of viewer independence and freedom in action – a far cry from the situation in Iraq. To this, one would have to reply: 'Yes, but no thanks to the BBC'. Both this qualitative analysis of *Panorama Interactive*, and quantitative analysis carried out at Cardiff University, indicate that those who criticised the BBC for its closeness to the Blair government's pro-war position, and for its attempts to influence the public in this direction, were correct. The Cardiff research shows that the BBC was more reliant than any of its rivals on government and military sources, and the least likely to quote Iraqi or independent sources. It also paid the least attention to Iraqi casualties, and to the Iraqi people's discontent with the invasion. The Cardiff researcher Justin Lewis concluded: 'Far from revealing an anti-war BBC, our findings tend to give credence to those who criticised the BBC for being too sympathetic to the government's pro-war stance' (*The Guardian* 4.7.03).

It might also be argued that this programme and its poll result contradicts the whole 'strong media effects' narrative that has built up over the case studies in previous chapters of this book. The answer is also: 'Yes. Perhaps something *is* finally changing, but this is scant evidence on which to predict a sea change'. This *Panorama* audience represented a small minority of mass media consumers with an evident interest in politics and world affairs, expressed in their choice to watch this programme over other distractions and activities available to them.

It was a telling synchronicity that Channel 4, just a few minutes after this *Panorama* had finished, started its programme *War on Iraq – which side are you on?* with the result of a poll which *it* had conducted, asking the surprise question: 'Do you think war on Iraq is inevitable?' This was, it seemed, a more scientific survey, based on a random sample rather than a self-selecting programme audience. The result was 'yes': 57 per cent, 'no': 35 per cent, and 'don't know': 8 per cent, almost an exact reversal of the BBC result. Order was restored.

Moments of Truth

The opening chapter of this book was entitled 'Moments of Untruth'. On 17 March 2003, as this final case study was being planned, the headlines of the UK and world press shrieked the words 'Moment of Truth', quoting unquestioningly the figurehead of the world's most powerful nation and military machine, G.W. Bush as he indicated that US/UK forces were about to start their assault on Iraq. His choice of words was a twenty-first century appropriation of 100 years of deceit, for this was an occasion possessing all the attributes of historic twentieth century 'moments of *un*truth', as traced throughout the preceding pages. The culmination of months of untruth and manipulation was being trumpeted across the world as a 'moment of truth'. 'Newspeak, doublespeak, the mutation of the past' (Orwell 1954:25), Orwell's Ministry of Truth would have been proud of this diametric inversion of meaning.

Why was this 'moment of truth' in fact a 'moment of untruth'? Following on from the other examples of effective hegemonic misleadership that have cumulated through this book, greedy and power-hungry economic, political and mass media elites are again seen to collaborate in manufacturing a *causus belli*, disguising their aggressive intent in a distorted Manichean morality tale. This deceit, they assumed rightly, would convince or confuse their media-besotted publics to the extent that most would ultimately accept the story and support or acquiesce in the action.

Rupert Murdoch's top selling UK daily, *The Sun*, part of his global News Corporation, was typical. For months, it had been building the credibility of the Bush/Blair case for attacking Iraq and embroidering on their stories of the Iraqi threat, its links with terrorism, its weapons of mass destruction, and the crimes of Saddam Hussein's diabolical regime. Similarly, it had been heaping opprobrium on the French, especially President Jacques Chirac, given his opposition to the Bush/Blair propaganda. On that day, 17 March, it gave, as usual, unqualified jingoistic support to its political friends. It knew as well as did the political leaders that this was no 'moment of truth', that is, no crucial moment of decision between war and peace. For one thing, the decision to invade Iraq had already been taken, and there was scarcely even an attempt to hide this by leaders or media. For another, the choice to name this particular moment the 'moment of truth' was arbitrary in terms of the threat posed by the country to be attacked. This was a case of the world's strongest military power picking and choosing the most strategically appropriate timing for its action and to declare that its patience was exhausted. The declared 'moment of truth' was thus already a double lie.

The lie that a diplomatic solution was still on the cards can be deduced from each of the seven full pages that *The Sun* devoted to the crisis that morning. On these seven pages, there are seven photographs of British soldiers carrying and aiming rifles. Page seven consists entirely of a cut-out photograph of a smiling soldier pointing his rifle at the reader against the background of the Union Jack, with the caption: '*The Sun* backs our boys', and the request to 'show your support for our troops by placing this poster in your window'. The photograph of Bush, Blair and Aznar at their Azores conference, supposedly making their last desperate bid for a peaceful solution, is surrounded by aggressive military images and the rhetoric of war.

The lie that a genuinely crucial point had been reached is wrapped up in the grave and bombastic vocabulary appropriate to the inflation of the moment into a dramatic climax. *The Sun*'s estimated ten million readers were treated to unquestioning support and admiration for Bush's hyperbole, designed to substitute for any genuine reason for immediate attack. Bush's words are quoted: 'The dictator of Iraq and his weapons of mass destruction are a threat to the security of the free world. He is a danger to his neighbours, he is a sponsor of terrorism and an obstacle to progress in the Middle East', but the irony that these words would be more appropriately applied to the man speaking them is missed. Meanwhile, *The Sun*'s editorial adds ponderously: 'Today is the moment of truth for the world, the day we determine if democracy can work. With those sombre words, President Bush began counting down to the first war of the twenty-first century'.

Any journalism with a claim to independence and to fulfilling the role of 'fourth estate' would be questioning Bush's soup of half-truth, empty assertion and distortion, and not trying to outdo him in mendacious pomposity. Had Murdoch's *Sun*, along with the rest of his news outlets, not been so intimately involved in Bush's brand of expansionist neo-conservatism, it would have pointed out that by 17 March, still no evidence of weapons of mass destruction (WMD) had been found; it would have made it clear that Iraq was a militarily and economically crippled country following the 1991 slaughter, subsequent sanctions and bombing; it might even have noted that the US's friend, Saudi Arabia, was, according to US intelligence, a far more serious source of terrorism, and that its other friend, Israel, was, by all accounts, a far larger obstacle to peace and progress in the region. *The Sun* could even have looked in on itself and asked whether the workings of democracy would be best served by genuinely independent and critical mass media, or whether they are deeply threatened by an unholy trinity of media, political and economic power elites. Such structurally inconceivable self-questioning could indeed lead to a 'moment of truth'.

Exposing the Ministry of Mendacity

Even if the mainstream media themselves are inherently incapable of carrying out radical questioning of themselves and their elite colleagues – the kind which goes beyond ephemeral personalities and issues – others are. The 18 months between September 2001 and March 2003 saw an upsurge of opposition and protest which announced the coming of age of a new resistance. To be sure, this did not halt or delay the juggernaut of discursive and military onslaught on Afghanistan and Iraq, or on the diffuse nightmares of 'terrorism' and the 'axis of evil'. It did, however, muster simultaneous massive demonstrations across the world on 15 February 2003, when at least 15 million citizens marched to express their deep opposition to the looming US-led attack on Iraq. This was unprecedented, and only one event in a longer and larger campaign.

Four factors contributed to this:

1. The crudity of US government positions on the 'war on terrorism' and 'anticipatory pre-emption' which led to deep divisions among international elites.
2. The reflection of these divisions in mainstream media output.
3. The volume and force of critical expression and analysis within the public sphere.
4. The internet.

When deep cracks in elite solidarity become evident (as opposed to the frequent superficial power squabbles, diversionary disputes, and jockeying for position among its members), the powerful undergo moments of relative weakness and vulnerability. On these quite rare occasions, normally hidden information seeps out through the fissures, and sometimes, dramatic measures, such as the sacrifice of a member of the higher echelons, are required to restore confidence and order.

The search for credible pretexts for invading Iraq was an example of elite failure to cover up real differences caused by arrogant US government posturing, and its failed bid to force other key countries into line behind its oil-stained bid for Middle East domination. The US propaganda pyramid, with Bush and Murdoch at its pinnacle, maintained adequate, though far from comprehensive, control of US public opinion, despite the resilient efforts of many thousands of activists, prominent figures ranging from ex-President Carter to Noam Chomsky and Michael Moore, and websites such as Z-Net. European publics were much more resistant. This was the case not only in countries like France and Germany, whose governments opposed the invasion of Iraq, but also in Spain and Italy, whose leaders offered support to the US government. In the UK, whose leadership provided dogged backing to the US position, the virtual media unanimity that had mustered substantial majorities behind the 1991 Gulf massacre, the 1999 Kosovo campaign and the 2002 Afghanistan bombardment showed significant cracks. A leading tabloid newspaper, the *Daily Mirror*, temporarily broke ranks, and the otherwise habitually fence-sitting broadsheet, *The Independent*, especially its Sunday editions, dared, at least some of the time, to live up to its name. Both of these papers on occasion went a step beyond the permitted mild dissent within the normal spectrum of consensus opinion, and the limited right of opposition afforded to licensed fools and court jesters that normally characterises mass media 'freedom' in pluralist democracies. This, combined with the largest parliamentary revolt within a ruling party for over a century, and ministerial resignations in the pre-invasion internal government splits, was cause for serious alarm in the highest places. Loyal ministers crowded the airwaves; the Prime Minister banked on his telegenic qualities and appeared before TV studio audiences to debate 'sincerely' and answer questions 'honestly'; MPs were subjected to heavy behind the scenes persuasion. The British government's immediate pre-war experience was a highly uncomfortable one, as Blair's hotly desired outcome, a second UN resolution, the figleaf which would provide international sanction for military action against Iraq and undermine internal opposition, collapsed in failure.

Once the invasion started, public support swung, with its usual reflex, behind the fighting forces. The *Daily Mirror* lost its nerve as its sales started to drop, and the feeling of a government in crisis was put on hold as blanket TV coverage of smoke-filled skylines, and all kinds of military activity except for the real business of killing, filled our screens. Many reporters were (physically and mentally) 'embedded' with US/UK fighting units, while others reported nervously from Baghdad hotel rooms. Still others, the most fortunate, just showed or repeated propaganda mouthed by military spokesmen behind the lines or at the no-expenses-spared Central Command media centre at As Sayliyah in Qatar, while, as one of them revealed, living at the six star Ritz-Carlton Hotel, which supplied a free buffet every afternoon and evening, complete with an open bar. No reporters were embedded with Iraqi families losing lives, limbs, homes and health to cluster bombs and depleted uranium shells.

However, imagination, compassion and the truth of war were, unusually, not entirely obliterated in the mainstream UK media. For example, articles by Robert Fisk appeared on the front page of *The Independent*. John Pilger was recalled to the *Daily Mirror*, and his work also appeared in *The Independent*. These were the two journalists in the forefront of opposition to this invasion, each with a lengthy record of war reporting and expertise in the region, and of investigative tenacity in uncovering the consequences of Western interventions there. Each was able, in the pre-invasion period, during the invasion, and into the post-invasion situation, to practise fourth estate journalism at its best, and to formulate radical critiques of US/UK government actions and their consequences. The number of critical column inches that they, and some others, had published in the mainstream press was tiny relative to the miles of sanitised reportage and belligerent comment which fitted within the pro-invasion government-media spectrum, but their visible presence did take a step beyond the habitual borders of repressive tolerance.

Two examples of this opposition discourse, published during the invasion within mainstream journalism will be recorded here as witness to the counter-currents which challenged the dominant newstoriography.

The first is Robert Fisk's report from Baghdad of 5 April 2003, published on *The Independent*'s website under the headline 'The Ministry of Mendacity Strikes Again'. A few days previously, a missile had exploded, causing dozens of casualties, in Shi'ala, one of the poorest quarters of Baghdad, populated by Shi'ite Moslems, oppressed by the Saddam Hussein regime, and its strongest internal opponents. These were precisely those whom the US/UK forces were purportedly liberating. The US/UK military were regularly bombarding Baghdad with intentionally 'awesome' intensity, whereas the Iraqi air force never got off the ground, and its missiles of this explosive power were, by all accounts, few and far between. Yet London's Ministry of Defence, indeed the Minister himself, Geoff Hoon, was insisting on the likelihood that it was an Iraqi missile which had caused the damage and the innocent civilian death and injury. It was an implausible claim, rendered incredible following Fisk's meeting with an old man who had found a piece of the fuselage of the missile stamped with a code which revealed that it had been made by Raytheon, the US Cruise missile manufacturers. Fisk reports: 'I collected five pieces myself, made of the same alloy, two of them dug out of the muck with my own hands'. Faced with this evidence, Hoon did not retract his story that it was an Iraqi missile, he implied instead that the pieces of Cruise missile fuselage had been planted at the site of the explosion by the Iraqi intelligence services to cover up the fact that it was their missile which caused it, and thus transfer the blame to the US. Fisk comments ironically:

> Poor old Geoff Hoon. It must be tough having to defend the indefensible when the Americans insist on plastering their missiles with computer codes that reveal their provenance even after they have blown the innocent to pieces [...]. Does the British Defence Secretary really think the Iraqi torturers have the ability to go about these hostile slums, burying obscure pieces of shrapnel for the likes of *The Independent* to dig up there?

He ends the article with this anecdote:

> I cannot help remembering an Iranian hospital train on which I travelled back from the Iran-Iraq war front in the early 1980s. The carriages were packed with young Iranian soldiers, coughing mucus and blood into handkerchiefs while reading Qr'ans. They had been gassed and looked as if they would die. Most did. [...]
>
> At the time I was working for *The Times*. My story ran in full. Then an official of the Foreign Office lunched my editor and told him my report was 'not helpful'. Because, of course, we supported President Saddam at the time and wanted revolutionary Iran to suffer and destroy itself. President Saddam was the good guy then. I wasn't supposed to report his human rights abuses. And now I'm not supposed to report the slaughter of the innocent by American or RAF pilots because the British government has changed sides.
>
> It's a tactic worthy of only one man I can think of, a master of playing victim when he is in the act of killing, a man who thinks nothing of smearing the innocent to propagate his own version of history. I'm talking about Saddam Hussein. Geoff Hoon has learnt a lot from him (www.independent.co.uk).

Such journalism, with its uncompromising contradiction of its own government's propaganda, its accusations of lying at ministerial level, and its final likening of the Minister to the leader of the enemy, is provocative in the extreme. Here is an investigative journalist literally unearthing evidence which points unequivocally to the fact that his government is deliberately covering up the truth and distracting the public with fabrications. Not only this, he is saying that this fits a pattern of deceit to which journalists are pressured to conform, whatever the contradictions and hypocrisies, and that this, if not resisted, leads to the propagation of an elite-controlled version of events and history, and an effective sabotaging of freedom of expression. It is self-evident that the publication of this article can be used as 'proof' that such practices are not taking place, and that is one good reason why Fisk and a few others can carry on publishing their material in a mainstream context. However, this kind of article normally only appears in a place where it passes relatively unnoticed, in the margins of the overwhelming conformist majority of mass media output.

The Independent has by some way the smallest circulation of all Britain's national dailies, and *The Independent on Sunday* occupies the same position in the weekend press. By Sunday 6 April 2003, it was virtually alone in its opposition to the attack on Iraq. It is from here that the second example is taken – an article by John Pilger, entitled: 'We see too much. We know too much. That's our best defence'. Pilger's vision is stark. The key conflict is now not between the 'coalition of the willing' and Iraq, nor is it the war on terrorism; it is between the government/economic/media elites as currently led by Bush and Blair, and the people of the world, among whom he counts 'journalists who see themselves as honourable truth-tellers' (*The Independent on Sunday* 6.4.03:25). Under precedents set at the 1946 Nuremberg Tribunal, he states, Tony Blair should stand trial at The Hague as a war criminal. The dominant mass media voices, he says later, are harmonised with the political leadership:

> Rupert Murdoch has been admirably frank. In lauding Bush and Blair as 'heroes', he said, 'there is going to be collateral damage in Iraq. And if you really want to be brutal about it, better we get it done now'. Every one of his 175 newspapers carries that sinister message, more or less, as does his American television network (ibid).

Thus Pilger perceives 'corrupt journalism' and 'successful propaganda', 'that consumes even our language' and 'writes the first draft of history' to be aligned against honest journalism and world publics:

> Since 11 September 2001, 'our' propaganda and its unspoken racism has required an imperial distortion of intellect and morality. The Iraqis are not fighting like lions, in defence of their homeland. They are 'cowardly' and subhuman because they use hit-and-run tactics against a hugely powerful invader – as if they have any choice. This belittling of their bravery and disregard of their humanity, like the disregard of thousands of Afghans recently bombed to death in dusty villages, confronts us with a moral issue as profound as the Western response to that greatest act of terrorism, the wilful atomic bombing of Japan. Have we progressed? In 2003, is it still true that only 'our' lives are of value? (ibid).

Pilger here points up the centrality of linguistic corruption to the construction of distorted newstoriography in the interests of Western power and domination over 'less valuable' parts of humanity, and indicates how this newstoriography is hardened into a historiography which in turn reflects back into a justification of present actions.

With regard to US-led 'war on terrorism' propaganda since 11 September 2001, however, Pilger discerns an increasing public scepticism. He quotes a *Time* magazine survey of a quarter of a million Europeans, in which 83 per cent see the USA as the country which poses the greatest threat to peace in 2003, as opposed to 8 per cent for Iraq and 9 per cent for North Korea. He believes that mass opposition to the invasion of Iraq influenced the way in which the military campaign was carried out:

> The killing of some 80 villagers near Baghdad last Thursday, of children in markets, of the 'chicks who get in the way', would be in industrial quantities now were it not for the voices of the millions who filled London and other capitals, and the young people who walked out of their schools; they have saved countless lives (ibid).

Although this statement is rhetorical (there is no evidence to prove or disprove it, not least because the number of short and long-term casualties of the invasion may never be known), it does reflect a revival of belief in mass citizen action, notably among the young, which had largely disappeared for most of the 1990s. To conclude his article, Pilger quotes approvingly Patrick Tyler of the *New York Times* who had a few days previously written that the new superpower confrontation was that between 'the Bush/Blair gang on the one side, and world opinion on the other' – a 'tenacious new adversary' and 'a truly popular force stirring at last and whose consciousness soars by the day' (ibid). This is undisguised manifesto language, designed to inspire, but it contains recognition of seeds whose real existence can be observed.

One such seed, which grew into a global grapevine, was the internet, a branch of which, by 2003, had burgeoned into a means of rapid worldwide organisation, and a major source of alternative information and analysis for the increasing numbers with access to it. This need not be exaggerated, since communications systems of previous generations had already permitted the co-ordination of mass international actions and the circulation of dissident debate (see Chapters 7 and 8). Yet the growth of instantaneous electronic messaging, and the popularity of a number of dynamic, radical and media-critical websites (again, a tiny frond within a tangled ecology of words and images) did provide an ease and speed of communication and real interactivity which was unprecedented. Whether or not it could have been done otherwise, e-mail became, *de facto*, the principal means of co-ordinating anti-war networks across the world. During the invasion of Iraq, the Baghdad blogger gained instantaneous global fame. US websites such as Truthout, and UK ones such as Media Lens gained substantial readerships for the kind of reportage and analysis which, apart from the significant few already referred to, could not be found in the mainstream mass media products.

For example, since coming on stream in Summer 2001, *Media Lens* (www.medialens.org) has been sending out regular Media Alerts, as well as establishing an archive of essays, book reviews and an interactive message board. Its Alert of 12 April 2003 takes this narrative forward in time to the immediate 'post-conflict' period, if one dutifully takes the manufactured media moment of victory declaration, the felling of the Saddam statue, as the 'official' end. Here, *Media Lens* writers David Edwards and David Cromwell, take a trenchant look at the jargon of war, and the way it separates words from meaning and people from their humanity. Certainly, the mainstream press had not entirely ignored the issue of war jargon. *The Guardian*, for example, ran an occasional series of columns entitled 'The Language of War. Decoding the Military Jargon' from 13 March onwards, through the period of US/UK seizure of Iraqi territory, and carried out some superficial analysis of misreporting in articles such as 'Facts, some Fiction and the Reporting of War' (*Guardian Media* 29.3.03). Such contributions did not, however, add up to a serious or coherent critique. The 'decoding' merely provided explanations of newly coined or appropriated terms such as 'embedding', 'supply nodes' or 'blue on blue' and contained only anodyne criticism of military euphemism. The reporting as fact of untrue and unverified propaganda stories was admitted, but not condemned as lying, rather explained away as 'premature' and a consequence of the 'rapidly changing environment' (ibid).

Media Lens, by contrast, understood the deeper cultural impact of misreporting and discursive corruption:

> It's Cartoon Time on ITN's Evening News. From a computer-generated street in Baghdad, a radiating signal from US 'Special Forces' attracts a cartoon Rockwell B-1B 'Lancer' bomber circling 'on call', like a doctor, overhead. Viewers could have been told simply that a bomber dropped four large bombs on the target, but ITN was kind enough to supply a few extra details: 'The B-1 drops four 2,000-pound, satellite-guided, JDAM "bunker-busting" bombs' (ITN, 8 April 2003).
>
> It's a sentence to enjoy – as with all fetishism, arousal is achieved through obsession with suggestive detail. We see the bombs arc down towards a computer-generated restaurant in the Mansour district of Baghdad. A couple of animated explosions flash on the building, which vanishes. There were no little cartoon people walking in the street, none sitting in the restaurant before the blast, and there are no cartoon dismembered limbs now. *The Guardian* quoted the version of reality of the pilot who dropped the real bombs: 'I didn't know who was there. I really didn't care. We've got ten minutes to get the bombs on target. We've got ten minutes to do it. We've got to make a lot of things happen to make that happen. So you just fall totally into execute mode and kill the target' (Julian Borger and Stuart Millar: '2pm: Saddam is spotted. 2-48: Pilots get their orders. 3pm: 60 foot crater at target' (*The Guardian* 9 April 2003).
>
> 'Special Forces', 'B-1 Lancers', 'JDAM Bombs', 'on-call' aircraft, 'execute mode', 'kill the target': this is jargon fetishising the manipulation of massive power over people and things. Phrasal verbs are used to the same effect: 'take out', 'take down', 'go after', 'blow away' all suggest immediate, decisive, all-powerful action.
>
> We have been made receptive to this worship of power by a hundred thousand Hollywood sermons. According to a study by the Glasgow Media Group, children can recall large sections of dialogue from the crime film *Pulp Fiction*: 'Many youngsters regard it as cool to blow people away', Greg Philo reports (*The Observer* 26.10.97). Young people regard the two hit-men in the film, Vincent and Jules, as the 'coolest' characters. A viewer explains why: 'Vincent was cool because he's not scared. He can go around shooting people without being worried'.
>
> After all, if power is possession of massive force, then ultimate power is the deployment of massive force with minimal effort and minimal emotion. This is what 'cool' means in our society; massive impact, no bother: 'So you just fall totally into execute mode and kill the target' (*Media Lens* Alerts 12.4.03).

The passage provides its own commentary, but it is quoted here as an exemplary demonstration that the world wide web has, among its multifarious other roles, become a significant space for alternative journalism, radical media-critical thought, and a source of non-mainstream cultural and political analysis in the post-11 September world. It is a new contributory phenomenon whose impact has yet to be evaluated.

In the current narrative, this concluding *Media Lens* extract can only be seen as a remarkable, but unwitting reprise of the Krausian cultural critique (see Chapters 3 and 4) and reformulation of his challenge, as relevant now as it was a century ago. The deadening of the imagination via the press that Kraus diagnosed as making possible the 1914-18 war here re-emerges in 2003 as the loss of compassion invoked by products of popular media culture. This leads to the possibility that not just pilots, but majority mass media publics are mesmerised into a virtual 'execute mode', unable to see the human truth behind the jargon and the sanitised computer graphics.

In the pre-invasion build-up, and during the military walk-over, it is true that more citizens than usual questioned and saw through mainstream government/media discourse, but they were still not powerful enough to upturn the massive propaganda exercise, the home-front version of the euphemistically named 'battle for hearts and minds'. Whatever small and unusable residue of WMD the Iraqi forces might have possessed, it really *did* happen that they never came near trying to use them. Rather, the world's greatest possessor and user of such weapons really *was* able to focus on the puny, putative Iraqi threat from them, and transform them into a justification for an invasion in which it did not itself hesitate to use a recognised and horrific WMD – depleted uranium. The word 'coalition' *was* really adopted to dignify the gang of invaders who were opposed in their action by the vast majority of the rest of the world. The claims of the 'success' of earlier maulings of almost defenceless countries, Serbia/Kosovo and Afghanistan, which served as oblique justifications for *this* adventure *were* made, and *did* remain unchallenged in the mainstream media. Images of rifles inscribed by their users with the phrase 'Killer Angels' passed rapidly without the shock of understanding the phrase or the mentality which could make use of it in that way. How many noticed the depth of inhumanity involved in the naming of Tomohawk missiles? What kind of twisted mockery did it take for the perpetrators of an earlier genocide to name their new military mass murder toy by stealing the word for an iconic cultural symbol of their victims? It has to be admitted that, despite a remarkable level of articulate opposition, the propaganda achieved its immediate aims.

Conclusion

What has emerged from this account is a picture of overall continuing hegemonic control, confronted nevertheless by a mass opposition which failed in its main objectives in 2002 and 2003, but which arguably had a greater impact on elite supremacy than the elite would readily admit in public. The 3,000 deaths in New York's Twin Towers have so far been avenged by at least ten times as many innocent victims in Afghanistan and Iraq, as the US government implements the 11 September tragedy to construct its twin murderous discourse towers, those of the 'war on terrorism' and 'anticipatory pre-emption', to distract an international media-consuming public from its global ambitions. The victors have named the 2003 invasion the 'Battle of Iraq', just one skirmish in the longer war against the 'axis of evil'. One may foresee more fighting, more propaganda, and more threatening, anti-democratic measures to quell internal opposition. Entwined media, government and economic elites will continue to wish to make history in their own interests and image, and will correspondingly manipulate and attempt to control publics with a judicious mix of friendly and unfriendly coercion. The nightmare that they wish to avoid at all costs is a massive, alert, media-wise alliance of articulate citizens who have seen through the genealogy of untruth that, as this book has demonstrated, has held sway since the beginning of the media age.

Chapter 13

Conclusion -
For an Active Audience

The sun had shifted round, and the myriad windows of the Ministry of Truth, with the light no longer shining on them, looked grim as the loopholes of a fortress. His heart quailed before the enormous pyramidal shape. It was too strong, it could not be stormed. A thousand rocket bombs would not batter it down. He wondered again for whom he was writing the diary. For the future, for the past – for an age that might be imaginary. And in front of him there lay not death but annihilation. The diary would be reduced to ashes and himself to vapour. Only the Thought Police would read what he had written, before they wiped it out of existence and out of memory. How could you make appeal to the future when not a trace of you, not even an anonymous word scribbled on a piece of paper, could physically survive? (George Orwell 1954).

Orwell's nightmare is the people's nightmare. It portrays a world where lies are truth, war is peace, and there is no prospect of reversing this oxymoronic upturning of word and meaning, since the powers controlling and distorting thought are invincible, the methods they use are, to most, invisible or too risky to contemplate.

The nightmare will prevail as long as there is no more powerful dream to counteract it, and envisaging such a dream as a real, liveable, eventually attractive process takes us to the point where critical analysis and diagnosis evolve into signposts for socio-cultural change and emancipatory activity. Radical criticism always, and rightly, provokes the challenge: 'What would you *do* about the mass media? What robust and realistic practices would you wish to see adopted to replace the present ones which you are rejecting?' Answers are far from fully developed, but start to run as follows.

Processes of change should advance in two areas:

1. Development of much greater critical and imaginative mass media wisdom among publics, linked to democratic citizens' activism within a re-defined public sphere.
2. Restructuring of the mass media to ensure genuine democratic plurality, incorporating world perspectives and priorities in the peoples' interests within a non-commercial, humanist discursive spectrum and a participatory ethos.

Both are far enough from current feasibility and fulfilment to appear utopian, but they would need to be progressed if twenty-first century humans wished to learn from and avert the tragic mistakes of their twentieth century predecessors.

Rather than lapse into impotent exhortations, I sketch out here a scenario which portrays critical and imaginative media-wise citizens of a coming generation whose media reception interacts with some public sphere activity, and who inhabit a world culture network in which, following successful struggles for social and legal media reforms, de-marketised and democratically restructured mass media are coming into operation. The scenario assumes a not too distant future in which many current socio-economic structures remain in place.

In line with the focus of the preceding case study, this story imagines a national government, backed by its military and pressurised by multinational arms manufacturers and other interested industrialists, which wishes to join its allies in a 'limited military action' to defend what it describes as 'essential national and international stability', and to 'fulfil its moral obligations' to lay low the 'evil' regime of a strategically placed, but still developing and resource-rich country which is failing to conform to the economic interests of the main advanced industrial powers.

The newly restructured, autonomous, democratically regulated mass media with their constitutionally defined rights and duties carry the government announcement, but they eschew nationalism, carry in full any counter-announcement from the other side of the conflict, set up thorough independent critical analysis of the history and context of the affair, and of both sides' activities and self-justifications leading to the current impasse. Taking views in a balanced fashion from both sides, as well as from neutral sources, the international community and the (democratically reconstituted) United Nations, they look at the rationale *for* turning to the last resort of violence, and look at the rationale *against* it. They probe into further diplomatic possibilities of mediation and compromise, involving impartial supranational conciliation. They show realistically what the foreseeable human and political consequences of fighting or not fighting would be, using unsanitised documentary material and testimonies from individual military and civilian citizens caught up in previous comparable wars and their consequences. Realistic best case and worst case scenarios for the post-war situation on both sides are debated with contribution from international aid and humanitarian agencies, and impartial lawyers, diplomats and reconstruction experts. This initial phase of information and contextualisation is carried through pluralistically by the range of broadcast, electronic and print outlets, in which comment and opinion are, via an enforceable code of practice, kept scrupulously distinct from news and information, and in which any special interests and political or commercial allegiances are prominently declared. A media-wise public will know that while the old commercial media invariably profited from wars, and the old public service corporations remained close to establishment orthodoxy, the new democratised media do neither of these things.

This is followed by broadcast parliamentary debate and a range of public sphere activities. A restructured democratic public sphere provides space for genuinely interactive broadcast media debates which, in response to public interest, take over peak viewing spots prior to moments of major decision making. It enables internet discussions, electronic, and face-to-face consultations with a broad range of experts and elected representatives. It encourages public meetings in work places, schools, universities, churches, pubs and other venues. It gives rise to public actions, and conferencing between citizens of participants in the conflict from all sides which could lead to joint actions from below to demonstrate views on the proposed violence.

In continuing media coverage, feedback from the public plays a prominent role; the use or encouragement of stereotypes, enemy images, xenophobia and racism is out of order in primary information sources as in debate. In reaction to all this, media-wise citizens and media-watch groups are constantly critically alert to the visual and verbal discourses of media output, seeking out and drawing the attention of others to abuses, distortions, contradictions and lapses from agreed requisite standards, while using statutory channels to exact immediate and prominent apologies and corrections from the offending source.

Active citizens form opinions and express, modify or change them in the light of public discussions. Where it emerges that human or civil rights abuses are occurring to fellow citizens on either side of the conflict, then joint citizens' campaigns are organised internationally to bring pressure to end them. The views of UN-approved international humanitarian organisations are given more attention than government spokespersons on either side of the conflict. Joint international action at institutional level (short of war) is urged and undertaken.

For immensely important life and death decisions, as in this scenario, such a public discussion process is more thorough and complex than on less portentous occasions, with a full range of alternative courses of action, and their consequences, taken into consideration. In this case, one can, using the example of the UK system, envisage key decisions being made after constituency meetings, in which citizens indicated the way they wished their Member of Parliament to contribute to and vote in a free parliamentary debate. One could also consider eventual use of an electronic referendum. Any government would have to have only the most pressing of subsequent strategic or constitutional reasons to change democratic decisions within a clearly defined legal framework, and such reasons would have to be submitted to full public scrutiny.

In the (unlikely) event of a decision to resort to violence resulting from such a process, following a failure of international mediation, and with Reformed United Nations approval, it would be made in full public awareness that it carried with it the renunciation of certain civil rights for the length of the military action, given the need for secrecy and rapid decision making in war. Yet the limits of such renunciation would also need to be defined and enforceable for governments, military commanders, media and public. During a war, autonomous media would broadcast clearly labelled official views from both sides, as well as uncensored, self-engendered reports and images from the scene of hostilities, always indicating without prejudice the source of the material. The war story would be told from the perspective of its victims, and those on all sides who found themselves on the receiving end of military action. Discourses encouraging hatred or dehumanisation of the opposing side would continue to be illegal. Specific war aims would be kept in the forefront of information distribution, and publicly established military codes of action operated, for which military citizens would be publicly answerable. Civilian public sphere activity during hostilities would involve continuing monitoring of media output, contributions to analysis and public debate, and participation in demonstrations. Via websites and e-mail, if in operation, the gathering and distribution of on-the-spot alternative information and reactions would occur, building, where possible, human contacts, understanding and solidarity across the battle lines, contributing to a minimisation of the length and intensity of killing and destruction, and to a less traumatic post-war recovery and conciliation process. There would never be any doubt that the resort to war, whatever the outcome, was the result of the *failure* of the governments concerned.

This brief scenario is sketchy and gives rise to countless questions. It involves a major retreat of the mass media from their current exercise of power over newstoriography and passivication, with a corresponding advance of citizen activity, and democratic as opposed to elite control of the discourses of information and public debate. This is unimaginable to those still caught under the spell of elite dominance of mass media structures and language. Let it be compared, however, with the chain of abuses described in the preceding case studies, and indeed with the many other twentieth century conflicts which have gone unmentioned here.

At several points in this narrative, there have been included quotations to the effect that if people really imagined and knew the realities of war, they would reject it, and it has been pointed out that, in the twentieth and early twenty-first centuries, it was the mass media and their discourses which played the key role in destroying imagination, distorting language and knowledge, and thereby reducing publics to passivity and conformism in such a way as to render war, barbarism, and insane armament and mass destruction normal and acceptable. Ultimately, despite the large volume of circumstantial evidence, the full testing of such views remains incomplete until such time as the models of activity, based on untruth, which dominated the twentieth and early twenty-first centuries are abandoned, and their utopian converse is imagined, formulated and attempted. Such would be a major part of a positive citizens' globalisation and a context in which, finally, war could become the first casualty of truth.

To progress, we must first, following Brecht, understand the concrete answer to the question: 'Why is this utopian?' That was the point of this book.

Bibliography

Achbar, M. (ed.) (1994) *Manufacturing Consent. Noam Chomsky and the Media*, Montreal, Black Rose Books.

Adorno, T. (1963) 'Resumé über Kulturindustrie', in *Ohne Leitbild. Parva Aesthetica*, Frankfurt.

Adorno, T. (1991) *The Culture Industry: Selected Essays on Mass Culture*, London, Routledge.

Adorno, T. & Horkheimer, M. (1972) 'The Culture Industry: Enlightenment as Mass Deception', in *The Dialectic of Enlightenment*, New York, Herder and Herder.

Althusser, L. (1984) 'Ideology and Ideological State Apparatuses', in *Essays on Ideology*, London, Verso.

Anders, G. (1987) 'Die Welt als Phantom und Matrize. Philosophische Betrachtungen über Rundfunk und Fernsehen' in *Die Antiquiertheit des Menschen. Über die Seele im Zeitalter der zweiten industriellen Revolution*, vol.1, Munich.

Ang, I. (1991) *Desparately Seeking the Audience*, London, Routledge.

Ang, I. (1996) *Living Room Wars: Rethinking Audiences for a Postmodern World*, London, Routledge.

Ash, T. (1989) *The Uses of Adversity. Essays on the Fate of Central Europe*, Cambridge, Granta.

Ash, T. (1990) *We, The People. The Revolutions of '89. Witnessed in Warsaw, Budapest, Berlin & Prague*, Cambridge, Granta.

Ash, T. (1993) *In Europe's Name. Germany and the Divided Continent*, London, Jonathan Cape.

Augstein, R. & Grass, G. (1990) *Deutschland, einig Vaterland? Ein Streitgespräch*, Göttingen, Steidl.

Barbero, J. M. (1993) *Communication, Culture and Hegemony. From the Media to Mediations*, London, Sage.

Barsky, R. (1997) *Noam Chomsky. A Life of Dissent*, Cambridge Massachusetts, MIT Press.

Barthes, R. (1973) *Mythologies*, London, Paladin.

Bell, A. (1991) *The Language of News Media*, London, Blackwell.

Bell, A. & Garrett, P. (eds.) (1998) *Approaches to Media Discourse*, London, Blackwell.

Benjamin, W. (1969) *Über Literatur*, Frankfurt, Suhrkamp.

Berry, D. (ed.) (2000) *Ethics and Media Culture. Practices and Representations*, Oxford, Focal Press.

Betz, F. (1994) *Das Schweigen des Karl Kraus. Paradoxien des Medienalltags*, Pfaffenweiler, Centaurus-Verlagsgesellschaft.

Biermann, W. (1973) *Warte Nicht auf Bessre Zeiten*, Frankfurt, CBS.

Billig, M. (1995) *Banal Nationalism*, London, Sage.

Bourdieu, P. (1991) *Language and Symbolic Power*, Cambridge, Polity.

Bourdieu, P. (1996) *Sur la télévision*, Paris, Liber-Raisons d'Agir. Translation: (1998a) *On Television and Journalism*, London, Pluto.

Bourdieu, P. (1998b) *Contre-feux*, Paris, Liber-Raisons d'Agir. Translation: (1998b) *Acts of Resistance*, Cambridge, Polity.

Bourdieu, P. (2001) *Contre-feux 2*, Paris, Liber-Raisons d'Agir.

Bouveresse, J. (2001) *Schmock ou le Triomphe du Journalisme. La Grande Bataille de Karl Kraus*, Paris, Collection 'Liber', Editions du Seuil.

Bowman, D. (1988) *The Captive Press*, Sydney, Penguin.

Brandt, W. (1989) *Erinnerungen*, Frankfurt, Propyläen.

Brecht, B. (1967) 'Der Rundfunk als Kommunikationsapparat' ('Speech on the Function of Radio') *Gesammelte Schriften 18*, Frankfurt/M. Also in: Pias *et al.* (1999).

Briggs, R. (1982) *When the Wind Blows*, London, Hamish Hamilton.

Bücher, K. (1906) 'Das Zeitungswesen', in: Hinneberg (1906).

Bücher, K. (1915/1917) *Die Deutsche Tagespresse und die Kritik*, Tübingen.

Cahnmann, W. (1973) *Ferdinand Tönnies. A New Evaluation. Essays and Documents*, Leiden, E.J. Brill.

Cahnmann, W. & Heberle, R. (eds) (1971) *Ferdinand Tönnies on Sociology*, Chicago, University of Chicago Press.

Carruthers, S. (2000) *The Media at War. Communication and Conflict in the Twentieth Century*, Basingstoke, Macmillan.

Castells, M. (1996) *The Rise of the Network Society. The Information Age: Economy, Society and Culture. Volume 1*, Oxford, Blackwell.

Castells, M. (1997) *The Power of Identity. The Information Age: Economy, Society and Culture. Volume 2*, Oxford, Blackwell.

Castells, M. (1998) *End of Millennium. The Information Age: Economy, Society and Culture*, Oxford, Blackwell.

Caute, D. (1988) *Sixty-Eight. The Year of the Barricades*, London, Paladin Grafton Books.

Chomsky, N. (1969) *American Power and the New Mandarins*, Harmandsworth, Penguin.

Chomsky, N. (1971) *At War with Asia*, London, Fontana/Collins.

Chomsky, N. (1989) *Necessary Illusions. Thought Control in Democratic Societies*, London, Pluto.

Chomsky, N. (1991a) *Deterring Democracy*, London, Vintage.

Chomsky, N. (1991b) *Media Control. The Spectacular Achievements of Propaganda*, New York, Seven Stories Press.

Chomsky, N. (1994) *World Orders, Old and New*, London, Pluto.

Chomsky, N. (1996a) *Class Warfare. Interviews with David Barsamian*, London, Pluto.

Chomsky N. (1996b) *Powers and Prospects. Reflections on Human Nature and the Social Order*, London, Pluto.

Chomsky, N. (1999a) *The New Military Humanism. Lessons from Kosovo*, London, Pluto.

Chomsky, N. (1999b) *Profit over People. Neoliberalism and Global Order*, New York, Seven Stories Press.

Chomsky, N. (2001) *9-11*, New York, Seven Stories Press.

Crowley, T. (1996) *Language in History. Theories and Texts*, London, Routledge.

Curran, J. (2002) *Media and Power*, London, Routledge.

Curran, J. & Seaton, J. (1991) *Power without Responsibility. The Press and Broadcasting in Britain*, London, Routledge.

Curtis, M. (2003) *Web of Deceit. Britain's Real Role in the World*, London, Vintage.

Dahl, H. (1998) *The Uses of Media History*, Keynote Address at 'Media History?' Conference, London, University of Westminster.

Dawes, J. (2002) *The Language of War*, Boston, Harvard University Press.

Debord, G. (1967) *La société du spectacle*, Paris. Translation: (1977) *Society of the Spectacle*, Detroit, Blach and Med.

Debord, G. (1990) *Comments on the Society of the Spectacle*, London, Verso.

Dennis, M. (ed.) (1987-88) *The GDR Approaches the 1990s. The View from Britain*, East Central Europe, vols 14-15, Bakersfield CA, California State University.

Eldridge, J. (ed.) (1993) *Getting the Message. Essays from Glasgow University Media Group*, London, Routledge.

Eldridge, J., Kitzinger, J. & Williams, K. (1997) *The Mass Media and Power in Modern Britain*, Oxford, Oxford University Press.

END Journal (1982-1989) Issues 1-37, London, END.

Enzensberger, H.M. (1970) 'Baukasten zu einer Theorie der Medien'. In *Palaver. Politische Überlegungen 1967-73.* Frankfurt/M. Published in *New Left Review* 12/70 as 'Constituents of a Theory of the Media'. Also in Pias *et al.* (1999)

Fairclough, N. (1989) *Language and Power*, Harlow, Longman.

Fairclough, N. (1992) *Discourse and Social Change*, Cambridge, Polity.

Fairclough, N. (1995a) *Media Discourse*, London, Edward Arnold.

Fairclough, N. (1995b) *Critical Discourse Analysis*, Harlow, Longman.

Fairclough, N. (2000) *Language and New Capitalism*, at: www.uol.es/humfil/nlc/LNC-ENG//nc-eng.html.

Federal Ministry for Intra-German Relations (1981) *Facts and Figures. A Comparative Survey of the Federal Republic of Germany and the German Democratic Republic*, Bonn, Bonner Universitäts-Buchdruckerei.

Foucault, M. (1971) *L'ordre du discours.* Paris. Gallimard. See Schapiro, M. (1982) for translation).

Foucault, M. (1980) *Power/Knowledge. Selected Interviews and Other Writings 1972-1977*, New York, Pantheon.

Fowler, R. (1991) *Language in the News. Discourse and Ideology in the Press*, London, Routledge.

Franklin, B. (1997) *Newszak and News Media*, London, Arnold.

Freire, P. (1972) *Cultural Action for Freedom*, Harmondsworth, Penguin.

Freire, P. (1972) *Pedagogy of the Oppressed*, Harmondsworth, Penguin.

Garnham, N. (1994) *Capitalism and Communication. Global Culture and the Economics of Information*, London, Sage.

Glasgow University Media Group (1976) *Bad News*, London, Routledge and Kegan Paul.

Glasgow University Media Group (1980) *More Bad News*, London, Routledge and Kegan Paul.

Glasgow University Media Group (1985) *War and Peace News*, Milton Keynes, Open University Press.

Golding, P. & Murdock, G. (1991) 'Culture, Communication, and Political Economy'. In J. Curran & M.Gurevitch (eds.) *Mass Media and Society*, London, Edward Arnold.

Golding, P., Murdock, G. & Schlesinger, P. (1986) *Communicating Politics. Mass Communications and the Political Process*, Leicester, Leicester University Press.

Gollin, G. & Gollin, A. (1973) 'Tönnies and Public Opinion', in Cahnmann (1973).

Gorbachev, M. (1987) *Perestroika*, London.

Gorbachev, M. (1999) *On My Country and the World*, New York, Columbia University Press.

Gramsci, A. (1971) *Selections from Prison Notebooks*, London, Lawrence and Wishart.

Grass, G. (1990) *Two States – One Nation. The Case against German Reunification*, London, Secker and Warburg.

Grass, G. (1992) *Rede vom Verlust. Über den Niedergang der politischen Kultur im geeinten Deutschland*, Göttingen, Steidl.

Grass, G. (1993) *Ein Schnäppchen namens DDR. Letzte Reden vorm Glockengeläut*, Munich, DTV.

Grosswiler, P. (1998) *Method is the Message. Rethinking McLuhan through Critical Theory*, Montreal, Black Rose Books.

Habermas, J. (1989) *The Structural Transformation of the Public Sphere*, Cambridge Massachusetts, MIT Press. German original (1962) *Strukturwandel der Öffentlichkeit.*

Habermas, J. (1998) *A Berlin Republic. Writings on Germany*, Cambridge, Polity.

Hahn, H. (ed.) (1995) *Germany in the 1990s*, Amsterdam, Rodopi/German Monitor.

Hall, S. (1972) *External Influences on Broadcasting: Television's Double Bind*, Birmingham, CCCS Occasional Paper 1.

Hall, S. (1980) Encoding/Decoding. In Hall, S. et al. *Culture, Media, Language*, London, Hutchinson.

Hartmann, F. (2000) *Medienphilosophie*, Vienna, WUV-Universitätsverlag.

Hergé (1930/1981/1988/2000) *Tintin au Pays des Soviets*, Paris, Casterman. (English Translation (1989) *Tintin in the Land of the Soviets.*)

Herman, E. (1992) *Beyond Hypocrisy. Decoding the News in an Age of Propaganda*, Boston, South End Press.

Herman, E. (1996) 'The Propaganda Model Revisited', in *Monthly Review*, July 1996.

Herman, E. (1999) *The Myth of the Liberal Media*, Frankfurt, Peter Lang.

Herman, E. & Chomsky, N. (1988) *Manufacturing Consent. The Political Economy of the Mass Media*, London, Vintage.

Herman, E. & McChesney, R. (1997) *The Global Media. The New Missionaries of Corporate Capitalism*, London, Cassell.

Hinneberg, P. (ed.) (1906) *Die Kultur der Gegenwart. Ihre Entwicklung und ihre Ziele*, Leipzig.

Hirsch, R. & Kopelev, L. (eds.) (1989) *Grenzfall. Vollständiger Nachdruck aller in der DDR erschienen Ausgaben (1986-87) Erstes Unabhängiges Periodikum*, Berlin.

Hobsbawm, E. (1994) *Age of Extremes. The Short Twentieth Century 1914-1991*, London, Michael Joseph.

Hofmann, M. (1991) 'The Unity Train.' In Nowell-Smith, G. & Wollen, T. (1991).

Horkheimer, M. (1955) *Die Soziologie der Gegenwart* (Radio Talk/Typescript), Vienna, Wiener Rundfunk.

Jackall, R. (ed.) (1995) *Propaganda*, Basingstoke, Macmillan.

Jenkins, R. (1992) *Pierre Bourdieu*, London, Routledge.

Kellner, D. (1995) *Media Culture. Cultural Studies, Identity and Politics between the Modern and the Postmodern*, London, Routledge.

Konrád, G. (1984) *Antipolitics*, London, Quartet Books.

Kraus, K. (1899) *Die Fackel, 5*, Vienna, Verlag 'Die Fackel'.

Kraus, K. (1905) *Die Fackel, 167*, Vienna, Verlag 'Die Fackel'.

Kraus, K. (1914) *Die Fackel, 404*, Vienna, Verlag 'Die Fackel'.

Kraus, K. (1918a) *Die letzte Nacht. Epilog zu der Tragödie: DieLetzten Tage der Menschheit*, Vienna, Verlag 'Die Fackel'.

Kraus, K. (1918b) *Die Fackel, 484-98*, Vienna, Verlag 'Die Fackel'.

Kraus, K. (1919/1926) *Die Letzten Tage der Menschheit*, Vienna, Verlag 'Die Fackel'. Also (1957) Munich, Kösel Verlag (1926 version).

Kraus, K. (1923) *Die Fackel, 632-639*, Vienna, Verlag 'Die Fackel'.

Kraus, K. (1925) *Die Fackel, 706-711*, Vienna, Verlag 'Die Fackel'.

Kraus, K. (1926) *Die Fackel, 712-716*, Vienna, Verlag 'Die Fackel'.

Kraus, K. (1928a) *Die Fackel, 781-786*, Vienna, Verlag 'Die Fackel'.

Kraus, K. (1928b) *Die Fackel, 777*, Vienna, Verlag 'Die Fackel'.

Kraus, K. (1929) *Die Fackel, 800-805*, Vienna, Verlag 'Die Fackel'.

Kraus, K. (1933) *Die Fackel, 888*, Vienna, Verlag 'Die Fackel'.

Kraus, K. (1934) *Die Fackel, 890-905 'Warum Die Fackel nicht erscheint'*, Vienna, Verlag 'Die Fackel'.

Kraus, K. (1952) *Die Dritte Walpurgisnacht*, Munich, Kösel Verlag.

Kraus, K. (1967) *Dramen. Werke, Band 14*, Munich, Albert Langen, Georg Müller.

Lakoff, R.T. (2001) *The Language War*, California, University of California Press.

Lassalle, F. (1874) *Die Feste, die Presse und der Frankfurter Abgeordnetentag. Drei Symptome des öffentlichen Geistes*, Berlin. See also Stremmel (1982).

Le Bon, G. (1895) *Psychologie des Foules*, Paris, Alcan.

Lippmann, W. (1922) *Public Opinion*, New York, Harcourt Brace.

Livingston, R. & Sander, V. (eds.) (1993) *The Future of German Democracy*, New York, Continuum.

Loyd, A. (2000) *My War Gone By, I Miss it So*, London, Anchor.

Marchand P. (1989) *Marshall McLuhan. The Medium and the Messenger*, Cambridge, MIT Press.

Marcuse, H. (1964) *One Dimensional Man*, London, Routledge and Kegan Paul.

Marx, K. (1959) *Selected Writings in Sociology and Social Philosophy*, ed. T. Bottomore and M. Rubel, London, Watts.

Mattelart, A. (1994) *Mapping World Communication. War, Progress, Culture*, Minneapolis, University of Minnesota Press.

Mattelart, A. (1996) *The Invention of Communication*, Minneapolis, University of Minnesota Press.

Mattelart, A. & Mattelart, M. (1995) *Histoire des théories de la communication*, Paris, Editions La Découverte. Translation (1998) *Theories of Communication. A Short Introduction*, London, Sage.

McChesney, R. (1997) *Corporate Media and the Threat to Democracy*, New York, Seven Stories Press.

McChesney, R. (2000) *Rich Media, Poor Democracy. Communication Politics in Dubious Times*, New York, New Press.

McChesney, R. & Nichols. J. (2002) *Our Media, Not Theirs*, New York, Seven Stories Press.

McLuhan, M. (1951) *The Mechanical Bride. Folklore of Industrial Man*, New York, Vanguard Press.

McLuhan, M. (1962) *The Gutenberg Galaxy. The Making of Typographic Man*, London, Routledge and Kegan Paul.

McLuhan, M. (1994) *Understanding Media. The Extensions of Man*. London, Routledge.

McLuhan, M. & Fiore, Q. (1967) *The Medium is the Message*, Harmondsworth, Penguin.

Miller, D. et al. (1998) *The Circuit of Mass Communication*, London, Sage.

Morley, D. (1988) *Family Television: Cultural Power and Domestic Leisure*, London, Routledge.

Morley, D. (1992) *Television, Audiences and Cultural Studies*, London, Routledge.

Morley, D. & Robins, K. (1995) *Spaces of Identity. Global Media, Electronic Landscapes and Cultural Boundaries*, London, Routledge.

Murdock, G. (1990) 'Redrawing the Map of the Communication Industries'. In: M. Ferguson (ed.) *Public Communication*, London, Sage.

Noelle-Neumann, E. (1984) *The Spiral of Silence*, Chicago, University of Chicago Press.

Nowell-Smith, G. & Wollen, T. (eds.) (1991) *After the Wall*, London, BFI.

Openshaw, S., Steadman, P. & Greene, O. (1983) *Doomsday. Britain after Nuclear Attack*, Blackwell, Oxford.

Orwell, G. (1946) 'Politics and the English Language', in *Shooting an Elephant and Other Essays*, New York, Harcourt, Brace and Company. Reprinted in Jackall (1995).

Orwell, G. (1954) *Nineteen Eighty-Four*, Harmondsworth, Penguin.

Park, R. (1972) *The Crowd and the Public*, Chicago, University of Chicago Press. (His doctoral thesis (1904) *Masse und Publikum*).

Peck, J. (ed.) (1988) *The Chomsky Reader*, London, Serpent's Tail.

Pfabigan, A. (1976) *Karl Kraus und der Sozialismus*, Vienna, Europaverlag.

Philo, G. (1990) *Seeing and Believing*, London, Routledge.
Philo, G. (ed.) (1999) *Message Received. Glasgow Media Group Research 1993-1998*, Harlow, Longman.
Philo, G. & Miller, D. (1998) *Cultural Compliance*, Glasgow, Glasgow Media Group.
Pias, C., Vogl, J., Engell, L., Fahle, O. & Neitzel, B. (eds.) (1999) *Kursbuch Medienkultur. Die maßgeblichen Theorien von Brecht bis Baudrillard*, Stuttgart, Deutsche Verlags-Anstalt.
Pilger, J. (1992) *Distant Voices*, London, Vintage.
Pilger, J. (1998) *Hidden Agendas*, London, Vintage.
Pilger, J. (2002) *The New Rulers of the World*, London, Verso.
Postman, N. (1985) *Amusing Ourselves to Death. Public Discourse in the Age of Show Business*, London, Heinemann.
Rai, M. (1995) *Chomsky's Politics*, London, Verso.
Rai, M. (2002) *War Plan Iraq. Ten Reasons Against War on Iraq*, London, Verso.
Rassak, J. (1927) *Psychologie de l'Opinion et de la Propagande Politique*, Paris, Librairie des sciences politiques et sociales, Marcel Rivière.
Reagan, R. (1981) *Papers of the Presidency*, Washington DC.
Reagan, R. (1984) *Papers of the Presidency*, Washington DC.
Richardson, K. & Meinhof, U. (1999) *Worlds in Common? Television Discourse in a Changing Europe*, London, Routledge.
Russell, B. (1961) *Has Man a Future?*, Harmondsworth, Penguin.
Said, E. (1996) *Covering Islam. How the Media and Experts Determine How We See the Rest of the World*, London, Vintage.
Shapiro, M. (ed.) (1982) *Language and Politics*, Oxford, Blackwell.
Schlesinger, P. (1987) *Putting 'Reality' Together: BBC News*, London, Methuen.
Schlesinger, P. (1991) *Media, State and Nation. Political Violence and Collective Identities*, London, Sage.
Smythe, D. (1977) 'Communication: A Blindspot of Western Marxism', *Canadian Journal of Political and Social Theory*, vol. 1, no.3.
Sobchack, V. (ed) (1996) *The Persistence of History. Cinema, Television, and the Modern Event*, London, Routledge.
Steiner, G. (1989) *Real Presences. Is There Anything in What We Say?*, London, Faber and Faber.
Steiner, G. (1996) *No Passion Spent. Essays 1978-1996*, London, Faber and Faber.
Stevenson, N. (1995) *Understanding Media Cultures. Social Theory and Mass Communication*, London, Sage.
Stevenson, N. (1999) *The Transformation of the Media. Globalisation, Morality and Ethics*, Harlow, Longman.
Stevenson, P. (2002) *Language and German Disunity. A Sociolinguistic History of East and West in Germany, 1945-2000*, Oxford, OUP.
Stevenson, P. & Theobald, J. (eds.) (2000) *Relocating Germanness. Discursive Disunity in Unified Germany*, Basingstoke, Macmillan.
Stremmel, J. (1982) *Dritte Walpurgisnacht. Über einen Text von Karl Kraus*. Bonn, Bouvier.
Tarde, G. (1901) *L'Opinion et la Foule*, Paris, Alcan.
Tarde, G. (1903) *The Laws of Imitation*, New York, Henry Holt. Translation of *Les Lois de l'Imitation. Etude Sociologique* (1901) Paris, Alcan.
Tarde, G. (1969) *On Communication and Social Influence*, Chicago, University of Chicago Press.
Tenberg, R. (ed.) (1999) *Intercultural Perspectives. Images of Germany in Education and the Media*, Munich, Judicium.

Theobald, J. (1987) 'The Image of the GDR in Britain. What the Students Think.' In Williams, I. (1987).

Theobald, J. (1987-88) 'Détente in the Classroom. A First Report on a Survey of British Students' Perceptions of the GDR.' In Dennis, M. (ed.) (1987-88).

Theobald, J. (1996) *The Paper Ghetto. Karl Kraus and Anti-Semitism*, Frankfurt/M, Peter Lang.

Theobald, J. (1999) 'Manufacturing Europhobia out of Germanophobia. Case Studies in Populist Propaganda.' In Tenberg (1999).

Theobald, J. (2000a) 'Radical Mass Media Criticism. Elements of a History from Kraus to Bourdieu.' In Berry, D. (2000).

Theobald, J. (2000c) 'Disgraceland GDR. Locating the Admirable amongst the Abject.' In: Stevenson, P. & Theobald, J. (2000).

Theobald, J. (2000d) 'Media Discourse and Balkan Wars.' In *Third Text* 51/2000.

Theobald, J. & Stevenson, P. (2000b) 'A Decade of Cultural Disunity. Diverging Discourses and Communicative Dissonance in 1990s Germany.' In Stevenson, P. & Theobald, J. (2000).

Theobald, J. & Zuber, G. (1993) 'Three Days in November. An Analysis of the British and French Press Coverage of the Opening of the Berlin Wall.' In *Journal of Area Studies* 2, 1993.

Theobald, J. & Zuber, G. (1995) 'Who Wanted Unification? The Forming of Public Attitudes in Britain and France.' In Hahn, H. (1995).

Thompson, E. (1963) *The Making of the English Working Class*, London, Gollancz.

Thompson, E. (1983) *The Defence of Britain*, London, END, CND, Merlin Press.

Thompson, E. & Smith, D. (eds.) (1980) *Protest and Survive*, Harmondsworth, Penguin.

Tönnies, F. (1922) *Kritik der Öffentlichen Meinung*, Berlin, Julius Springer.

Tönnies, F. (1957) *Community and Society*, East Lansing, Michigan State University Press. Original German text (1887) *Gemeinschaft und Gesellschaft*, Stuttgart.

Tunstall, J. (1996) *Newspaper Power. The New National Press in Britain*, Oxford, Clarendon.

Turner, G. (1996) *British Cultural Studies. An Introduction*, London, Routledge.

Van Dijk, T. (1988) *News as Discourse*, New York, Erlbaum.

Walker, M. (1994) *The Cold War and the Making of the Modern World*, London, Vintage.

Wallraff, G. (1977) *Der Aufmacher. Der Mann, der bei bild Hans Esser war*, Cologne, Kiepenheuer & Witsch.

Wallraff, G. (1979) *Zeugen der Anklage. Die 'Bild'-beschreibung wird fortgesetzt*, Cologne, Kiepenheuer & Witsch.

Wallraff, G. (1981) *Das BILD-Handbuch bis zum Bildausfall*, Hamburg, Konkret Literatur Verlag.

Williams, I. (ed.) (1987) *GDR. Individual and Society*, London, Ealing CHE.

Williams, R. (1974) *Television, Technology and Cultural Form*, London, Fontana.

Williams, R. (1978) 'The Press and Popular Culture: an Historical Perspective' in G. Boyce, J. Curran & P.Wingate (eds.) *Newspaper History*, London, Constable.

Winter, J. (2002) *Mediathink*, Montreal, Black Rose Books.

Wodak, R., de Cillia, R., Reisigl, M. & Liebhart, K. (1999) *The Discursive Construction of National Identity*, Edinburgh, Edinburgh University Press.

Wuttke, H. (1875) *Die Deutschen Zeitschriften und die Entstehung der öffentlichen Meinung*, Leipzig.

Zograf, A. (1999) *Bulletins from Serbia. E-mails & Cartoon Strips from Behind the Front Line*, Hove, Slab-O-Concrete Publications.

Newspapers and Magazines

Daily Mail
Daily Mirror
Daily Telegraph
Der Spiegel
L'Express
Le Figaro
Le Monde
Le Monde Diplomatique
Le Nouvel Observateur
Le Point
Libération
New York Times
The Guardian
The Independent
The Independent on Sunday
The Observer
The Sun

Broadcasts and Video Materials

BBC1 (2001) 'Panorama'.
BBC1 (2002) 'Panorama'.
BBC1 (2003) 'Panorama'.
BBC2 (1995) 'Jerry Building'.
BBC2 (1999) 'Kosovo: How the War was Spun'.
BBC Radio 4 (2000) 'Between Ourselves', 13 June.
ITV (1997) 'Paul McKenna Show'.
Referendum Party (1997) Election Campaign Video.
Spiegel TV (1990) 'Protokoll einer Deutschen Revolution'.

Websites

www.bbc.co.uk
www.guardian.co.uk
www.independent.co.uk
www.indianexpress.com
www.mango.org
www.medialens.org
www.tintin.be

Index

academic freedom 97
Achbar, Mark 40
Adie, Kate 11
Adorno, Theodor 26, 29, 31, 32, 34, 69
  and culture industry 33
Afghanistan 171, 181, 182, 185, 195,
  196, 202
Al Qaida 182, 187
Alfaro, Rosa Maria 50–1
Althusser, Louis 32, 35, 36
  and ideology 34
Anders, Günther
  and mass media 32–3
  pessimism of 33
Andreotti, Giulio 146
Andropov, Yuri 87, 89
Anglo-German relations 14–15
  and British Germanophobia 159, 161–
  6
antipolitics, and peace movement 113
appeasement 180
  potency of 154
Ash, Timothy Garton 119–20
audiences
  and culture industry 33
  and mass media 24–5
  and the public sphere 48–9
  and radical media criticism 39
  seduction of 139
  and triumph of untruth 33
Aznar 194

Baghdad blogger 200
Bahr, Egon 95
Barbero, Jésus Martín 9, 39, 47, 48
  *Communication, Culture and
  Hegemony* 50
Barsky, Robert F. 42
Barthes, R 32, 36
Baudrillard, Jean 34, 37, 39
BBC, *see* British Broadcasting
  Corporation (BBC)
Belgrano 58
Bell, Martin 175

Benedikt, Moriz 57, 58, 64
Benjamin, Walter 29, 31
  on Kraus 26
Berlin Wall 98, 130
  demolition of 144
  and end of Cold War 141
  and media discourse 141–2
  myths surrounding 143–4
  opening of 14, 129, 143-4
Bertrand Russell Foundation 118
Biermann, Wolf 109
bin Laden, Osama 181, 182, 183, 185,
  186
Birmingham Centre for Contemporary
  Cultural Studies (BCCC) 36, 39
Black, Conrad 160
Blair, Tony 154, 169, 173, 188, 193,
  194, 196, 200
  and United States 181
  as war criminal 199
Boehme, Ibrahim 133
Bohley, Bärbel 132
Böttger, Martin 134
Bourdieu, Pierre 6, 7, 9, 35, 39
  Contre-feux 43, 45
  and determinism 43
  and dispossession 44
  and emancipation 44–5
  and language 43
  Language and Symbolic Power 43
  The Power of Journalism 44
  as radical thinker-activist 43–6
  On Television 43, 44
Bowman, David 46
Brandt, Willy 95, 124–5, 126
Brecht, Bertolt 35, 208
Brezhnev, Leonid 87
Briggs, Raymond 115
Britain, *see* United Kingdom
British Broadcasting Corporation (BBC)
  47
  as Anglo-US propagandist 182, 183,
  186
  and German language courses 95–6

and Gulf War (2003) 181
Kosovo: How the War was Spun 168–75
Panorama 16
  New York-Islamabad programme 182–6
  Panorama Interactive programme 187–93
Brown, Ken 173
Bücher, Karl, on influence of press 28, 29
Burlatsky, Fyodor 80–1
Bush, George W. 72, 180–1, 183, 184, 187, 188, 194, 195, 196, 199, 200

Campaign for Nuclear Disarmament (CND) 114
  growth of 117
  Sanity 118
Campbell, Alistair 169, 173
Campbell, Nicky 182, 184
Canclini, Nestor García 39, 47, 48, 50
Carter, Jimmy 196
cartoons, and discursive challenge 135–7
Castells, Manuel 9, 39
  and informational economy 51
  and a public sphere 52
censorship
  and dispossession 44
  and dominant opinion 27
  and mass media 12
Chamberlain, Neville 154
Charter 77 121, 135
Chechnya 142
Chirac, Jacques 194
Chomsky, Noam 9, 29, 39, 40–1, 43, 46, 49, 196
  and European tradition 42
  Propaganda Model 41
Churchill, Winston 154
cinema 29
civil defence, and *Protect and Survive* 115
Clark, Wesley 172, 173
cliché
  Kraus on 26, 60–1
  and Nazis 71–2
  Orwell on 31
  and war on terrorism 180
Clinton, Bill 173
Cold War 118

and attitude formation 97–108
and Cuban missile crisis 80–1
deception of 93
détente 95, 96
and deterrence 94, 115
and discourse transformation 79–80
and dominant discourse 91, 92–3, 108, 112
as dubious term 14, 80
and German-German relations 95
and mass media 94, 109, 114
and 'middle of the road' conformism 92–3
and passivication 108–9
public acquiescence in 81
Reagan era 85
Western propaganda 80, 81, 83, 108
communication
  history of 20–1
  and industrial revolution 21
Cook, Robin 183, 184, 186
Corbyn, Jane 188, 190
Critical Discourse Analysis (CDA) 9–11
  Foucault's influence 34–5
Cromwell, David 200
Crowley, Colonel P J 173
Cruise missiles 114, 115, 120, 121, 122, 123
Cuban missile crisis 80
culture, and radical media criticism 39
Curran, James 29, 39, 42

Dahl, Hans Fredrik 19
Davis, Evan 192
de Gaulle, General Charles 82
Debord, Guy, as radical media critic 9, 35
Degrelle, Leon 82
Delors, Jacques 147
democracy, and mass media 25
détente 95, 96
determinism, and Bourdieu 43
deterrence 94, 115
  Thompson on 117
Diebold, Bernhard 74
Dienstbier, Jiri 135
Dimbleby, David 183, 184, 185
discourse 97
  alternative 119, 121, 130
  counter-hegemonic 13, 15–16, 30, 112, 114, 138, 140

and radical media criticism 39
  see also dominant discourse
dispossession, and censorship 44
dominant discourse 29–30, 91
  and Cold War 91, 92–3, 108, 112
  containability of opposition 102
  and elites 91–2, 112
  impact of education 97–108
  and 'normality' 92
  overthrow of 138
  power of 106
  and Soviet Union 129
  see also discourse
Douillet, Joseph 83

Eastern Bloc
  mass media 138–9
  triumph of alternative discourse 130
  and Westernisation 142–3
Eatherly, Claude 81
education, impact on attitudes 97–108
Edwards, David 200
Einstein, Albert 126
Eldridge, John 39
Eliot, T. S. 37
elites
  challenges to 111–12
  and deception 56
  and dominant discourse 91–2, 112
  and end of Cold War 142
  and Gulf War (2003) 194, 196
  and mass media 20, 41
  and media discourse 12, 15
  and media distortion 58
  Pilger on 199
  rejection of 138
Enduring Freedom, Operation 182
Engell, L 19
Enzensberger, Hans Magnus, and public
  action 35–6
Esler, Gavin 188, 189, 190, 192
Europe, Cold War division of 120–1,
  122
European Nuclear Disarmament (END)
  16, 114
  activities of 117–18
  END Journal 117–26
    appropriation of ideas 123–6
    and peace movement aims 120–3
European Union 155
  and British Europhobia 155, 159, 160–6

British media and 14–15
eyewitness accounts 57

Fairclough, Norman 9, 10, 11, 26, 30,
  35, 39, 43
  influence of Kraus 26
  and language 46
  and media discourse 10
Falklands War 58, 155
fascism, and media discourse 68–76
Federal Republic of Germany 88, 95
  and German unification 142, 145, 146
  peace movement 16
  see also German Democratic Republic;
    German unification; Germany
First World War
  and journalism 55–6
  and Kraus 13, 56–65
Fischer, Werner 132, 133
Fisk, Robert 173, 176
  and Gulf War (2003) 197–8
Foucault, Michel 10, 32
  and discourse 34
  influence of 34–5, 46
Fowler, Roger 9
France
  and German unification 147–8
  and Gulf War (2003) 187, 196
  opposition to US policy 181
Frankfurt School 9, 26, 29, 48, 49
  and cultural pessimism 31–2
Franklin, Bob 39, 46
Frei, Matt 192

Gadaffi, Muammar 157
Galtieri, Leopoldo 154
Galeano, Eduardo, and mass media 20
Garnham, Nicholas 29, 39
Gemeinschaft 27
German Democratic Republic 88, 95
  and alternative media 16
  attitudes towards 97–108
  collapse of 14, 137
  and counter-hegemonic discourse 130
  end of travel restrictions 144
  German unification 145, 146
  Grenzfall 130, 131–8
    and environmental issues 134
    and German unification 132, 135,
      136
    graphics used in 135–7

and human rights 135
  preoccupations of 132
  publication history 131–2
  and socialist democratisation 132–4
  and solidarity 134–5
nature of 130
opposition in 130–1
reform protest 145
representation of 95–6, 148–51
surveillance apparatus 131
and United States 148
and Western discourses 139
and Westernisation 142–3
see also Federal Republic of Germany;
German unification; Germany
German unification 14
  and *Die Letzten Tage bis zur Einheit*
    148–51
  and East German protestors 145
  French views on 147–8
  and *Grenzfall* 132, 135, 136
  and media discourse 141–2
  myths of 143–6, 148–51
  opposition to 146
  stage-managed nature of 148
  symbolism of 146–7
  and West Germany 146
  see also Federal Republic of Germany;
German Democratic Republic; Germany
Germany
  and Gulf War (2003) 187, 196
  opposition to US policy 181
  see also German unification
Gesellschaft 27
Glasgow University Media Group 39, 46
Goebbels, Joseph 73, 92
Goethe, J.W. von 62
Golding, Peter 29, 39
Goldman, Lucien 36
Goldsmith, James 162
Gorbachev, Mikhail 87, 89, 118, 120,
  122, 123, 125, 126, 129, 132, 133, 134,
  146, 148
Gramsci, Antonio 9, 29, 34, 42
  background 29
  and counter-hegemonic discourse 30
  and dominant discourse 29–30
  influence of 30, 36–7, 46
Grass, Günter 146
Great Britain, *see* United Kingdom
Greenham Common 114

Grenzfall 131–8
  and environmental issues 134
  and German unification 132, 135, 136
  graphics used in 135–7
  and human rights 135
  preoccupations of 132
  publication history 131–2
  and socialist democratisation 132–4
  and solidarity 134–5
Gulf War (2003) 48, 155
  and the BBC 187–93
  and elites 194, 196
  Fisk's reporting on 197–8
  and the internet 200–2
  and mass media 194–5
  'moment of truth' as a lie 194–5
  as moment of untruth 194
  opposition to 195–6, 197, 199–200
  Pilger's reporting on 199–200
  and weapons of mass destruction 187,
    190, 191, 195

Habermas, Jürgen 9, 29, 37, 39
  A Berlin Republic. Writings on
  Germany 49
  and the public sphere 42, 48–9
Haeger, Monika 133
Hall, Stuart 9, 24, 30, 34, 39
Havel, Václav 118–19, 135
Hawley, Caroline 191–2
Hayden, Nicki 184, 185
hegemonic discourse, *see* dominant
  discourse
Hergé (Georges Rémi)
  and Germany 85
  and Tintin
    Assemblée Nationale debate 82
    context of 82–4
    popularity of 82
    Tintin in the Land of the Soviets 14, 82,
    90, 115
      anti-Soviet themes 83
      economic failure 87–9
      fake factories 85–6
      luxury goods 89
      phoney elections 86–7
      publication history 82, 83
      and the secret police 84–5
      symptomatic character of 89–90
    wartime collaboration 82, 83
Herman, Edward 9, 29, 31, 39, 40–1, 46

and European tradition 42
and mass media vulnerability 41–2
Propaganda Model 41
Hewlett, Steve 175, 176
Hiroshima 93
Hirsch, Ralf 132, 134
historiography 7
and newstoriography 7
history
nature and role of 4–5
and role of media 5–6
Hitler, Adolf 68, 73, 77, 84, 154, 157,
163, 180
Kraus on 69, 71
and propaganda 67
Hobsbawm, Eric 1, 119
Hofmann, Michael 146–7
Hoggart, Richard 36
Honecker, Erich 150
Hoon, Geoff 197–8
Horkheimer, Max 26, 29, 31
and culture industry 33
Hussein, Abida 183, 184
Hussein, Saddam 154, 157, 180, 181,
187, 190, 192, 197

ideology, and Althusser 34
Independent Commission on
Disarmament and Security (Palme
Commission) 124–5
industrial revolution, and communication
21
information, media monopoly on 12
Initiative Frieden und Menschenrechte
(Peace and Human Rights Initiative)
130, 131, 134, 135, 136–7
Innis, Harold 37
internet, and Gulf War (2003) 200–2
Iraq 17, 181, 194, 195, 199, 202
and weapons of mass destruction 187,
190, 191
Iraq war, *see* Gulf War (2003)
Israel 195

Jenkins, Richard 43, 44
Johnson, Paul, 'In Praise of Being
British' 155–9
journalism
Bourdieu on 44
criticism of 23
and First World War 55–65

function of 6
and the internet 201
Kraus on 26, 70
and meaning 3
as misleader 1
and newstoriography 6–7
journalistic discourse
acceptance of 7–8
and passivication 8
role of 15
Juillard, J 147–8

Kaldor, Mary 119, 122–3
Kellner, Douglas 39
Kennedy, John 80
Kierkegaard, Sören, as media critic 22–
3, 76
Kinkel, Klaus 163
Khruschchev, Nikita 80, 87
Koch, Ed 185
Kohl, Helmut 93, 111, 121, 130, 161,
162, 163
and German unification 146, 148, 149
Konrád, George 113, 115
Kopelev, Lev 132
Korean War 80
Kosovo 155, 202
and BBC on media coverage 168–75
bombardment of 167, 196
eyewitness accounts 170–1
and mass media 15, 167, 173–6
and NATO pilots 170, 172
and NATO propaganda 169, 170, 172–5
Kraus, Karl 2, 22, 24, 32, 35, 37, 40, 47,
51, 94, 168, 169, 175
background 25
on clichéd language 26, 72
death of 77
Die Dritte Walpurgisnacht 75
Die Fackel 25, 58, 59, 69, 173
epitaph of 76
and First World War 13, 56–65
and international capitalism 59–60
opposition to 56
role of press 60
use of language 60–1, 62
and war reporters 62–4
importance of 21
influence of 26
on journalism 26
and language 60–1, 62, 68

The Last Days of Humanity 13, 56–65,
    67, 76
  and newstoriography 76
  and Orwell 30–31
  and passivication 76
  press criticism of 25–6
  Press Song 67
  and propaganda 67
  and rise of fascism 68–76
    and barbarism 75–6
    elite reassertion 69–70
    on Hitler 69, 71
    and language 71–3
    on lies 76
    Nazi literature 74–5
    the press 70
    silence of 68–9
  working methods 58
Krenz, Egon 150

Labour Party 114
Laity, Mark 174–5
language
  Bourdieu on 43
  and cliché 26, 31, 60–1, 71–2, 180
  distortion of 199
  Fairclough on 46
  and Kraus 26, 68
    and the First World War 60–1, 62
    and rise of fascism 71, 72–3
  and mass communications 2
  and meaning 1, 2, 30–1, 68, 205
  Orwell on 30–1
  Pilger on 48
  and political change 21
  and power 7
  and radical media criticism 39
  Thompson on 115–16
  and war jargon 200–1
Lassalle, Ferdinand, as media critic 23–
    4, 27
Latin America, and radical media
    criticism 50–1
Le Bon, G, and the crowd 24
Leaf, General 169
Leavis, F.R. 36, 37
Lenin, Vladimir 157
Lewis, Justin 193
Ley, Robert 166
liberal democracy, power structure 15

lies
  durability of 8–9
  and Gulf War (2003) 194–5
  and journalism 55
  Kraus on 76
  and mass media 33
Lippmann, Walter 29
Litynski, Jan 135
Livingston, Robert 145
Lloyd-George, David 55, 56, 65
Lockhart, Joe 173
Loos, Adolf 69
Loyd, Anthony 168, 175–6
Ludendorff, General 71
Lukács, George, 36

McAlpine, Alastair 163
McChesney, Robert 9, 29, 39, 40–1
  and commercialisation of media 41
  and European tradition 42
  and mass media vulnerability 41–2
McKenna, Paul 163–5
McLuhan, Marshall 9, 32, 42
  as radical media visionary 37
MacNamara, Robert 80
Major, John 154, 161, 162
Malraux, André 82
Mao Tse Tung 157
Marcuse, Herbert 32, 35, 42, 48
  and emancipation 34
  One Dimensional Man 33
market economy, and mass media 12, 20
Marx, Karl 19, 34
mass communications 2–3
mass culture, and culture industry 33
mass media
  as actors or agents 6
  and censorship 12
  commercialisation of 41
  and consumer acceptance 92
  and democracy 25
  development of 11–12, 21
  Eastern Bloc 138–9
  and elites 20, 41
  expansion of 38
  and information monopoly 12
  the internet 200–2
  and market economy 12, 20
  and news 5
  overthrow of 138

and passivication 8
and powerlessness 3, 13
as provocateurs 77
and the public sphere 49
radical criticism of 19–20
restructuring of 205–6
and totalitarianism 49
and trust 6
and truth 13, 21–2
vulnerability of 41–2
and war 12–13, 176, 208
Mattelart, Armand 2, 9, 40
and history of communication 20–1
and sociology of communications 19
Mattelart, Michèle 40
meaning
and journalism 3
and language 1, 2, 30–1, 68, 205
and the public sphere 49
media discourse 1
as commodity 130
and creation of events 7, 77
and creation of history 6
and elites 12, 15
Fairclough on 10
and historical events 3
and moments of untruth 7
nature of 3
and passivication 15
and rise of fascism 68–76
Media Lens 200–1
Meitner, Captain John 170, 172, 173, 175
Michnik, Adam 135
military-industrial complex 94
Milosevic, Slobadan 154, 157, 169, 173
Mitterrand, François 85, 93, 146, 147
Molesworth 114
Moore, Michael 196
multiculturalism 155
multinational companies 144
Mumford, Lewis 37
Murdoch, Rupert 42, 47, 58, 160, 165, 167, 194, 195, 199
Murdock, Graham 29, 39
Mussolini, Benito 180
Mutually Assured Destruction 80, 81
Myrdal, Alva 140

Nagasaki 93
national identity, British 153–9

nationalism
and Anglo-German relations 14–15
and British Germanophobia 159, 161-6
and myth 153–4
NATO, *see* North Atlantic Treaty Organisation
Nazis
media discourse and rise of 68–76
use of mass media 31
neo-liberalism 111
and Bourdieu 45
news
commodification of 57, 176
and moments of truth 5
nature of 5
newspapers
criticism of 23–4, 27–8
growth of 21
newstoriography 6–7
and historiography 7
and Kraus 76
and passivication 8–9
Nichols, John 41
Noelle-Neumann, E 27, 92
non-governmental organisations, role of 120
normality, and dominant discourse 92
North Atlantic Treaty Organisation (NATO), and Kosovo 169, 170, 172, 173, 174, 175
Northcliffe, Lord 161

Orwell, George 2, 29, 40, 42, 46, 181, 194, 205
Politics and the English Language 30–1

Palme Commission 124–5
Palme, Olaf 118, 124, 126
Park, Robert E 25, 29
passivication 7–9
and Cold War 108–9
and inevitability 142
and journalistic discourse 8
and Kraus 76
and media discourse 15
and newstoriography 8–9
Thompson on 116
Peace and Human Rights Initiative, *see* *Initiative Frieden und Menschenrechte*
peace movement 16, 112, 114
and alternative discourses 119, 121

and antipolitics 113
appropriation of ideas 123–6
and E.P. Thompson 114–17, 127
and European Nuclear Disarmament
    (END) 117–26
extent of 118
fulfilment of specific aims 120–3
and Gulf War (2003) 195–6
impact of 113, 119–20, 122–3
Perle, Richard 183, 184, 185–6
Pershing 2 missiles 114, 120, 121, 122,
    123
Philo, Greg 39
Pias, Claus 40
Pilger, John 9, 39, 42, 43, 49, 65, 173,
    197
    background 46
    discourse manipulation 47–8
    and Gulf War (2003) 197, 199–200
    Hidden Agendas 47–8
    and language 48
    on media saturation 55
    radical perspective of 46–7
    role of 48
Pillai, Nisha 182, 188, 189, 191
political economy, and mass media 26–7
Poncet, Jean-François 147
Ponte, Lisa 184, 185
Poppe, Gerd 133, 134
Poppe, Ulrike 133
popular culture 36
Postman, Neil 9, 31, 37, 39, 51
power
    and language 7
    and media discourse 8
    worship of 201
powerlessness, and mass media 3, 13
Project for the New American Century
    181
propaganda
    and Cold War 14, 80, 81, 83, 108
    Hitler on 67
    and Kraus 67
    NATO and Kosovo 169, 170, 172–5
    nature of 153
    and Nazi party 31
public discourse
    and Cold War 93
    commodification of 4
    forces shaping 3
    impact of 3

power of 111
subordination of 21–2
public opinion
    and mass media 25
    Tönnies on 27, 28
public service broadcasting 139
public sphere 112
    and Castells 52
    Habermas's concept of 48–9
    and meaning 49
    restructuring of 206–7
public sphere networks
    counter-hegemonic 16
    and radical media criticism 39
publics
    and mass media 24–5
    see also audiences

radical media criticism 19–20
    development of 38
    meaning of 20
    and restructuring proposals 205–7
    the first generation 21–9
    the second generation 29–32
    the third generation 32–7
    the fourth generation 38–52
        context of 39–40
        as thinker-activists 38
radio 29
Raguillo, Rosario 50
Rassak, Jules 25
Reagan, Ronald 79, 93, 95, 98, 101, 111,
    120, 121, 124, 126, 180
    and the 'evil empire' 86
    world vision 85
Referendum Party 162–3
regionalism 155
Rémi, Georges, *see* Hergé
Richard, Cliff 164
Riefenstahl, Leni 149, 151
Roda, Roda 62–3
Rovan, J 147
Runnymede Trust, *The Future of Multi-
    Ethnic Britain* 155, 157
Russell, Bertrand 42, 126
    Has Man a Future? 80
    and Western propaganda 81

Saïd, Edward 39
Saki (H. H. Munro) 161
Saudi Arabia 195

Schalek, Alice 11, 62
Schmidt, Helmut 121
Scott, C.P. 55, 56, 65
Search for Common Ground 77
sequence, notions of 5
Shakespeare, William 1
Shea, Jamie 169, 173, 174
Shukman, David 190
Simpson, John 188, 190, 192
Smythe, Dallas 39
Soviet Union
  anti-Soviet propaganda 14, 90
  collapse of 112, 129
  and dominant discourse 129
  see also Hergé (Georges Rémi), *Tintin
    in the Land of the Soviets*
Stalin, Joseph 83
Steiner, George 1, 2, 12, 26, 39, 49, 87
  influence of Kraus 26
  on Orwell 30
Stevenson, Nick 40
  media transformation 11–12
Stourton, Edward 170
Strategic Defence Initiative 85, 118
Sun, The 58, 160, 167, 194–5
Swift, Jonathan 21, 92

Tairov, Tair 125–6
Taliban 182
Tarde, Gabriel 9, 22, 26, 27, 32, 33, 49
  importance of 21
  L'Opinion et la Foule 24
  and media publics 24–5
  and public opinion 25
technology
  and mass media 11–12
  and radical media criticism 39
  subjugation of 168
television 32
  Bourdieu on 44, 45
  and German unification 146
  and portrayal of Germany 160
Templin, Wolfgang 133
terrorism, war on 16–17, 180, 196, 199,
    202
  and anticipatory pre-emption 180
  as nonsense 180
  and regime change in Iraq 187
Thatcher, Margaret 93, 95, 98, 101, 111,
    114, 121, 146, 148, 154
Thompson, Edward 36, 46, 111, 134

The Defence of Britain 126–7
  and deterrence 117
  and European Nuclear Disarmament
    (END) 113–14
  and language 115–16
  and peace movement 122, 127
  Protest and Survive 114–17
Thompson, J.B. 43
Tintin, *see* Hergé (Georges Rémi)
Tönnies, Ferdinand 9, 29, 3222
  importance of 21
  Gemeinschaft und Gesellschaft 27
  Kritik der Öffentlichen Meinung 27
  political economy perspective 26–7
  press as capitalist enterprise 27–8
  public opinion and the press 27, 28
totalitarianism, and mass media 49
Trujillo, Adelaida 50
trust, and the media 6
truth
  concepts of 3
  and culture industry 33
  and lies 8–9
  and mass media 13
  moments of 5
  notions of 5
  subordination of 21–2
Truthout 200
Turner, Graham, on Frankfurt School 31
Tyler, Patrick 200

Uhl, Peter 135
United Kingdom
  and British superiority 155–9
  civil defence 115
  and Cruise missiles 114, 115
  and European Union 155, 159
  and Europhobia 160–1, 162–6
  Germanophobia 159, 161–2, 163–6
  and Gulf War (2003) 187, 196
  and multiculturalism 155
  nationalist myth 153–5
  peace movement 16, 187
  regionalism 155
  and United States 181, 182, 187
United Nations 187
United States 113, 187
  appropriation of World Trade Centre
    attack 179, 182
  foreign policy 180–1
  and German unification 148

see also Bush, George W.; Gulf War
  (2003); Reagan, Ronald; terrorism,
  war on; World Trade Centre terrorist
  attack
untruth, moments of 1, 3, 17, 76, 90
  and commodification of public
  discourse 4
  concepts of 3
  and Gulf War (2003) 194
  and media discourse 7

Veritas, Operation 182
Vienna, press in 24
Vietnam War 80
Vogel, J. 19
Voltaire 92

Walker, Martin 79, 119
Wall Street Crash 83
Wallez, Fr Norbert 82
Wallraff, Günther 39, 43
war
  and mass communications 2
  and mass media 12–13, 176, 208
  and restructured mass media 206–8
war reporters, Kraus and 62–4
Ward, Colin 47
Watkins, Peter 94

weapons of mass destruction 93, 112,
  187, 190, 195, 202
Williams, Raymond 30, 32
  influences on 36–7
  as radical media critic 36–7
Winter, James 39
Wintonick, Peter 40
Wodak, Ruth 9, 10, 11, 26, 35
  and Critical Discourse Analysis (CDA)
    10
  influence of Kraus 26
Wollenberger, Vera 132
World Peace Council 125
World Trade Centre terrorist attack 16–
  17, 72, 179, 202
  appropriation by US government 179,
    182
  and axis of evil 180
  and mass media 182–6
  media coverage 179–80
  see also terrorism, war on
Wuttke, Heinrich, as media critic 24

xenophobia, and British Germanophobia
  14–15, 159, 161–2, 163–6

Zograf, Aleksandar 170–1, 176